The Categorical Impulse

The Categorical Impulse

Essays in the Anthropology of Classifying Behaviour

Roy Ellen

Berghahn Books
New York • Oxford

First published in 2006 by

Berghahn Books
www.berghahnbooks.com

First paperback edition published in 2008

Library of Congress Cataloging-in-Publication Data

The categorical impulse : essays on the anthropology of classifying behaviour / Roy Ellen.
p. cm.
Includes bibliographical references and index.
ISBN 978-1-84545-017-5 (hbk.); 978-1-84545-155-4 (pbk.)
1. Ethnology--Classification. 2. Human behavior--Classification. 3. Ethnopsychology--Classification. I. Ellen, R. F., 1947-

GN345.3 .E45 2005
305.8'001'2--pcc 22 2005040611

British Library Cataloguing in Publication Data

A catalogue record for this book is available from the British Library.

Printed in the United States on acid-free paper.

ISBN 978-1-84545-017-5 hardback
ISBN 978-1-84545-155-4 paperback

For the begetters (Nancy and Gerald),
and for the begotten (Philippa and Olivia)

Contents

Preface

The essays collected here (all written since 1975) explore various aspects of the anthropological engagement with the problem of the category and of classification, as my own ideas have progressed over three decades. Most of them draw on Indonesian fieldwork data for illustration and inspiration, and especially examine constructions of the natural world. All, however, reflect general issues at the interface of anthropology and cognition, as these have been discussed in recent years, and draw upon experience in teaching courses in 'Culture and cognition' and 'Language, categories and culture' at the University of Kent over a period of twenty years. The essays are not only interlinked in terms of the problems which they address, but have now been revised and edited to show explicitly how they connect up with general theoretical trends. To these have been added an entirely new introduction, which not only provides some background to the major ideas discussed, but also reviews select developments in cognitive anthropology since the time the first papers were written, outlining how these have impacted on classification studies.

I have arranged the chapters in a logical rather than a chronological order. Thus, the short encyclopedia article dated 1996 appears as Chapter 2, before a more discursive essay (Chapter 3) first published in 1978. The original location of the papers is also reflected in their style: whereas Chapter 2 exhibits the compactness – even terseness – required of its genre, Chapter 6 dispays the conventions of a Festschrift, while Chapter 9 was written as a lecture to be spoken. The other chapters are more conventional in their formats. Chapters 1, 2 and 3 are all general overviews of classificatory studies in anthropology, but each very much indicative of the issues at the times when they were written. Chapters 4, 6 and 8 are studies of various aspects of Nuaulu classifying behaviour, while Chapters 5, 9 and 10 incorporate Nuaulu data as key illustrations, but rather emphasise underlying universal features of cognitive process: body partonymy, the process by which perception is culturally modified through reification, and the basic cognitive propensities underlying the varying constructions of nature.

Chapter 1 is written especially for this collection, though it draws upon a number of published and unpublished papers. Chapter 2 first appeared as: 1996 'Classification', in *Encyclopedia of Social and Cultural Anthropology*, A. Barnard and J. Spencer (eds) (London: Routledge, pp. 103–6), and is reproduced with the permission of Routledge Taylor and Francis. Chapter 3 first appeared as: 1979 'Introductory Essay', in *Classifications in their Social Context*, R.F. Ellen and D. Reason (eds) (London: Academic Press, pp. 1–29), and is reproduced with the permission of Academic Press. Chapter 4 first appeared in 1975 as 'Variable constructs in Nuaulu zoological classification', in *Social Science Information* 5(14), 201–28, and is reproduced here with the permission of the editors. Chapter 5 first appeared in 1977 as 'Anatomical classification and the semiotics of the body', in *The Anthropology of the Body*, John Blacking (ed), Association of Social Anthropologists Monograph No. 15 (London: Academic Press, pp. 343–70), and is reproduced here with permission of the Association of Social Anthropologists and Academic Press. Chapter 6 first appeared in 1991 as 'Grass, grerb or weed? A Bulmerian meditation on the category "monote" in Nuaulu plant classification', in *Man and a Half: Essays in Honour of Ralph Bulmer*, A. Pawley (ed.) (Auckland: Uniprint, pp. 95–101), and is reproduced here with the permission of The Polynesian Society. Chapter 7 first appeared in 1998 as 'Palms and the prototypicality of trees: some questions concerning assumptions in the comparative study of categories and labels', in *The Social Life of Trees*, L. Rival (ed.) (Oxford: Berg, pp. 57–79), and is reproduced here with the permission of the editor and the publisher. Chapter 8 first appeared in 1998 as 'The inedible and the uneatable: totemic and other restrictions on the use of biological species among the Nuaulu', in *Old World Places, New World Problems: Exploring Issues of Resource Management in Eastern Indonesia*, S. Pannell and F. von Benda-Beckman (eds) (Canberra: Australian National University, pp. 243–66), and is reproduced here with the permission of The Australian National University Press. Chapter 9 was the Curl Lecture for 1987 and first appeared in 1988 as 'Fetishism' in *Man (N.S.)* 23(2), 213–35, and is reproduced here with the permission of the Royal Anthropological Institute. Finally, Chapter 10 was prepared for the 1995 conference of the European Association of Social Anthropologists and first appeared in 1996 as 'The cognitive geometry of nature: a contextual approach', in *Nature and Society: Anthropological Perspectives*, Philippe Descola and Gisli Palsson (eds) (London: Routledge, pp. 103–23), and is reproduced with the permission of the European Association of Social Anthropologists and Routledge Taylor and Francis.

In putting this collection together I have been assisted by Susi Soemarwoto and Caroline Grundy, who I must thank for their efficiency and infinite patience. Some of the costs incurred during editing have been supported by Economic and Social Research Council grant R000 239310, 'Frequency and periodicity in Nuaulu ritual regulation'.

Roy Ellen
Canterbury

List of Figures

List of Tables

CHAPTER 1

Introduction: Categories, Classification and Cognitive Anthropology[1]

An overview of the anthropological study of classifications and classifying behaviour during the twentieth century, especially attempts to differentiate and then reconcile the role of cultural, psychological and biological processes.

Philosophy is a graveyard of 'isms' (Edelman 1992: 158)

Categories are those entities which the human mind creates in order to make sense of the diversity of experience, by grouping things, attributes and phenomena on the basis of similarity and difference. Categorisation, therefore, is the means by which 'the uniqueness of each experience is transformed into the more limited set of learned, meaningful categories to which humans and other organisms respond' (Varela et al. 1993: 176). By comparison, classification is here understood as the way in which categories are related to each other, and the means by which particular cultural patterns are produced. Neither categorisation nor classification are cognitively autonomous processes, and in this book the emphasis is on how both articulate with cultural input in social contexts. The title 'The Categorical Impulse', suggests, with quite deliberate ambivalence, that not only is our capacity to create and manipulate categories impulsive (something which is deep-seated and driven) but that it is 'categorical' in the sense simultaneously of 'referring to categories' and 'asserting absolutely'. In this respect it is consistent with the rationality of propositional logic, which can only be achieved by imposing systematic cultural conventions.

Categories and classifications have been the subject of interest within philosophy, mathematics, logic, linguistics, cognitive psychology, anthropology, and more recently neurobiology and interdisciplinary cognitive science (via artificial intelligence and computing), for much of the twentieth century. Classification, as an object of recent anthropological scrutiny came to prominence during the 1960s, exemplified in the British (constructionist) tradition by the writings of Mary Douglas, and in the American ethnosemantics (cognitive) tradition by the likes of Harold Conklin and Brent Berlin. Both schools shared roots in cultural relativism, though an influential strand of the American lineage was subsequently to turn relativism on its head. This historical background is explored here in Chapters 2 and 3. What I wish to do in this introductory chapter is to situate what follows by summarising some of the significant developments that occurred in the study of categories and classification during the period that the essays first appeared in print, that is between 1975 and 2001, a period which has seen a revolution in our understanding of the interrelationship between language, categories, culture, social behaviour and the mind. When Chapter 3 was first published, the constructivist and cognitive approaches seemed almost irreconcilable, to exist, as it were, in parallel universes, in much the same way as scientific and postmodernist approaches have done more recently. However, over the last thirty years we have witnessed both a reinvigoration of classification studies and a cross-fertilisation of these once antagonistic approaches.

My own work has always tried to bridge this divide and develop a more embedded and processual approach. In particular, I have used the detailed empirical analysis of people's categorisation of natural kinds as a portal through which to achieve an understanding of how classifying behaviour in general works, engaging with the ideas of both anthropologists and psychologists. This tendency to see the merits of both the cognitivist and social approaches has led some, with good reason I think at the time, to chide me for being 'equivocal' (Friedberg 1995: 210). Douglas, as late as the early 1990s (1993: 161–5) continued to warn us against compromise and the 'eclectic muddle' which must inevitably follow. She offered just three alternatives to the study of classification – naturalism, idealism and constructivism – denying the validity of all but the last, which she deemed essential to provide 'a general framework' (ibid., 182). Such stark polarity looks distinctly out of kilter in the light of contemporary rethinking of conventional nature (innate) – nurture (acquired) arguments, in both biology (Ridley 2003) and anthropology (Ingold 2001: 129–33). Indeed, for many it is no longer necessary, when speaking of cognition, to choose between the 'chicken position' (an approach which assumes a world with pre-given qualities) and the 'egg position' (where reality is simply the reflection of internal laws of the system). It seems that we can, after all, negotiate a middle path (Varela et al. 1993: 172).

I have focused predominantly on studies of categorisation in anthropology, and yet in the development of the interdisciplinary field of cognitive science the absence of an obvious and continuous anthropological contribution has often seemed a mystery (Boden, forthcoming). Despite the formative inputs into the theory of cognitive science made by the likes of Bruner, Bartlett, Bateson and Wallace, and more contemporary work on distributed cognition and schema theory, much anthropology between the 1960s and 1990s actively resisted making connections between culture and the mind, and in recent decades has positively seemed to marginalise even the cognitive anthropology within. While we can share Geertz's disquiet with what he calls 'the cognitivist fallacy' (1973: 12), the idea that culture consists primordially of mental phenomena, it is manifestly absurd that culture might exist 'primordially' elsewhere, devolved perhaps in inter-subjective social space. It is increasingly difficult to determine where a boundary between the internal world of mental representation and the external world of cultural practice might lie. The conceptual boundary between mind and brain is no longer as conveniently maintained as was once possible, some preferring to use the term 'mind-brain' to express this uncertainty (Laughlin et al. 1992), and questions are posed as to whether we should include our external sensory perceptors – our eyes, ears, even our hands, as part of the spatially devolved mind. The body, in a word, encompasses the function of the brain which, when it experiences itself through interaction with other mind-bodies and things in its perceptual field, is what we understand by consciousness. For Bruner (1996) culture has long been as much a precondition for the development of human cognition as human cognition has been for the development of culture, and work in brain science and cognitive anthropology has now begun to show us the beginnings of how this might work empirically. The consequence has been the return of cognition to the centre of anthropological theorising, using both neo-Darwinian (e.g. Sperber 1996; Atran 1998; Boyer 2001) and non-Darwinian (e.g. Holland and Quinn 1987; Bloch 1991; d'Andrade 1995; Whitehouse 2001; Reyna 2002) approaches. But increasingly this is a cognition which is 'experientialist' or 'embodied' (Lakoff and Johnson 1980: 178), and one which relies crucially on a concept of culture which by definition is interactive and intersubjective, enculturating the different brains it inhabits. This trend has been accompanied by a recognition that the boundary between shared and individual representations is difficult to maintain (Sperber 1985), and that therefore semantic organisation at the personal as well as at the shared cultural level is a proper focus of anthropological scrutiny (Strauss 1992).

I Words and the Structure of Categories

Most studies of classification continue to approach the subject linguistically, and the beginnings of cognitive anthropology are indeed to be found in the application of linguistic models, most notably as formal semantics. This is understandable, for the obvious reasons that most data acquired in fieldwork settings are generated through interviews and by hearing people talk about what they think, perceive and experience; because this is how most people themselves share classificatory knowledge; and because many classificatory strategies are revealed through language. However, it has long been recognised that words are not always a good guide to the existence of categories: there may be several words which label the same category (synonyms), and the same word can be used for quite different ideas. Moreover, some categories may exist without being labelled.

The nomenclature for labelling categories tells us something both about classificatory knowledge and about the attributes which people find important in distinguishing different entities, attributes and phenomena. Labels provide us with evidence of more inclusive categorising strategies: for example, plant binomials often indicate two categories linked by a *kind of* relationship. Thus for Nuaulu, *sinsin msinae*, 'red sinsinte' (a kind of croton, *Codieum variegatum*), is a binomial. In this case the more inclusive category is identified not only by its priority but because it has been lexically-reduced: thus *sinsinte* becomes *sinsin*. Local linguistic conventions have to be carefully observed, and it is important to note, for example, that *kasipi sinsinte* is not a kind of *sinsinte*, but rather a variety of manioc, *Manihot esculenta*. In this linguistic context *sinsinte* becomes, instead, an adjectival qualifier. The kinds of adjectival qualifiers used vary, from descriptions of diagnostic visual attributes, uses, smells, to sounds, depending on the semantic domain. The important thing is not that something has a fixed name, but that the percept is registered through continual and repeated perceptual events, reinforced over the longer term and transmitted between individuals. A shared name, however ad hoc, might be the outcome of such a process, but it need not be.

Early attempts by anthropologists and linguists to understand how categories are established and used employed a distinctive feature model, in which category A was thought to be distinguished from category B in terms of a number of key characteristics. For example, birds have wings, feathers, beaks and fly, in contrast to fish, which swim and have fins. This model was largely drawn from lexicography and logic (Conklin 1962). However, it was noted that the condition of contrast required for this model to work was not always evident. Thus category A might be linked to category B by one common attribute, and category B linked to category C through a different common attribute, thus linking categories A and C even though they had nothing in common: this is known as 'polythetic classification' (see Chapter 3). As work on classification (particularly ethnobiological classification) expanded it became obvious that the digital distinctive feature model was inadequate, and that a better way of modelling the cognition of basic and more inclusive categories might be in analogue terms, as cognitive prototypes. In this model the brain has an image of, say, 'birdness' or 'treeness' or 'cup-ness' to which incoming perceptual images are matched; the presence or absence of particular features is not an overriding consideration, only closeness of match (Rosch 1977). In this core-periphery model an image could be a close match or a marginal match. Thus in British English classification of birds a robin would configure closely the core prototype, but an ostrich would be marginal, whereas in the folk classification of crockery a mug is a kind of cup, but only peripherally so. As it happens, this critique of functionalist views of cognition has been recently reinvigorated by work at a neurobiological level (Edelman 1992: 233), to which I shall return below. Of course in practice, both the notion of contrasting features and cognitive prototypes are necessary to understand how classifications work in detail.

The difficulties of assigning things to categories may be made easier, then, by imposing culturally agreed boundaries, or indeed by creating these inadvertently or deliberately through genetic and other physical manipulations of the natural world e.g. breeding varieties of plant which emphasise phenotypic difference for aesthetic reasons or planting trees individually to display their architecture in ways which are often occluded in natural settings. Because parts of our experience of the world are complexly continuous, it is occasionally necessary to impose boundaries to produce categories at all, for example in certain parts of the colour spectrum. Sometimes these can be quite arbitrary, and even in such an apparently technically precise area as engineering design it is now evident that the scope for cultural arbitrariness over technical necessity is considerable (e.g. Lemonnier 1992).

II The Relations between Categories

It has become conventional, following the analytical procedures of cognitive anthropology, to begin any analysis of classificatory knowledge by establishing a cognitive or semantic domain or field (Frake 1962). The domain in question can be established at varying degrees of classificatory inclusiveness: thus it might de determined as 'all genealogically specified relatives', 'all living things', 'furniture', 'plants', 'trees', 'rice', depending on the focus of the analysis. Although the domain may be isolated for analytical reasons, and is to this extent arbitrary, its boundaries are generally understood to reflect distinctions which are empirically important for the population who share them. Thus if a population has no concept of 'fish' then such a category cannot be established as a cognitive domain. On the other hand, as we have noted, categories do not need to be labelled in order to exist, even at the level of domain. Where a cognitive domain has been established, it is usually understood that most categories which subdivide it will be labelled, and a domain or field identified in terms of its labels is usually known as a lexical field. Of course, the lexical field, for say plants, may not correspond with the cognitive domain, because of the existence of covert categories (see Chapters 4 and 7) at various levels of inclusiveness.

The earliest work on cognitive domains modelled the internal subdivisions largely in terms of a taxonomic model: that is, in terms of a hierarchical model of contrast and class inclusion. This is partly because this form of classifying is so dominant in the literary and scientific tradition of the West, and particularly because of the precedent of Linnaean taxonomy. The work of Brent Berlin (1972, 1992; and Berlin et al. 1973, 1974) developed the taxonomic idea further, putting forward a strong claim for it to be considered the general way in which at least ethnobiological classification works cross-culturally, hypothesising that a series of levels could be established, broadly reflected in the main ranks of the Linnaean scheme: unique beginners, life-forms, intermediates, generics, specifics and varietals.

I have stated my own views on the adequacy of the taxonomic model in *The Cultural Relations of Classification* (1993). In brief, I agree that the principle of taxonomy is a persuasive one as a universal classifying strategy. There can be little doubt also that people classify living things into increasingly inclusive groups, and that this provides a powerful inductive framework for making systematic inferences about the properties of organisms. But this need not imply taxonomy in the formal or domain-specific sense. Systematic contrast and class inclusion are present across a number of domains. It is particularly striking in plants and animals because of their 'thinginess' (Chapter 10) and because they are the outcome of an evolutionary process which is reflected in patterned physical and behavioural resemblance. In the domain of living kinds these tendencies converge in a special way, not obviously because of the character of the mind which does the classifying, but because of regularities in the objective world which is classified and to which the mind responds.

Some cultural profiles encourage taxonomic thinking as a way of representing relationships between things more than others (see e.g. Lancy and Strathern 1981), and some subcultural contexts encourage it more than others (e.g. formal literary-based operations in classroom contexts). Moreover, because of the propensity of most anthropological researchers to rely heavily on a taxonomic approach embedded in Western science, it is easy to yield taxonomies in patterns of data collected from non-literate informants. In asserting a universal 'abstract taxonomic structure' the methodology all too often seems to be one in which inconvenient features of peoples' classifying behaviour which do not fit the expected pattern are systematically ignored or explained away as exceptions, until a suitably 'taxonomic' pattern is obtained. But if we accept instead the centrality of prototypical thinking and polythesis in classifying activity, it is not at all surprising that it is often difficult to establish systematic and consistent hierarchical relationships between superordinate and subordinate categories (Edelman 1992: 236).

III Classifying Strategies and Cultural Universals

When Chapter 4, which looks at evidence for the different ways in which the Nuaulu classify cassowaries and marsupials, was first written (1975), studies of local variability, flexibility and consistency in classifying behaviour were unusual. Consequently, claims to the universality of certain patterns and, therefore, of cognitive determinism were easier to sustain. However, studies of variability are now numerous (Berlin 1992: 199–231) and provide strong evidence of the role of social and situational factors, challenging the validity of some key assumptions regarding sharing characteristic of the first phase in the development of cognitive anthropology (Lave 1988: 10–11).

One universal, however, the existence of which few would now deny, is that all classifications display some concept of basic category: that logically all classifications start from a hypothesised 'level', series or group of percepts or concretised entities or things, the segregates of which are then either aggregated or disaggregated. These basic categories may refer to biota (or things in nature, or natural kinds), people, social groups or other types of object or entity. But there is less agreement as to how consistent such a level of basic categorising is cross-culturally. When applied to natural kinds, Haudricourt (1973: 268) noted that in many vernaculars it is the genus that gives us the basic level for plants, and that species only obtain priority with Linnaeus. This view is echoed by Berlin, though more recently there has been doubt expressed as to the level at which basic categories of natural kinds might be found (Ellen 1993: 67–71). The issue is also taken up in places in this book, including especially Chapters 9 and 10.

More problematic has been the notion of taxonomy, to which I have already referred. Brent Berlin has consistently argued in favour of the universality of taxonomy for ethnobiological schemes, but this only really works if we also assert the clear separation of general-purpose from special-purpose schemes; that is, those that are logical and 'natural' from those that arise to meet particular cultural requirements. This distinction is discussed further in Chapters 2, 3, 4 and 6 below. Indeed, the effective demonstration of the empirical primacy of taxonomy depends on the extent to which categories are linked in a particular way, although we know that they are often flexibly connected in numerous different ways, ways which undermine implicit taxonomic levels and contrasts and the general-purpose/special-purpose distinction. It also depends upon the ease with which ethnographers can elicit transitivity statements (of the kind *a* is a *b* and *b* is a *c*, therefore *a* is a *c*). It is, then, fundamentally an appeal to our common (cultural) sense.

Atran (1998: 563) no longer thinks that folk taxonomy defines the inferential character of folk biology as suggested in his *Cognitive Foundations of Natural History*, and his recent findings do not uphold the customary distinction between general-purpose and special-purpose classifications. This is consistent with the results of my own ethnobiological ethnography (Ellen 1993: 123–4). Nuaulu, like Itzaj Maya, do not 'essentialise ranks', which would violate their primary concern with 'ecological and morpho-behavioural relationships' in favour of abstract properties. The development of worldwide scientific systematics has until recently explicitly required rejecting such relationships with their cross-cutting classifications (Atran 1998: 561–2). I believe that one of the problems central to the methodology that we use to generate so much of our ethnobiological data is not knowing quite how independent the system of ranks that we discover is from the kinds of concepts with which we start. On the whole, it is my experience that data from long-term ethnographic research are more consistent with the notion of a holistic and dynamic conception of the relations between categories, one which allows for the generation of particular 'classifications' depending on context. Thus, the variable position of 'palms' in comparative ethnobotanical schemes and the nebulousness of its position as a 'life-form', intermediate or 'unaffiliated generic' (Chapter 7), is an excellent example of the preeminence of local ecological and cultural considerations, but also of some general fundamental ambiguity. On balance, I agree with what I understand to be Atran's current position, that the more dense our knowledge the more we deviate from the general model, and that in a very real sense taxonomies are the result of 'degenerate knowledge': that is they only become possible by simplifying experiential complexity in ways which make knowledge less useful. Thus the failure to integrate the classification of plant and animal domesticates into general accounts of the working of classifications of the natural world, given the practical importance of such classificatory knowledge for most humans, is a major problem in this sense, since it cannot easily be rejected as a 'special case'. I also find the idea that cultural selection of domesticates makes taxonomy possible by heightening the differences between categories of cultivars a neat and fertile one, and one which reinforces the interpretation of other current work (e.g. Shigeta 1996).

Irrespective of the degree to which we can accept a single, common, non-cultural model for classification, we can agree, I think, that folk classifications of biological species at least coevolve with the plants and animals that are their subject. We can, therefore, in the most general sense, agree with Boster (1996) that at the level of clearly discriminated prototypes of natural kinds, humans 'carve nature at the joints': there are certain discontinuities that are so protean, so much part of the lives of so many human populations, that they can be said to be universal. I believe this to be true for natural kinds as a phenomenal type, but also 'unique beginners', such as plant or animal. One is reminded here of the position adopted by Reed (1988), that 'animacy' or 'animality' is not simply an end-product of classification based on multiple cognitive discriminations, but relates to a fundamental ability of the brain to distinguish an organic form that registers a particular kind of saliency which matches objective phylogenetic features. Since hominids have evolved in environments which display a particular phylogenetic and phenomenal discontinuity, it is not entirely surprising that they should demonstrate a capacity (a) to utilise a notion of natural kind which assists the management of diversity, and (b) to recognise more diffuse prototypes in non-cultural ways (e.g. 'animal', 'plant', perhaps 'tree', 'bird', 'fish'). The argument for some unique beginners (plant, animal, person, artefact) having non-cultural roots is also supported by negative evidence, that it is difficult to see how cultural and developmental factors in themselves could generate such salient if sometimes lexically covert categories (Boyer 2001). However, such artifacts of cognition are logically different from 'life-forms' in the sense developed by Berlin (e.g. Berlin et al. 1973). These latter vary cross-culturally, but do not always partition 'the living world into broadly equivalent divisions' (Atran 1998, note 5). Thus, though the basic image prototype of 'tree' may have existed for millions of years (see section 1.6 below), the life-form category and term seem relatively recent (Witkowski et al. 1981), while its earliest labelling appears to have involved functional considerations reflected in tree/wood polysemy (see Chapter 7). Indeed, Brown's work (1984) confirms the variability of many life-forms as much as it has demonstrated the universality of a few. Chapter 6 examines one Nuaulu plant life-form which is difficult to explain in universalistic terms.

Much emphasis (e.g. Boster 1996; Brown 1984) has been placed on the roots of natural kind classification in evolutionary psychology when there is equal reason to believe that classifications which cut across morphologically 'natural' classifications, such as 'edible-nonedible' and 'dangerous-nondangerous', may also be in part a consequence of non-cultural recognition abilities. Thus, humans may not see 'stones' but they may well perceive objects in their environment with the properties of stones which can serve a particular purpose, and be grouped accordingly (Ingold 1992). Hence function may precede classification, and it is not essential to classify in order to use. We certainly need to investigate further the extent to which 'affordance based' classification can operate independent of cultural inputs or context, but my own view is that these cognitive propensities are so abstract as to tell us relatively little about how people classify in their everyday lives, at less inclusive (and more functional) levels of discrimination. On the whole, non-cultural input operates in terms of the process of categorisation, rather than underpinning particular categories, while certain regularities may be the product of general mechanisms operating across different and very varied domains, constrained by the data being organised.

IV Category Formation in Different Kinds of Semantic Domain

Many aspects of rule-governed category formation and classification work in the same way irrespective of cognitive or semantic domain, but there are also significant differences which we must note, some of which have major theoretical and methodological implications. If we consider four different domains – colour, kinship, biodiversity and the body – we can note that all are qualitatively different in terms of the 'things' classified. Colours are not really 'things' at all, but rather properties of things, measurable along the dimensions of hue, saturation and brightness (Kay and Kempton 1984); while kinship classes are part of social deixis (those aspects of language which vary with the occasion, time and location of utterance, and with the identity of speaker and hearer), and refer to the properties of the relations between things. Bodies are clearly bounded entities, but the way we divide them up into parts-through analytic (that is partonymic) classifications-involves some degree of arbitrary grouping, despite a large degree of cross-cultural conformity. Of the three domains only natural kinds map directly on to real, discrete objects in an objective world. But even with biodiversity, some gaps between purportedly discrete kinds and objects are bigger and more salient than others, in most environments, and therefore serve as more widespread (even universal) markers in classifying behaviour. Our experience, in many diverse environments, does not mean that we automatically recognise, for example, a 'tree' as a clearly separate bounded kind of thing, as we can see in any photograph of a stretch of forest. Trees often merge imperceptibly into bushes, are polythetic in definition, single features being neither essential to group membership nor sufficient to allocate an item to a group. It may seem, therefore, that categories vary according to the complexity of their definition, rather than simply the scope of their content.

In an important sense, then, the objective 'thinginess' of the biota sets it apart from many other semantic domains (Chapter 10), and what separates it from other domains which classify objects (say, cultural objects) is the degree to which we can organise it according to its plausibly conjectured evolution. Thus classifying natural objects a and b together is more likely to indicate (though not always) natural historical affinities (common origin) than, say, a classification of furniture. We underestimate the difficulties of categorising the natural world precisely because it consists of concrete entities with utilitarian referents. But to speak of the thinginess of the natural world is simply to acknowledge the universal human imperative to turn the natural world into things and to think of the things so prehended in terms of their essential qualities. This is not to say that such a capacity is innate in the sense of springing into action from the first moment of postpartum development: it is simply to recognise the existence of a process that takes place over time, a consequence of interaction between normal developmental processes and environmental stimuli.

The operations of categorisation and classification work equally in terms of unmodified sense data or their cultural representations. In this sense the cognitive and cultural tools available to do this do not distinguish between the social world and the non-social world, though in the analysis of classification this has become a conventional distinction. Similarly, classification can treat its subject in a pragmatic and mundane way or by using various symbolic allusions. Since so much of what we sense and experience is mediated by social consciousness, and since the boundary between the mundane (technical) and symbolic is often unclear, it has sometimes been difficult, in practice, to know how to divide these two axes. It seems to me that there is more consensus on the principles of categorisation than on the status of patterns of categories which are the outcome.

The distinctions between symbolic and mundane classifications, and between those of the social and non-social worlds, cannot always, therefore, be neatly drawn: symbolic things are in an important sense practical, and practical classifications of the non-social world often rely on metaphors which are ultimately social, as in the use of the terms 'genus' and 'family' to organise plants and animals. In totemism, touched on briefly in Chapter 4 and discussed in more depth in Chapter 8, we usually find biological distinctions being used to make sense of social groupings. But on the other hand we also use forms of intelligence which appear to have evolved to cope with social interaction between humans to make sense of the natural world. In other words, we 'anthropomorphise' nature through 'cognitive fluidity', through the merging and transposition of different kinds of thought process. And we all know that many semantic domains overlap not simply in the way they are used to describe another, but in their empirical content. One striking example of this is the essential unity and continuity of natural and supernatural, of visible and invisible forms, highlighted in the ambivalence shown by Nuaulu over the correct classification of numerous monsters in myths and stories (Ellen 1993: 176–8). Another is the impossibility of making sense of many Austronesian terms and categories for 'bird/chicken', 'mammal/meat' and 'tree/wood' without considering utilitarian and symbolic criteria.

Although there have been several attempts to force a marriage between cognitive and symbolic anthropology in the way these data would seem to require (beginning with Colby et al. 1980), all have so far met with questionable degrees of success. Those who espouse extreme formulations of the universalistic (formal)-relativist (symbolic) divide sometimes claim that they are engaged in separate kinds of endeavour, and that one body of work should not invalidate the other. This is, I think, the view which Mary Douglas has defended for the symbolists (e.g. 1993: 161–5), and Brent Berlin for the formalists. However, though I notice no inclination on the part of Douglas to shift ground in the face of recent evidence and arguments, Berlin (1992) does appear to present a moderated version of his early views in *Ethnobiological Classification*.

The truth is that we cannot keep semantic domains separate. Quite apart from anything else, no one domain can be represented in its own terms: it needs to be translated into some other domain in order to be understood. Thus metaphorical and symbolic thought are central to cognition. Given what we know about the role and dominance of the social intellect in primate evolution, it is understandable that this might have influenced classifications of the material world. Thus the material is explained in terms of the social, and the social in terms of the material. The material-social distinction is, of course, anyway empirically arbitrary, and in one sense entrenches through cognition the methodology of Cartesian dualism. Like Newtonian physics, though we know it to be ultimately a distortion, it does work sufficiently well for most of the time for us to rely upon it for practical purposes. Or to put it another way, the subjective and objective can be the same thing, depending on your position (Reyna 2002: 49): every categorical instance, every event must be understood as a simultaneity (Ardener 1989), both category and 'category'.

When we classify as humans, not only do we use codes established in one domain to make sense of another in ways which distort aspects of experience, we systematically repress or forget or ignore certain characteristics and associations of particular natural things, and exaggerate and foreground others. Any one species, entity, idea or percept presents too complex an aggregation of traits to take into account in routine practical memory storage and information handling. This is why, for example, numerical taxonomy does not provide a good model for understanding how human minds process data – it is just too multidimensional. Sometimes this simplification results in more naturalistic classifications, sometimes it results in more symbolic ones, or a combination of the two. This is very clear when we look at graphic icons for natural species in different aesthetic and writing traditions. Thus in Britain a child is likely to see a picture of a 'teddy-bear' before it sees a real bear. I think that on the whole I am rather suspicious of theories claiming that we should always try to conflate or aggregate all meanings of nature and natural things in order to achieve some inductive understanding of the whole. When we do, we often generate cognitive contradictions that pose spurious interpretative problems for those scholars seeking an overall synthesis. Perhaps it is the ability to cope with these contradictions, to separate out potentially awkward representations of the same perceptual reality, that is itself some kind of universal mechanism of the mind.

V The Biological Basis of Classification: Old and New Versions

For an earlier generation, the biology of categorisation meant only our genetic propensity to classify in particular ways, and the way in which the brain was organised to facilitate this: the legacy of Cartesian mind-body dualism (Harré 1986). Recent research has confirmed some of this. There can be little doubt, for example, that gene interactions responsible for neurobiological organisation (a) govern what Rosch (1977) calls 'cognitive economy', the propensity to store information in ways which make best use of the perceptual and cultural resources available; (b) provide templates with which to model 'fuzzy' concepts and 'core' prototypes, some of which even prompt predictable behavioural responses (see section 1.6, below); (c) permit recognition of 'animacy'; (d) allow for registration of some kinds of natural discontinuity on a pan-human level with some life-forms more salient than others; and (e) generate a repertoire of artefacts through the physiology of perception which themselves can be used to organise perceptual and symbolic data such as phosphenes (McDougall 1977).

None of this should be unexpected as our sense organs are, after all, products of an evolutionary selection process. Although such ideas had a pre-life in the work of some psychologists and animal ethologists working in the 1960s and 1970s, they were to be translated during the 1980s and 1990s into the language of modularity (Fodor 1983), whether the 'Swiss penknife' model of domain-specific modules (Barkow et al. 1992), including the derivative 'cathedral architecture' analogue developed by Steven Mithen (1996), or the memetic theories of others inspired by Dawkins (1976). Whereas previous commentators treated apparent biological predispositions as discrete emanations of general intelligence, the modularists sort to group them into generic kinds of cognition (e.g. intuitive physics, natural history intelligence, social cognition) which themselves reflected neurobiological organisation. The difficulty for anthropologists and psychologists alike here has been in identifying cultural and cognitive traits of sufficient discreteness to be accepted as unitary modules or memes in the first place, and the ways in which the human mind unhelpfully interferes with the conventional forces of selection by reforming such units, linking them together in novel ways and attributing to them new (and sometimes contradictory) linkages and meanings (Aunger 2000). If natural history knowledge – say – is a meme, and if Bruner (1996: 101) is correct in his claim that the intersubjective, the actional and the normative probably all have biological roots in the genome, then science and folk, or indigenous, knowledge are cognitively closer than we might think.

Anthropological interest in neurobiology, rather than cognitive or evolutionary psychology, has been minimal until the last decade, when new technologies for viewing the living brain have generated more interest in the link between social action, cultural constructs and physiological processes. One figure whose work was seriously in advance of other developments, but who has been otherwise marginalised, is Robin Fox. Fox is a British-trained social anthropologist, much influenced by the work of animal ethologists and the early neo-Darwinian sociobiology, who also found inspiration in the late work of Victor Turner (1983). Fox begins with the anthropological truism that a major characteristic of humankind is the formulation of rules about things which are crucial to effective reproductive strategies – food, sex and violence – and that we need to categorise collectively useful behavioural tendencies in order to interact socially. He argues that we do this by reinforcing category boundaries through the use of emotional resources. Fox accepts the neurological hypothesis that this is an engagement between the prefrontal cortex and the limbic system through the hippocampus (Fox 1986: 32; also 1980: 194). Drawing on the work of Mark, Ervin, Winson and their associates, Fox (1980: 253, n.19) notes that one function of the hippocampus is short-term memory processing, and that people with lesions in this part of the brain cannot remember anything from one moment to next and live in an 'eternal present'. But the hippocampus is also involved in long-term memory storage, and those with lesions can still remember things they learned much earlier. It seems that a three-year cycle is necessary for experiences to enter long-term memory, but once they are entered they are resistant to loss (Fox 1986: 35), reinforced through slow-wave rapid eye movement (REM) sleep which we associate with dreaming. Items assembled in the prefrontal cortex are repeatedly 'rehearsed' by passing them through the limbic system, which is also the centre for emotional facilitation and control. Dreaming, it is suggested, triggers biochemical changes at 'neuronal gates'.

Through this mechanism, logical statements such as '1 + 1 = 2' are emotionally reinforced through notions of 'rightness'. Similarly, a tendency to right-handedness is amplified strongly by cultural stories about right being good and left being bad. In other words, 'is' statements become 'ought' statements: emotion reinforces rules (Skoyles and Sagan 2002: 133; Holland and Quinn 1987). The crucial distinctions of social classification, such as whether something can be eaten or not, or whether something is dangerous or not, are therefore established physically through changes in the size and shape of synapses. No wonder we react with anxiety (even pain) to threats to our classifications. More challengingly, Fox (1979: 136) also argues, this time drawing upon the inspiration of componential analysis and Lévi-Strauss's structuralism, that such mechanisms are sufficient to cope with the complexities of kinship categories. This is because, of the ninety-four combinatory types possible, surprisingly few actually occur, and because logically the minimal elements necessary to generate the possibilities are few in number (generation, sex, affinity, collaterality, bifurcation and polarity).

What Fox had discovered was a theory of 'cognitive fluidity', which contrasted markedly with the modular theories that were to become more influential but are really too rigid to account for what we now know, especially given the short time-scale of human evolution. He was able to demonstrate a plausible way in which social intelligence could make sense of natural difference, and vice versa, and of how mental processes of individual humans might derive from collective social processes. In this he even appeared to reconcile psychology with Durkheimian collective consciousness (Fox 1980: 183, 188; cf. Skoyles and Sagan 2002: 134–5), to show how a cognitive model might provide a mechanism for integrating shared patterns of acquired behaviour (Donald 1993: 9).

The neurobiological work which so stimulated Fox has subsequently grown into a more widely held view of cortical function as an emergent phenomenon, rather than as hard-wired cyto-architectonic circuitry (Donald 1993: 5). Current work suggests that cognitive fluidity is materially rooted in neural plasticity (Buonomo and Merzenich 1998; Skoyles and Sagan 2002: 26–7), that is, in the capacity of neurons to change the spatial and volume location in the brain devoted to particular functions, to undertake new, reordered functions and activities during development, or in response to changed environmental stimuli (for example, following injury, disease or pain). This is, in effect, a theory of neuronal group selection (Edelman 1992), in which software routines are programmed and continually reprogrammed by each of us extrasomatically. Although such 'mindware' (Skoyles and Sagan 2002: 21) of the prefrontal cortex is particularly important in modulating, coordinating and organising routines originating elsewhere in the cortex, some cognitive functions (e.g. language) historically associated with certain regions, are most likely distributed throughout the 'triune' brain (MacLean 1973), that is, between its ontogenetically reptilian, mammalian and neocortical components.

Such mindware 'booting' may occur through play or, for language acquisition, through an infant repeating overheard sounds, the meaning of which can be explored in later verbal exchanges. The human brain is at its most receptive to this kind of moulding during the first ten years of life, but retains much flexibility throughout life. Thus, through social experience, the human brain is quite literally 'enculturated': culture constraining and actively restructuring the brain (Donald 1993: 14) by configuring the arrangement of neurons, as much as the brain constraining and determining culture. It therefore follows – and this is the radical implication for a comparative anthropology – that since the potential input is highly localised, culture colonises the brain in different ways in different places. Our understanding of this process of individual neural enculturation has itself borrowed from observations of somatic processes of cultural selection and simplification. Thus for some, neuronal selection is comparable to the way in which a child establishes competence in a native language by selecting an appropriate phonemic infrastructure from the vast array of biologically phonetic possibilities. And the fact that such a process of 'syllabic attrition' is as evident in learning birdsong as in human speech acquisition (Changeux 1985) suggests that the mechanism is phylogenetically widespread and therefore probably primitive from an evolutionary standpoint.

What I have just described constitutes the basis for 'neuroanthropology' or 'neurohermeneutic theories of culture', espoused by, amongst others, Reyna (2002: 13, 156, 180), and Whitehouse (2001). In its most recent form these draw largely on the inspired synthesis of Edelman (1992), but also owe much to, for example, Changeux. The central idea is of selection pressure being exercised over epigenetic neuronal development to produce a distinctive topobiology and neuroanatomy, which then serves as the basis for experiential selection resulting in actual rather than potential synaptic connections. This in turn allows for 're-entrant mapping', the interactive process between firing patterns which coordinates different parts of the brain involved in perception, some patterns being reinforced through experience, while others are weakened or eliminated. In such a model, 'classification of the environment is not a process of *instruction* (as in conventional cognitivism) but of *selection*' (Edelman 1992: 210). Edelman (p. 211) uses the example of an automaton which distinguishes objects with characteristic A and objects with characteristic B, which through a process of experiential selection can learn to distinguish those which are both A and B and those that are just A or just B. In this model, categorisation therefore involves a minimal unit of two functionally different maps connected by re-entry, though they may separately receive signals. Over time, re-entrant signalling strongly connects active combinations of neuronal groups in one map with those in another, through the strengthening and weakening of the synapses, establishing a 'dynamic loop' (pp. 87–9) that continually matches a percept's characteristics (for example, the gestures and postures of an animal) to the independent sampling of several kinds of sensory signal. As with Fox's borrowing from an earlier generation of neurobiologists, 'an emotionally stimulating configuration of firing patterns has a greater chance of being repeated than a neutral configuration'. Categorical decisions are consequently based on 'the statistics of signal correlations' over time (p. 90), and interpretation might be said to operate simultaneously with classification (Reyna 2002: 112). This process can be elaborated at the non-neurological level as one of cognitive 'resonance', whereby bodies of cultural data, schemata and cultural models tend to harmonise or modify over time through mutual interaction in contexts of use.

An important part of the mechanism linking the cultural with the cognitive involves the role of memory, which for Edelman (1992: 102) 'is the specific enhancement of a previously established ability to categorise'. Following Tulving (1983), it has now become conventional to distinguish episodic from semantic memory, the difference between the remembering of past events, and remembering cultural rules and the meaning of abstract concepts, including their linguistic manifestations. In one sense, the establishment of categories in the brain is ultimately rooted in particular experiential events, but over time the brain works on the episodic real-time data to generate semantic memories through the kinds of mechanism discussed so far in this section. Although our first perceptions of a particular segment of the world are often stored in deep memory and inevitably influence our perception of the same or similar stimulus on a subsequent occasion, memory (semantic as much as episodic) is a work of 'imaginative reconstruction' (Bartlett 1932). It is unlikely, therefore, that we can understand perception independent of previously accumulated mental images (that is, cultural representations), not only those which we store in individual brains but also those distributed (through multiple brains and artifacts) in intersubjective space. The alarming consequence of this idea is therefore that when we think we 'see' something, our first impressions at least are highly influenced by previous occasions when we have seen the same or a similar stimulus. Most of what we sense, interpret, say, or do, such as linguistic utterance, is unconscious: for most of the time we are on 'automatic pilot'. The 'act' of perception is like joining up the dots in a children's puzzle, and every act of perception involves a central role for this kind of imagination, which is no more than drawing on reserves of memory and socially distributed information to interpret a present sensory experience. Indeed, we now know that the areas of the brain used in imagining are identical to those areas involved in actual sensing or doing, though imagination may require more blood and energy (Skoyles and Sagan 2002: 36). And this role of imagination is not by any means restricted to categorical perception. We imagine what others feel about us, and we imagine amputated limbs as if they were there. Since that memory will make all kinds of connections between phenomena with degrees of resemblance, whether perceived at first hand or acquired from someone else, one can see how imagination easily connects the symbolic with the material.

The danger in such persuasive theories as these, which at last seem to have achieved the anthropological Holy Grail of linking cultural particulars with neurophysiological process, which seem to provide a justification for epigenetic permissiveness, is that they reduce everything to neuronal firing patterns. It is important to remember that while biology is not just about genetic propensities, neither is cultural cognition just about brains. Quite apart from anything else, genes are not equal in what they express phenotypically. They influence the process of ontogenetic development and phenotypic expression through complex organism-environment interaction (Ingold 2001: 121–5), while the human genome project has revealed that it is not the number of genes which is important so much as the number of combinatory possibilities achieved during neoteny. Indeed, what engages with the environment to generate classificatory activity is not just the brain but the body. We experience not the world but interaction with the world through our bodies (Bateson 1973), and the materiality of the human body presents us with the context in which classification works. Indeed, a brain without sensory and motor interfaces cannot possibly have consciousness. While we have a genetic propensity towards right-hand asymmetry which is amplified culturally, right and left asymmetry are also influenced by our direct experience of living in a particular three-dimensional world (Needham 1973; McManus 2003); the very shape of the body and our disposition towards the principle of symmetry directs the selection of anatomical semiotica (Chapter 5); part-whole schemas originate in bodily experience; and the zero-to-infinity principle is attributable in part to the canonical forward posture and upright movement of human beings (Clark 1973). Thus categorisation and classification are embodied and experienced, not just imposed or constructed (Edelman 1992: 236; Skoyles and Sagan 2002: 162–3): they proceed as synesthetic processes, combining all our senses (Varela, Thompson and Rosch 1993: 172–7).

Thus in the new neurobiology brains do not come pre-equipped with tight genetic specifications, hard-wiring or modules for classifying the world, for acquiring grammars in terms of the memorability of representations, or for any other mental function; rather, they have 'a mass of ever-changing circuitry' which is capable of endlessly creating new maps (and new configurations of maps). Genes work *with* neural plasticity, as revealed, for example, in twin studies, by laying down the basic linkages rather than the detailed blueprints. Put slightly differently, our brains 'are programmed for nothing except to explore the potentialities of our bodies and environments via a process of learning by neuronal group selection' (Edelman 1992: 212); they are 'programmed to get us programmed'

(Skoyles and Sagan 2002: 34–5). Moreover, the brain is continuously recategorising data, and although such brain-based memory is inexact and probabilistic when compared with, say, computers and other cultural artefacts, it is capable of great degrees of generalization (Edelman 1992: 102–4), making theories of cognitive semantics, such as those of Lakoff, more consistent with current neurological research, than the deep structures of Chomsky. And since the most stimulating aspects of the human environment are social, we must 'envisage all processes of transmission in terms that are simultaneously sociological, psychological and neurological (Whitehouse 2001: 217)'.

VI The Evolution of Hominid Categorisation Processes

We have evidence for neuronal plasticity and for the 'flexible learning' that it permits in the simplest of organisms (Ridley 2003), and may reasonably conclude that the kinds of processes explored in the previous section have a long evolutionary history. However, it is the macroscopic organisation of the brain found in much higher chordates which made possible both the increasing use of cultural transmission, and categorical thinking. It is the macroscopic organisation of the brain which, fortunately, we can trace through fossil evidence. Nevertheless, we can reasonably infer that as the reptilian brain gave rise to the old mammalian 'limbic' brain, and through it the new mammalian 'cortical' brain, so new parts were not simply added, but more elaborate functions emerged which connected the microanatomy of all existing structures.

As far as we know, non-human animals do not consistently construct categories in a way we would instantly recognise; even less so do they classify. However, we have already noted some of the evidence for genetically encoded image prototypes in non-human vertebrates which trigger characteristic behavioural responses, such as aversion behaviour with respect to predator-like images. It has even been suggested that such behaviours; which evolved early in the evolution of terrestrial vertebrates; have left traces in highly encultured human categories: for example, 'dragons' imaginatively combine the prototypical aversion characteristics of three types of predator which threatened early humans: big cats, big snakes and raptors (Jones 2002). More prosaically, Herrnstein (1985) performed a much-reported set of experiments on pigeons that were shown pictures of all kinds of trees, as well as trees in different contexts, and could selectively differentiate these from non-trees (see also Cheney and Seyfarth 1990: 87). As discrimination did not appear to be based on a single set of perceptual criteria, the experiments are usually interpreted as providing evidence for the existence of a concept of 'treeness' as a general cognitive prototype, an idea which has been subsequently explored further (Orians and Heerwagen 1992: 4559). In the realm of social intelligence too, non-human primate studies yield evidence that individuals can classify others according to their pattern of association (Cheney and Seyfarth 1990: 86). Comparative studies of different species of non-human primates have now demonstrated the cognitive importance of an ability to compose two or more objects into sets, in other words to achieve minimal classifying, though they have yet to show good evidence of more advanced hierarchic cognitions such as comprehensive taxonomising, or of developing synchronically with notions of causality (Langer 1993). For Premack (1983; Cheney and Seyfarth 1990: 88) abstract categories require the kind of language training which some chimpanzees have undergone, while other chimps can achieve the same end using an 'imaginal' code. Chimpanzees can also classify functionally, as well as according to perceptual criteria, grouping, for example, pips and fruit rather than apples and pears (Premack 1976, 1986; Cheney and Seyfarth 1990), though it is still unclear whether these kinds of operation are realised in routine behaviours in natural settings, or are simply pre-adapted potential evident in experimental situations only. Nevertheless, we can be sure, as suggested by Fox (1986: 24), that categorical thinking does not in itself separate humans from other animals, and we probably share an array of biological prompts which help us make sense of the world, combined with some more specific genetically encoded image-response patterns. The tendency to categorise the world and then act on this redefinition is itself, therefore, an evolved and ancient natural function.

In the preceding paragraph I provided undifferentiated examples of categorising from both natural history and social intelligence for non-hominids. In all apes and hominids these processes are achieved through advanced neural plasticity of the prefrontal cortex, augmented by 'fission-fusion' mind skills, and somatic sensory and motor skills (Skoyles and Sagan 2002: 77–9). Since their popularisation by Fodor, our understanding of the evolution of the hominid brain has been much influenced by modular theories (domain specificity), which stress the differential development of categorising abilities in different functionally discrete domains (language, mathematical ability, intuitive physics and so on). The evidence for this in part comes from our understanding of those brain pathologies we label autism, where certain kinds of intelligence may be very sophisticated and other cognitive skills (say those associated with social intelligence) impaired (e.g. Sacks 1995). Such approaches have allowed for a sophisticated modelling of cognitive evolution, but as we have already seen, in the light of the new neurobiology, this view of the brain, with its computational and algorithmic representation, is increasingly incompatible with what we now know of brains and bodies and how they interact with the world.

Whether or not the modular view can be sustained, we can agree that early hominid environments were more risky than they are now and that food resources were irregularly distributed, all of which exerted selective pressure in favour of ways of more efficiently using increasing numbers of kinship connections and extended social links beyond the immediate present. What Daniel Dennett has called 'the great encephalisation' was, therefore, driven by the size of social groups (Dunbar 1993), the demands of increased sociability, the need to handle social complexity (including fission and fusion of relationships), and a broad-spectrum food-getting strategy. Such an argument emphasising the selection of systems of social categories and symbolism in order to handle and maintain kin and relationship recognition over time and space, even when the relevant individuals are absent, again reminds us of Fox.

If we link these developments to what we now know of culture-brain interaction, we can see that these conditions were the forcing house for what Reyna (2002: 128) calls the 'neurohermeneutic system', which involved a shift from a predominantly episodic memorate culture to one which was predominantly mimetic, but one also reinforced and modified episodically (Donald 1993; Reyna 2002: 65). As far has we can judge from the fossil evidence, these developments took place between 2 and 0.5 million years BP, beginning at least with *Homo habilis*; and were complete with the appearance of anatomically modern humans. The ability to develop mindware based on symbolism – abstract notions which stand for other entities in non-mechanistic ways – was a capability which already characterised Lower and Middle Pleistocene *Homo erectus* groups. This phase witnessed the emergence of a more complex language capacity from proto-language of the kind displayed by chimpanzees, perhaps encouraged by sexual selection on the part of those individuals who were the most effective communicators and thereby the most adept social manipulators. Neurologically it was mirrored in the developing ability of the cortex to construct maps of its own activities, not just responding to external stimuli, and recombining these maps in different ways. Concept formation, therefore, involved percept categorisation, adjusted by the memory of previous similar perceptual events (resemblance), and augmented by learning, language and intention (Skoyles and Sagan 2002: 109–10). Even language competence itself, Edelman (1992: 129) suggests, emerges through a self-learning process that he calls 'semantic bootstrapping', in which as a lexicon grows and sentences are experienced the categorisation of the experience leads to syntax.

In understanding how somatically distributed and shared cognition evolved, the palaeo-skeletal evidence is helpfully biased, for, after the brain, no organ has been subject to as much debate concerning its role in hominisation as the hand. We have already noted that other parts of the body are integral to the process of cognition, and that category mechanisms work through a kind of mapping which necessarily involves our bodies and our personal histories (Edelman 1992: 152). But the evolution of the hand, and with it the tool, brought about a transformation in the relationship between hominids and their own body, a greater level of physical self-awareness and sense of self. The whole human organism became, as it were, an instrument to solve problems, establishing an exponential 'virtuous circle of self-consciousness and agency' which was to drive cognitive evolution thereafter (Tallis 2003).

With the appearance of the first anatomically modern humans, around 130,000 years ago, mindware networks had evolved a potential to encompass abstract processes, operations and extended symbolic systems, the manipulation of which enables individuals to carry out complex operations, greatly enhancing cognitive power. For Skoyles and Sagan (2002) symbols are not just 'propagated arbitrary associations' but 'active shapers of the very substrate by which we act, think and feel. Symbols, working together with our prefrontal cortex and neural plasticity, transform our minds and the character of our consciousness.' The uncontestable evidence for this transformation first appears with the technological specialisation, art and decoration of the Upper Palaeolithic, though there is recent African evidence suggesting that it may have begun much earlier, or at least that the potential for such developments could be much older.

The development of second-order representations, images of images, is certainly crucial. The generalisation of percepts until this point was in the form of material inscriptions only in the minds of individual humans. The abilities to first describe those images to others through language, and secondly to materially inscribe visual representations graphically, were to have a profound consequence because they allowed people to share those same images – brains could communicate with other brains in ways that had not been previously possible. The integration of abstract concepts through socially transmitted visual and other categorical images involved processes of cognitive simplification, reification, iconification and anthropomorphisation, and new kinds of explicit rules to maximise shared understanding. Put in diachronic evolutionary terms, this is essentially the same logical and ontogenetic model developed in Chapter 9 below to account for the process by which categories become more detached from the percepts which initially prompted them, through constant reinforcement by engagement with the material world, achieved through mapping one thing on to another in a different domain. The influence of the acquisition of effective language made classifying much easier but more arbitrary, enforcing boundaries and the general rule-governed dimension.

VII Changing Category Systems in Anatomically Modern Humans

Classifying behaviour, as it evolved in early anatomically modern humans, was the consequence of practical engagement in everyday life, constantly reinforced by experience. Its adaptiveness stemmed from the multiplicity of ways it could reorganise perceptual data and from the redundancy built into this process. The classifications which resulted were fluid and negotiable, produced as well as reproduced. As we know from contemporary ethnographic studies, although particular kinds of empirical knowledge might focus on particular individuals and might achieve a degree of coherence in rituals and other symbolic constructs, the distribution of classificatory knowledge is always fragmentary. It does not exist in its totality in any one place or individual, despite the extraordinary oral encyclopaedism of the likes of Alonso Ton Mendez (Berlin 2003) or Saem Majnep (Marcus 1991). Indeed, to a considerable extent classificatory knowledge has become increasingly devolved not in individuals at all, but in cultural artefacts, and in the practices and interactions in which people themselves engage.

Because we know that people vary in the consistency with which they label and use categories, in the degree to which they share both labels and categories within a given population and deploy names and categories flexibly in response to particular cues and contexts, it is obvious that they are in a constant state of change. We now have good descriptions of how classifications change in the short-term through category extension (as reflected in, for example, lexical marking behaviour), category obsolescence, the way ranks grow in particular ways, and how new life forms are added to natural history knowledge (Berlin 1972; Brown 1984). But for as long as classifications were oral and shared they were constantly being reinforced by cognitive limitations of the brain and body. Johnson-Laird (1982), for example, claims that storing knowledge as causal hypotheses (or models) is efficient because humans (and we might add, relying on oral culture and low levels of division of labour) do not have sufficient memory to make the right responses by induction alone.

Specialisation, the creation of visual images, and the written word permitted the long-term storage of classifications, which were not limited by (even distributed) memory, and could be manipulated in new ways. Social distribution of knowledge and increasing specialisation led to specific semantic domains and classifications having a semi-autonomous history of their own, and to the 'emergent' generation of categories within a completely cultural framework unconstrained by ecological experience and cognitive limitations. Folk classifications generally organise knowledge which is orally transmitted, that is through imitation and demonstration. The corollary of this is that writing it down changes some of its fundamental properties. Writing, of course, also makes it more portable and permanent, reinforcing the dislocation that arises when knowledge rooted in a particular place and set of experiences (i.e. local or indigenous), and generated by people living in those places, is transferred to other places (see Chapter 2). Thus, 'lion' could be imagined as a category and transmitted between generations even where lions had never existed; and people could agree on categories even where there was apparent disagreement over descriptions of what were to be put in them. Consider, for example, what Heppell has to say about the basilisk in medieval and early modern writings:

> descriptions and illustrations of the basilisk are abundant. There was little consensus about the basilisk's appearance. It is represented with either two or eight legs, or even none, and is sometimes winged and sometimes not. Its head resembles that of a snake, a bird, or a horse, and its tail tapers to a point, or is forked. How then does a one recognize a basilisk? (Heppell 1990: 13)

An excellent example, you might think, of a Sperberian 'half understood concept'. At the same time, culture permitted degrees of complexity in the arrangement of categories which individual brains could not cope with. Thus although in terms of global linguistic comparison there is a strong association between meat and mammal-like categories, David Knight's (1981: 25) description of the emergence of the highly culturally specific mammal life-form in European languages suggests that its ultimate acceptance as a folk concept was largely a result of the development of modern scientific taxonomy:

> in natural history, throughout the eighteenth century in Britain and in France, our own class of mammals was generally described as the quadrupeds, and indeed this was the term used by Cuvier in his great works on living and fossils mammals published in republican and Napoleonic France. Most mammals are indeed quadrupeds, but man is not and nor are seals, dolphins or whales; while on the other hand lizards and frogs are quadrupeds but not mammals. By a rather different process, the terms 'reptile', which in the eighteenth century meant anything creepy-crawly (and therefore made an excellent term of abuse), was narrowed down so as to exclude invertebrate creatures like centipedes by the end of the century. And 'amphibia' was similarly refined by the middle of the nineteenth. 'Insect' in the eighteenth century had been synonymous with 'reptile', as in Lawson's *History of Carolina*, 1709; and it still was in Victorian railway taxonomy, for Frank Buckland the naturalist found that he must pay for a monkey which counted as a 'dog', but not for a tortoise which was an 'insect'. (Knight 1981: 25)

In France, language dynamics were different. This is partly exemplified by the way in which Latin scientific names influenced French but not English vernaculars, including the priority given to genus over species in nomenclature (Haudricourt 1973). Indeed, the conflict between proponents of alternative scientific classification systems during the eighteenth and nineteenth centuries was often heated (Ritvo 1997: 1–50). But although there has been a constant interaction between general (folk) and specialist (scientific) classifications throughout history, the differences are being constantly reinvented. What are we to make, for example, of the groupings in medieval bestiaries? Are they 'special-purpose' or 'general-purpose'?

Categories, then, have detailed cultural histories, which have a bearing on their current usage but which also reveal much of past classificatory practice. Thus, 'animal' is hardly used in English as a norm before the end of the sixteenth century, according to the *Oxford English Dictionary*, and is not found in the Authorised (1611) Version of the English Bible. The word used commonly before this was 'beast', and for 1513 we find under animal 'beyn contenyt all mankynd, beist, byrd, fowll, fisch, serpent, and all sik thingis'. Part of the problem faced by European folk classifications after 1500 was exposure to an increasing diversity and quantity of species which did not always fit easily into established categories based on European endemic wildlife, and in this respect European classifications faced the same problems as those routinely reported in ethnolinguistic accounts of how novel species are assigned to categories (Ritvo 1997: xiii–xiv).

To move from the sublime to the ridiculous, a rather different history is attached to the category 'adhesives'. We now live in a world where most of these are synthesised chemically, but until the 1930s all were based on natural products: 'pastes' were sticky mixtures of flour and water, 'gums' oozed from trees, 'cements' were rubber dissolved in solvents (or latterly burned clay mixed with lime) and 'glue' was a sticky solid made by boiling bones. Now we tend to call them all 'glue', or use some of the terms interchangeably for products to which they were originally never meant to apply. Such terms and categories change informally to reflect subgroup dynamics, but in some cases classification may be the subject of legislation, ecclesiastical or secular. Many famous British law cases revolve around decisions to distinguish clearly between one thing and another, for example 'male' and 'female' (Douglas 1973: 115–17). A more mundane distinction was the subject of some discussion in 1972 in the House of Commons, as a result of damage caused to trees by grey squirrels. One Member of Parliament wanted their name changed to 'tree rats' to promote a less friendly image. The idea was rejected by a Government Under Secretary on the grounds that squirrels were *Sciuromorpha* and not *Myomorpha*. In this instance, a supposedly morally neutral taxonomic legitimation was used to support a pre-existing folk classification which triumphed in the face of a morally charged but probably more useful folk innovation.

Thus the liberation of the process of category formation from cognitive and ecological constraints and their semi-autonomous development in intersubjective space led to the creation of kinds and degrees of complexity that had not hitherto been possible. But while it is evident that categories do vary in their complexity, to date little attention has been paid to how we measure this. Complexity, for example, might refer to density of content, range of content, number of distinguishing features, extent of polythesis, absence or presence of a cognitive prototype, whether a category is 'perceptual' or 'symbolic' (material or metaphysical), the degree to which members of a population share definitions, the degree to which definitions are context-bound, and the range of contexts in which a category works. In each case we must ask whether the complexity lies in the categories of the classification or within the context of the classification.

One criterion for distinguishing simple from complex categories is the type of specification required to distinguish a member (or instance) of the category. The simplest case is where a single feature is required for the distinction. More complex are multiple features. More complex still is the inclusion of optional features – x and y and z or q. In all but the latter case there is implicit subcategorisation of the first type: the presence of a category is sufficient to limit the possibilities inherent in the assignment of a case to a category. This principle of inherent subcategorisation has been amply used to justify the taxonomic type of classification, as well as the feature tree specification, the former summarising the relationships between categories in a two-dimensional format, the latter as a two-dimensional projection of an n-dimensional classification space. In these terms, a more complex type of category is one in which there is no useful subcategorisation by the use of features: the presence or absence of a particular feature value by itself yields far less than one piece of information in the classification scheme. In some sense this is true of all classification schemes, as the information inherent in the classification of features themselves is a neglected one; the act of imposing more inclusive ('higher-level') order over sets of category alternatives itself adds a large amount of information to the scheme; indeed, this is one of the reasons why we strive to produce classification schemes in the first place.

Another potential difference between 'simple' and 'complex' categories is the apparent unboundedness of the latter, in the sense that complex, symbolically derived, categories can be constructed in an enormous number of ways. If, as shown in Chapter 4, variability is apparent in 'simple' folk-zoological classifications, then it is much more so in complex ones. While complex categories might have a large number of possible cognitive forms, culturally these must conform within specific boundaries in any given context over an interval of time. While there may not be strict determinism of an individual's model of a category, use as a social device requires that a condition of structural stability must be reached; a restriction in the range of variation. Symbols must not only be constructed, they must be identifiable and identified, if not on physical precepts (such as a tree) then on symbolic ones (such as a basilisk).

VIII Distributed Models, Cognitive Process and Prehension

Early anthropological models of category formation were heavily constrained by adherence to linguistically defined entities and a language-based interpretation of how classification worked, even if formal recognition was given to the separation of category and label. This model has been described by some (e.g. Bloch 1991) as the 'linear-sentential' model of culture. With a shift away from the use of distinctive features, emphasis on core-periphery models and cognitive prototypes, and with a growth in the use of psychological approaches at the expense of linguistic ones, greater recognition has been given to how we might classify and engage with differences in the world without necessarily using language as an intermediary.

Problems arise when the process of classifying (the cultural and cognitive mechanisms by which the assignation of objects, concepts and relations to categories is achieved) is conflated with classifications (the linguistic, mental and other cultural representations which result). To speak of 'classifications' is to run the risk of reifying schemes as permanent cultural artefacts or mentally stored old knowledge, when they are more often properly understood as the spontaneous and often transient end-product of underlying processes in an individual classifying act. We might call such an error 'the classificatory fallacy' (see Chapter 2 below). In view of this, I should perhaps add that when I use the phrases 'classifying act' or 'an act of classification' here I do so purely as a rhetorical device, and I fully accept that in real life acts of classification are embedded in real situations and hardly separable from what goes before and what comes afterwards. Indeed, the 'act' may evolve, be reinforced or rescinded, over a period of time, as in, for example, drawing a person's attention to an object .

To extend this distinction, and make it more productive, it is useful to employ the model of agency and structure (structuration) which we owe in its sociological form to Anthony Giddens (e.g. 1986). Thus the relationship between classifying as a cognitive and cultural process and 'a classification' as a representation is recursive and dialectical: you cannot have one without the other. The classifying process is always situated in, and assumes some context of, previous classifications, while itself modifying the context for the next time a classifying act takes place. As this largely operates within the constraints of human culture and memory it is clearly a matter of degree, depending on the knowledgeability of the classifier, the variability of the contexts and the entities being classified (Ellen 2003a: 53, fig. 2.1).

Rather than documenting taxonomies or other kind of classification and category as so many butterflies (Leach 1961: 21), it is important to focus upon the processes which generate them – not detached cognitive processes, but those rooted in particular situations. In a review of ethnobiological classification published in 1986 (republished with modifications as pp. 229–31 of Ellen 1993) I introduced the term 'prehension' as a framework for discussing these problems.[2] Prehension, literally from the Latin *prehendere*, 'to grasp', suggests that classification is not only an act, but a process that is contextually bound: the sum total of those empirical processes determined by the interaction between knowledge, context, purpose and the cognitive architecture which give rise to particular classificatory outcomes. Prehension:

(a) refers to those processes which through various cultural and other constraints give rise to particular classifications, designations and representations;
(b) entails a process which integrates the context of the classifying activity, including the interactive interplay with others in that context (and even the elicitory techniques of an ethnographic interview), and diverse information derived from past experience;
(c) emerges from a sequence of individual 'acts' of perception, but is not (and cannot be) confined to them;
(d) is a model that can cope explicitly with imperfect processing and communication of information, and with the capacity of humans to adapt and modify their store of information and the interrelations between that information;
(e) suggests that there can be no adequate model of classification that attempts to separate the structure of classification from its context and content.

Whereas cognition and perception suggest purely cerebral processes, prehension recognises, without the necessity of qualification, the difficulty of distinguishing mind from matter, thinking from doing or speaking, individual from group, cerebral from social, natural from cultural. Category formation and classifying behaviour are inherently adaptive processes, and must incorporate facilities for relating those instances of the present with those of the past, but provide a structure of stability over a context of chaos. All of this echoes Varela, Thompson and Rosch (1993: 173), who emphasise how sensory and motor processes, perception and action, are fundamentally inseparable in lived cognition, having coevolved. They argue that 'mind and the world together arise in *enaction* [italics added], [though] their manner of arising in any particular situation is not arbitrary' (p. 177); while knowledge, located at 'the interface between mind, society, and culture, rather than in one or even in all of them ... does not preexist in any one place or form but is enacted in particular situations' (p. 179). Classificatory engagement with the physical world involves not only interlection but sensation (to use an Ingoldian distinction); and prehension involves the whole person as he or she moves around the world in space and time.

We can only begin to approach a realistic understanding of categorisation and classifying behaviour if we begin by observing people assigning items to categories and using names in natural ethnographic settings as well as in experimental ones. People bring to situations in which classifying activity takes place, and from which verbal statements about classifying behaviour result, information of diverse kinds acquired through both informal and formal socialisation experience, of the world in general and of earlier classifying situations. How they then classify depends upon the interplay of this past knowledge (including prescriptions and preferences with regard to particular cognitive and linguistic idioms) with the material constraints of the classifying situation, between conscious and subconscious, the purposes of the classifying act, and the inputs of others. Thus thinking, saying and doing are not separate activities but interpenetrating ones, while the same cognitive bricolage provides us with both models 'of' and models 'for' in terms of Geertz's (1966) distinction. Classifications of all kinds connect culture, psychology and perceptual discontinuities of the concrete world, and as we can now see, also aspects of brain organisation through neural plasticity. Confusion has arisen in the past from failure to distinguish clearly between individual instruments of cognitive process and the collective medium in which these operate, comprising belief, cultural representations and social practice, between information storage and representation, and between abstract knowledge of the world and the pragmatic schemata we use to negotiate our way through it. Our propensity to classify in the ways we do certainly involves the possession of innate cognitive skills, but is mainly an ability to organise our perceptions through culture (aided by language) based on models drawn from somatic experience, and from social and perceptual experience of the material world. The form a particular classification takes will sometimes be a culturally defined whole, but as often as not will be the outcome of interaction in particular circumstances – the interplay of past knowledge, material context and social inputs. Classifications as *things*, therefore, are not the inventions of individuals, but arise through the historically contingent character of cultural transmission, linguistic constraints, metaphorical extensions and shared social experience in relation to individual cognitive practice.

Notes

1. This chapter includes material first developed in 'How complex are complex cultural categories? Distributed and global models in cognitive anthropology', presented with Michael Fischer at a Cambridge seminar organised by Pascal Boyer in 1990. Some of the text also draws on Ellen 2003, and Ellen 2003a.
2. For a somewhat different use of the same term see Tallis (2003: 32–43, 279), for whom 'modes of prehension' appears to refer quite explicitly to the range of sensory and cognitive implications following from the evolved human hand, between manipulative function and the growth of intelligence.

CHAPTER 2

Anthropological Studies of Classification (1996)

A short introduction to the subject offering some basic definitions and explaining differences between symbolic classifications which articulate social space-time, symbolic classifications which order non-social phenomena, non-symbolic means of organising social space and non-symbolic means of ordering non-social phenomena. The usefulness and problems associated with such a typology are addressed.

Introduction

Classification is that activity in which objects, concepts and relations are assigned to categories; classifying is the cognitive and cultural mechanism by which this is achieved; and classifications are the linguistic, mental, and other cultural representations which result. Problems arise when the adjectival and nominal status of the root 'class' are conflated. This reifies schemes as permanent cultural artifacts or mentally stored old knowledge, when they are more properly understood as the spontaneous and often transient end-product of underlying processes in an individual 'classifying act'. We might call such a misinterpretation 'the classificatory fallacy', and there is every reason to believe that it is potentially evident whenever anthropologists try to make sense of their data, whether these be tables of symbolic oppositions, animal folk taxonomies or kinship relationship terminologies.

We cannot think about the world unless we assign it to categories. Categories also help us act within the world, but are probably not essential to all kinds of activity. It is a matter for debate whether categories for thinking and for acting differ. The discussion which follows concerns classifications as objects of intellectual scrutiny (for the most part, folk classifications) rather than the classifications which anthropologists use to order their data, though these latter are ultimately subject to the same generalisations.

Ways of Classifying the World

Classification as an object of anthropological analysis effectively begins with the publication of *Primitive Classification* by Durkheim and Mauss in 1901–2. This work (almost as if in passing) establishes a distinction between 'mundane' (technical, descriptive) and 'symbolic' (ritual, explanatory) schemes which well-reflects, and partly determined, the subsequent history of classification studies. Before going any further it will be helpful to examine this distinction.

Humans classify the world about them by matching perceptual images, words and concepts (Ohnuki-Tierney 1981: 453). The operations work equally in terms of unmodified sense data or their cultural representations. The cognitive and cultural tools available to do this do not distinguish between the social world and the non-social world, though in the analysis of classification this has become a conventional distinction. Similarly, classification can treat its subject in a pragmatic and mundane way or by using various symbolic allusions. Since so much of what we sense and experience is mediated by social consciousness, and since the boundary between the mundane and symbolic is often unclear, it has sometimes been difficult, in practice, to know where to divide these two axes. It may help to set out the dimensions as a matrix:

	Social	<——————>	Non-social
Symbolic	1		2
Mundane	3		4

Classifications of type 1 involve the use of symbolic devices to partition and articulate social space and time: the use of material objects to represent wife-givers and receivers in certain kinship systems, or the punctuation of time through significant ritual events, are good examples of these. Classifications of type 2 use symbols to make sense of non-social space, as in representations of the cardinal directions in Javanese thought by colours (Pigeaud 1977). Classifications of type 3 include descriptive ways of partitioning social space, as with pronouns and kinship terminologies. Classifications of type 4 include much of what passes for biological classification, including Linnaean scientific schemes. The distinctions cannot always be neatly drawn: symbolic things are in an important sense practical, and practical classifications of the non-social world often rely on metaphors which are ultimately social, as in the use of the terms 'genus' and 'family' to organise plants and animals. Attempts to bring these aspects of classifying behaviour together have met with varying degrees of success. Those who espouse extreme formulations of the universalist (practical)–relativist (symbolic) divide sometimes claim that they are engaged in separate kinds of endeavour, and that one body of work should not invalidate the other. On the other hand, some have stressed the empirical connections between the two, and envisage an ultimate convergence of cognitive and symbolic anthropology (Colby et al. 1980). The distinctions are entrenched and not wholly avoidable. Here I first discuss some general principles of categorisation and then examine mundane and symbolic schemes separately.

Principles of Categorisation

Categories may be constructed either by reference to their semantic focus, their boundaries or some combination of the two. In the first case, focus is based on some exemplary instance or cognitive prototype (Rosch 1977): thus a sparrow is a focal member of the category 'bird'. Other instances may be non-focal (peripheral) members of their category: as with 'emu', an egg-laying feathered biped which does not fly, and is described in English as a 'bird'. But not all content assigned to categories consists of physical things. Content may include attributes (colour, sound, shape, size ...) and abstractions such as time. The visual sense, however, is dominant and there is a tendency to objectivise even the most intangible. The difficulties of assigning things to categories may be made easier by imposing culturally agreed boundaries. Because parts of our experience of the world are complexly continuous, it is occasionally necessary to impose boundaries to produce categories at all.

Many categories are 'monothetic', meaning that the defining set of features is always unique, either coded in some binary way or in terms of the clustering of criteria. Others are 'polythetic': single features being neither essential to group membership nor sufficient to allocate an item to a group. It may seem, therefore, that categories vary according to the complexity of their definition, rather than simply the scope of their content. Many social categories are held to be complex in this sense, though the fact that they are often vague and general (as in Polynesian *tabu*) might also suggest that they are semantically primitive.

The relationship between categories and words varies, although the overall developmental primacy of categories over labels is now generally accepted. Language exists within culture and society, but determines the outer parameters of neither. This highlights a major methodological impediment in the study of classification: we rely on language data as the main way of discovering classification, yet words do not always provide an accurate guide. One of the most obvious disjunctions between language and classification is represented by the existence of unlabelled or covert categories. We know that these exist at various degrees of inclusiveness. Thus, many languages have no words for 'plant', yet there is plenty of evidence to suggest that the category exists. Similarly, many varieties of rice may be recognised by a people who do not consistently label them.

Any consideration of the internal structuring of categories quickly merges into a consideration of how categories relate to one another. In many cases the definition of any one category must be understood in relation to others ('black, white'): the part must be related to the whole. What this whole is need not always be clearly distinguished, as in the case where polythetic criteria apply. In some situations the whole may simply be two categories which mutually define each other; in others more inclusive and complex classificatory space which we describe as a 'semantic' (or 'cognitive') domain. Some domains are defined by their physical boundaries, such as a house or the human body. Here the internal classificatory architecture is 'analytic' in the sense that it decomposes a greater physical whole. The terms which label categories in such classifications are called 'partonyms' ('windows', 'doors'; 'arms', 'legs'). Other domains are culturally and cognitively derived from perceived shared resemblances. These we can call 'synthetic', and are exemplified by domains such as 'animals' and 'plants'. Some are clearly defined emically (that is, articulated by local people themselves), others are vague, and it is here that anthropologists are most tempted to impose etic (that is, scientific or analytic) distinctions, either through ignorance or convenience. Knowing whether or not to treat kinship categories apart from other social deietics represents a problem of this kind.

The organisation of categories within a domain may vary. Many can be represented in terms of 'class inclusion' and contrast, that is, as 'taxonomies'. In other cases non-hierarchical models are more appropriate. Brent Berlin (1992) has consistently argued in favour of the universality of taxonomy for ethnobiological schemes, but this only works if you also assert the separation of general-purpose from special-purpose schemes, that is, those that are logical and 'natural' from those that arise to meet the needs of particular cultural requirements. Despite its prevalence, the principle of taxonomy is better represented among some populations than others. Its effective demonstration depends on the extent of linkage between categories in (often flexible) ways, which undermine implicit taxonomic levels and contrasts and the general-purpose/special-purpose distinction. It also depends upon the ease with which ethnographers can elicit transitivity statements (*a* is a *b* and *b* is a *c*, therefore *a* is a *c*).

Mundane Schemes

The systematic analysis of mundane schemes was first initiated during the 1950s, and in its formative phase is associated with ethnoscience methodologies (e.g. Sturtevant 1964). It is typified by a rigorous formal analysis of semantic domains. Early work emphasised the role of distinctive features in the allocation of things to categories and class inclusion as the means of ordering segregates. More recent work has shown a preference for core-periphery models and cognitive prototypes. The kinds of classificatory schemes analysed in this way have been varied (colour, disease types, firewood, soil, and so on), though most work has focused on ethnobiological schemes. The model for work of this kind was established by Harold Conklin and later Brent Berlin. Their pioneering studies have been swiftly followed by much attention to the evolution of such schemes, the examination of their underlying taxonomic character, regularities in the order of appearance of different degrees of inclusiveness (ranks), and in the order of appearance of life-forms. Much of this work has sought to show the extent to which folk and scientific categories correspond and the relationship between features of a classification and kinds of society. It has also addressed the proposition that plant and animal categories at a particular classificatory level are more salient (basic) than others and have a logical primacy, though there is some dispute as to whether this operates at a consistent level between different natural kinds and across cultures.

Symbolic Schemes

Symbolic classification occurs when we use some things as a means of saying something about other things, such as when totemic species stand for different social groups. It serves to express formally metaphysical and cosmological speculation, and may be translated into technical procedures which permit the efficacious manipulation of the world, as in ritual and divination. Symbols enhance the significance of important categories, such as those involved in social control ('prohibited, non-prohibited'). In this sense, categories imply rules and rules imply categories.

The study of symbolic classification embarked upon by Durkheim and Mauss was given new impetus in the 1960s by the work of Lévi-Strauss and a group of influential British anthropologists, notably Edmund Leach (1964), Mary Douglas (1973) and Rodney Needham (1979). This work emphasised the centrality of 'binary opposition' (dualism, polarity) as a principle of social thought. With this basic human organising idea, best exemplified by the oppositions 'right' and 'left', 'male' and 'female', the elements are usually complementary but sometimes ambiguously asymmetric. Binary opposition is reflected in symbolic schemes where even numbers above two are used as an organising principle. Classifications partitioning semantic space by three may also be important, as in the colour triad (red-white-black) (Turner 1966) or in dual classifications where a third (mediating) element has been added. Classification based on the principle of five is exemplified by the Javanese division of the cosmos into four cardinal directions plus a mediating centre (Pigeaud 1977). Here, each dimension integrates a large number of different levels of experience (time, colour, state of mind, number, and so on). The case illustrates another pervasive feature of symbolic classification, namely analogy, which explicitly occurs in some cultural genres as semantic parallelism (Fox 1975). Apart from opposition and analogy, symbolic schemes often display principles of transition (as in marking rites of passage), exchange and transformation (such as the inversion of left and right in the interpretative logic of the Javanese shadow-play). Transformation is often a way of signifying the ambiguous, which may also be marked by anomaly. Anomalies are a means by which significant differences can be highlighted (as in the categories underlying Jewish dietary laws). However, boundaries are not always considered dangerous or polluting, and anomalies are not a necessary result of classificatory process.

Conclusion

While some symbolic classifications strongly reflect social groupings (binary opposition and dual organisation, quaternary schemes and Kariera marriage section systems), the view that all classification (or even symbolic classification) finds its roots in social institutions is now generally considered untenable. Certain features of symbolic classification may evolve autonomously, reflecting underlying general principles of cognition. What is always striking is the consistent multivocality and economy of symbols, the same oppositions occurring again and again, amongst different peoples.

Classifications of all kinds connect culture, psychology and perceptual discontinuities of the concrete world. Confusion has arisen in the past from failure to distinguish clearly between individual instruments of cognitive process and the collective medium in which these operate, comprising belief, cultural representations and social practice. It is also crucial to distinguish information storage from representation, abstract knowledge of the world and the pragmatic schemata we use to negotiate our way through it. Our propensity to classify in the ways we do results from the possession of certain innate cognitive skills (some of which we share with non-human primates), plus an ability to organise our perceptions through culture (aided by language) based on models drawn from somatic experience (such as right and left and bodily rhythms), and from social and perceptual experience of the material world. The form a particular classification takes will sometimes be a culturally defined whole, but often as not will be the outcome of interaction in particular circumstances: the interplay of past knowledge, material context and social inputs. Classifications as things, therefore, are not the inventions of individuals, but arise through the historically contingent character of cultural transmission, linguistic constraints, metaphorical extensions, and shared social experience in relation to individual cognitive practice.

CHAPTER 3

Classifying in its Social Context (1979)

A pioneer attempt to document the differences between symbolic (social constructivist) and formal universalist-evolutionist approaches to understanding classification. Notions such as arbitrariness, expression of inclusiveness, and structural complexity are introduced and the problems of comparative study explored. A critique of each tradition is offered and proposals are made to reconcile them, in part by shifting the emphasis from classifications to classifying.

> Throughout nature, wherever man strives to acquire knowledge he finds himself under the necessity of using special methods, 1st, to bring order among the infinitely numerous and varied objects which he has before him; 2nd, to distinguish, without danger of confusion, among this immense multitude of objects, either groups of those in which he is interested, or particular individuals among them; 3rd, to pass on to his fellows all that he has learnt, seen and thought on the subject. Now the methods which he uses for this purpose are what I call the *artificial devices* in natural science, – devices which we must beware of confusing with the laws and acts of nature herself. (Lamarck 1963: 19)

I

The above quotation, drawn from the *Zoolological Philosophy* of Jean-Baptiste Pierre Antoine de Monet de Lamarck, indicates succinctly a perennial problem in anthropology: the confusion of the order of nature with that imposed upon it by humans. It is a problem which it shares with other sciences, but (as with sociology) is posed in a uniquely complex way. Historically, the problem of classifications in anthropology arose from the desire to assign physical and social humanity to groups arranged both spatially and through time. Underlying this has generally been some kind of evolutionary paradigm. The objections to such an enterprise are legion, but they commonly revolve around the accusation of stasis, the legitimacy of particular defining characteristics and categories, and the errors which arise from the assumption that groups with similar characteristics have a common origin. But whatever the complaint and however vigorous the assault, such classifications persist and for some workers remain a supreme objective. This is because they cannot be explained simply as indications of the primitive development of a science: they persist because they are necessary.

While we may defend classification as the logical prerequisite of comparison, generalisation and explanation, it is difficult to justify some of the notions and theoretical underpinnings that have been perpetuated. Despite the sophistry, the objectives, procedures and problems still betray their intellectual origins in pre-modern natural history (Hempel 1965; Ember 1973). This approach is well illustrated in Radcliffe-Brown's conception of a natural science of society, where implicit evolutionism is obscured by social physiology (Radcliffe-Brown 1957).

Radcliffe-Brown was positively pre-Lamarckian in his idea of species reflecting some basic immobility of nature. In terms of the history of science, he had much more in common with Tournefort and Linnaeus than with either Bonnet, Benoit de Maillet or Diderot, who viewed species as being more plastic (Foucault 1970: 127). For Radcliffe-Brown, natural species and human societies were alike; both were closed, ongoing self-perpetuating systems. In each case it was quite possible to arrive at correct descriptions and arrange them in valid typological relations, through observation, classification and generalisation (Leach 1976: 14, 17). Edmund Leach has parodied this kind of classificatory activity, and the comparativism associated with it, in an elaborate, museological metaphor bridging fifteen years. For him it is 'butterfly-collecting', an antiquarian approach drawn from 'fossils, rocks, insects, stuffed-birds ... fixed entities, changeless, everlasting' (Leach 1976: 8; 1961). We expect to find such things juxtaposed in the rigid spaces of cabinets, herbaria and zoological gardens, not in real life. It is a view founded in a set of ideas that is pre-genetic, pre-Darwinian and pre-molecular.

For Leach and for many others there is a lack of fit between the ideal categories of classifications and the empirical discontinuities of nature. Paradoxically, this is a view which had its own origins in natural history rather than biology. Buffon, Bonnet and Lamarck all saw species simply as the end-products of applying the rules of taxonomic method. Like Aristotle and the Chinese Mohists of the Chou dynasty before them (Peck 1965: vii, *passim*; Needham 1962: 165–84), they recognised the difficulty of working out the principles of *natural* classification and the social element involved in fixing terminology and nomenclature. They were concerned with logical and artificial systems. That this is, in fact, the case, and that clear boundaries between species are not found by straightforward inference from empirical facts, has been amply confirmed by recent work in genetics and statistical biology. It is the very idea of species that is inherently imprecise. 'The species of empirical reality lack objective homogeneity and are blurred at the edges; what is allocated to them is determined by definitions' (Leach 1976: 17). And while all this finds more than an echo in the work of Lévi-Strauss, Foucault,[1] Mary Douglas, Leach himself, and their various acolytes, it seems to have gone unrecognised by Radcliffe-Brown.

II

The classifications so far considered, and the sense in which Radcliffe-Brown was employing them, have been described variously as observers', interpretative, operational, analysts', scientific and 'etic'. They attempt to divide up the real world as perceived by the investigator. They are assumed to be objective and may be either the tools or end-product of a research project. It was only with the publication of 'De quelques formes primitives de classification', published in the *Année Sociologique* for 1901–2, that classifications themselves really became a legitimate subject for ethnographic, philosophical and historical research. On this occasion the key terms for categories were cognitive, cognised, perceived, conscious, native, 'home-made' or 'emic' (see e.g. Harris 1969: 568–604).

Although there are grounds for insisting that indigenous categories of kinship had earlier been subject to systematic analysis (Needham 1971: xxi–xxii), it is not simply a matter of convenience that we should see the contribution of Durkheim and Mauss as representing an important theoretical landmark. Few would now accept the extreme view that society, not the mind, is the prime model for the classification of nature; but that classifications generally express the societies within which they are elaborated is an inescapable verity. Over and above this, however, the importance of the work was to isolate classification as an aspect of culture worthy of sociological analysis (Needham 1963: xi).[2]

The ideas of Durkheim and Mauss on this subject have influenced contemporary thinking along two paths. The first is through the collective consciousness of the intellectualist Oxford tradition, by way of Lévy-Bruhl, Hocart and Evans-Pritchard; the second is via Lévi-Strauss. Among those writers who have consumed varying mixtures of this scholarly diet must be counted Leach, Douglas and Rodney Needham. I shall label these the 'sociologists' or 'social constructionists'.

In the meantime, ideas in America were shaping up rather differently. Boasian particularism and rigorous anthropological linguistics contrasted sharply with the general lack of interest in the categories of language (with the notable exception of Malinowski) in the British School (Ardener 1971: ix). Via the descriptive linguistics of Sapir and Whorf there developed a formal approach that was both detailed and, in its own terms, rigorous. This is usually termed 'ethnoscience', and among its most important exponents must be listed Conklin, Goodenough and Berlin (see Conklin 1972). It has been characterised by an interest in semantic universals and general classificatory principles.

The results of research in these two areas have been as inadequate in some fundamental respects as they have been intriguing and stimulating in others. Those that have been sociologically sophisticated have often been technically and empirically weak, and those that have been technically and linguistically rigorous have frequently been sociologically naïve. The 'sociologists' have paid attention to social concomitants with varying degrees of care, but have gone astray with the analysis of actual classificatory structures. They have made assumptions about 'total' taxonomies, the existence of anomalies and semantic hierarchy where the evidence is unclear. On the other hand, the formalists have concretised words and categories, treating them as the only hard facts worthy of study; accessible reality is seen as items in abstracted classificatory systems which represent the mind in its pure state (Schneider, quoted in Douglas 1975: 120). Sadly, we seem to know as little of the empirical details of Lele ethnozoology as we know of the sociology of Tzeltal botanical categories.

There have been two fairly recent developments which suggest some resolution of these stark alternatives. Firstly, classifications are being examined in a wider intellectual context with conscious attempts to link superficially distinct research problems: the history of ideas, structuralism, developmental psychology, phenomenology and ethnomethodology, social anthropology, language studies, theoretical biology and mathematics. Such tentative interconnections which do exist, largely as a result of a linguistic phase in social science, have by no means gelled into a recognisable and dynamic research network or distinctive field. It was partly the task of the seminar for which this chapter was originally written to examine whether or not this putative convergence was likely to be fruitful and realisable, or if it was no more than a pious wish. Secondly, in a much more restricted anthropological sphere, there is some evidence that the formalists and social constructionists are beginning to come to terms with each other. In the field of ethnobiology, to which I shall largely restrict myself here, this is evident in the work of Ralph Bulmer, who has combined an almost pedantic concern for folk-zoological detail and accuracy with a sophisticated treatment of both the structure of categories and their social context (Bulmer 1967, 1970; and e.g. Bulmer and Tyler 1968).[3] It may not be too optimistic to hope that these trends will nurture what Mary Douglas (1975: 21) has described as the synthesis of classificatory logic and transactions.

III

Much of the work on folk classifications of animals has been concerned with showing the extent to which they are similar to, or different from, phylogenetic schemes, in their structure, extensiveness and attention to detail. Perhaps motivated by assumptions concerning the psychological unity of mankind, both folk and scientific classifications are attributed with hierarchical taxonomic structures, suggesting common cognitive processes (Conklin 1962; Kay 1971). At the same time, and increasingly, other workers have shown that in this and other respects they are in fact very different. Now, it seems to me that this has got us into something of a muddle, of much the same kind as that which has arisen over the degree of attribution of Western rationality to non-Western beliefs. Not only do such puzzles stem from false, or unhelpful, assumptions about the characteristics of particular systems; they also occur because the categories 'folk classification' and 'scientific classifications' are themselves problematic. This is well illustrated by the debate over the distinction drawn by Berlin and his associates between special purpose and general purpose schemes (Berlin et al. 1966; Bulmer 1970; Berlin, 1974). Attempts to set out the general principles of classification and nomenclature in folk biology (e.g. Berlin et al. 1973: 215–16) are certainly useful for particular systems, but to make empirical generalisations about certain types assumes that variability is according to a limited number of well-understood criteria along parallel axes. What are the conditions which indicate the transformation from a folk classification to a scientific one, for example, and what are the characteristics of systems that cannot easily be assigned to either? Specifically, what of the criteria for classificatory systems falling outside the simple models of the formalists?

The restricted checklist approach exemplified by the early work of Berlin and his associates cannot, then, cope with the wider dimensions of variation between systems. It tends not only to reify a particular kind of classification (that which we call 'taxonomic'), but seems to claim that a large number of semantic fields are at all times similarly organised. That this is patently not so is made ridiculously obvious in the beautiful passage from Jorge Luis Borges which stimulated Foucault to write his *Les Mots et les Choses*. The reference is to 'a certain Chinese encyclopaedia' which divides animals into categories:

> (a) belonging to the Emperor, (b) embalmed, (c) tame, (d) sucking pigs, (e) sirens, (f) fabulous, (g) stray dogs, (h) included in the present classification, (i) frenzied, (j) innumerable, (k) drawn with a very high camel hair brush, (l) *et cetera*, (m) having just broken the water pitcher, (n) that from a long way off look like flies. (Foucault 1970: xv)

That the example is either a complete fiction, or poorly translated from the original, or undecipherable through lack of knowledge of cultural context, may all be plausibly suggested. Equally, its authenticity might be attested to by seeing in it the scepticism of such sages as Chang Ping-Lin, for whom all possible classifications were unreal (Needham 1962: 196). Strangely enough, and with all its logical paradoxes and Foucault's astonishment, the arrangement has a familiar ring for an anthropologist. Virtually all the animal categories and many of the combinations find parallels in known ethnographic schemes. The exception is 'included in the present classification', and even this may exist in the perceived world with the aid of either mystical symbolism, the graphics of Maurits Escher, or the metaphysics of Borges himself. I am not being deliberately obscure here: I am trying to make the simple point that there are substantive areas and dimensions to classificatory space which remain unexplored (and perhaps unexplorable) by our present limited techniques, but which are nevertheless appropriate subjects for analysis.

What is required is some kind of meta-theory, or at least a meta-framework, which will bring order to this dizzy scene. But this is easier said than done. Some writers have already distinguished formally between different kinds of classificatory constructs: taxonomies, indices, keys, paradigms and typologies (Conklin 1964: 39–40), analytical (part-whole) and synthetic (class inclusive) forms (Conklin 1962: 131–2; Chapter 5 in this volume) and so on. Others (e.g. Hunn: 1976; Ellen 1993) have worked on non-hierarchical models of organising classificatory space. But many classifications combine several of these different forms. Further, such abstract analyses make little reference to features of the substantive context with which they might vary concomitantly. This requires a somewhat different perspective, and the key variables are not necessarily those emphasised in formal studies.

IV

In this section I look briefly at seven variables or groups of variables which may begin to provide us with analytical links between formal structures and social context. The list is incomplete, extremely provisional and many of the points have already been discussed in the literature, individually and in slightly different ways. They are: variability; arbitrariness; expression of inclusiveness; anomaly; structural complexity; terminology, nomenclature and taxonomy; and integration in semantic fields. They are discussed here with examples drawn from ethnobiology, but the generalisations can probably be applied more broadly.

Variability

Cognitive variability generally refers to relations between three variables: lexical items, the content of categories in scientific or other 'objective' terms, and informants. Further elements could be added, such as knowledge of uses, but as yet this is an aspect which has not widely been considered. Moreover, although the incongruity between words and categories is well understood, it is generally assumed that the lack of congruence and the existence of covert categories can, in most cases, be ignored, or must inevitably be so if measurement is to be possible. Given this proviso we can distinguish between three basic kinds of variation:

(a) variation in the relationship between lexical items (or categories) and scientific notation;
(b) variation between individuals;
(c) variation according to rules appropriate to specific contexts.

These can be described, respectively, as consistency, sharing and flexibility (Ellen 1979).

Consistency and sharing vary according to the material or social significance of the categories involved, the available aids for storing and arranging information – such as filing systems, libraries, training methods, catalogues, indexes, specialists, reference collections and illustrations, and the actual variations and complexities of fauna and flora. They are related to the social importance of conformity, either practically (Ellen 1978a) or ideologically, and maintained through the process of social communication. Flexibility varies according to differing social and perceptual contexts within a society: classificatory structures in particular may vary according to the different purposes being served on separate occasions. It does not usually represent individualistic or deviant behaviour, but reflects social rules (e.g. Chapter 4 below).

Arbitrariness

Classifications can be ordered according to degree of arbitrariness. An arbitrary criterion, following Saussure, is one that is unmotivated. Thus to classify dogs on the basis of their colour is less arbitrary than to do so on the basis of an alphabetical ordering of their names, for names are only signs. Here I extend this idea, so that by a less arbitrary classification we understand one that more adequately identifies a category vis-à-vis all others in the same set. So, for example, to classify dogs solely on the grounds of colour is more arbitrary than to include also size and shape.

In practice, no classifications (limited as they are by material and cognitive space) can be formulated in terms of *all* natural discontinuities. Classifying requires the selection of features on the grounds of manageability and significance. The number of distinctive features used in a classification varies according to information-handling techniques. To a large extent, folk classifications appear to be built up according to generalised conceptions of particular species (Ellen 1979). But even here particular characteristics must be selected for emphasis, and those that are chosen vary for social and perceptual reasons. In his botanical taxonomy, Tournefort employed certain differentiae, not because they were the most obvious and useful parts of the plant, 'but because they permitted a numerically satisfying combinality' (Foucault 1970: 141). More arbitrary still are alphabetical classifications and other simple notations (such as numerals) based on abstract signs, including those not derived from the form of the species itself, but which are characteristics rather of the word or other sign used to denote it. Although some of these types are as old as written language itself, others are very recent innovations in European thought.

The fewer features considered, the more arbitrary, in these terms, the classification. If we can employ a single feature the classification is logically most satisfying: all men classified by unique proper names, all animals classified by their diploid number of chromosomes, all plants classified according to the alphabetical order of their name: these are socially and cognitively efficient. They are aesthetically pleasing, too. Anomaly is excluded a priori. The problem is, of course, that the fewer the features adopted to distinguish categories, the less they reflect what is actually seen. But then that is not always the purpose of classifications. Some do purport to reflect reality (phylogenetic schemes), others simply to act as economical data-retrieval systems (such as library codes), and yet others to deliberately obscure it. Most classifications are, in fact, a bit of each.

The problems posed by single-feature schemes logically give rise to attempts to introduce schemes based on multiple features. Instead of employing a single feature which has different values for each item $(x\ (=a)_1$, $x\ (=b)_2$, etc.), a number of different features are chosen:

A

	1	2	3	4	5
x	V1	V2	V3	V4	V5
y	V2	V3	V4	V5	V1
z	V3	V4	V5	V1	V2

B

	1	2	3	4	5
x	+	+	–	–	–
y	–	–	–	+	+
z	+	–	–	–	+

In any case, a decision has to be made as to whether the values assigned to them for each item are on a continuous scale (*A*) or whether they are to be listed on a simple binary (or conceivably ternary) basis (*B*). The first alternative is difficult to implement in non-written systems, and is avoided in written systems wherever possible. It is easier to talk of 'winged' in contrast to 'legged', rather than degrees of 'wingedness' or 'leggedness'. But even a continuous scale must be divided up into classes at some point, and this will always generate a binary structure. Such models have been the main means by which ethnographers, at least, have interpreted indigenous classifications. It is an approach which derives from formal treatment and has permitted the development of a rigorous, if largely unproductive, componential analysis.

In classifying items in which the number of utilised variables is large, the multiple-feature approach meets with difficulties. Isolating only a small number of characters might be misleading, and considering large numbers presents technical problems. In many folk classifications the problem of manageability is overcome by differentially rejecting certain attributes for each item, and I will discuss this matter further. In interpretative scientific schemes, modern hardware, such as the computer, has allowed the utilisation of large numbers of attributes. Numerical taxonomy of this kind has been used by both biologists and archaeologists (Sokal and Sneath 1963; Clarke 1968). While such devices may reduce the complexity of a system, they are subject to finite limitations in the amount of information that can be encoded. The fallacy inherent in the phylogenetic system, then, is precisely this: that it seeks to reduce to linear order something which is, in fact, a complex reticulum virtually impossible to reduce to signs on a piece of paper. Indeed, among theoretical biologists doubts still exist as to whether or not there is an ideally perfect classification which may be accepted as the aim of taxonomy; and again, whether or not phylogeny can ever be fully expressed in classification. Clearly, here is a dilemma between a valid scheme and a useful one. Perhaps the best we can hope for is that different classifications should reflect different aspects of reality, as in the distinction between the evolutionary arrangement of homologous structures for the purposes of comparative morphology and the grouping of organisms in an order of presumed evolutionary descent (McLean and Ivimey-Cook 1956: 2121–2).

The classifications considered so far in our discussion of 'arbitrariness' have all been what Sneath has described as 'monothetic', i.e. the defining set of features is always unique (Sokal and Sneath 1963: 13). Given the discriminatory inadequacy of those classifications made up of limited features and the impossibility or doubtful validity of those employing large numbers, contemporary biological taxonomies are something of a compromise. However, this is also true of what we know of folk classifications. One way in which we might distinguish the two is by the level at which the compromise has had to be made: folk classifications tend more towards the single-feature end of the continuum than do the scientific ones.

Given the necessity of using some form of multiple-feature scheme, it is nevertheless clear that (a) the selected features are not always relevant or helpful for a particular discrimination and (b) it is difficult to operate schemes with a large number of attributes for each item. This, of course, is less so with written systems. Many folk classifications only become manageable through selectively rejecting attributes. Here, categories are not defined with reference to a limited set of features characteristic of and unique to each category, but are semantically primitive (Hunn 1975a: 19); what Sneath has suggested we describe as 'polythetic'. Such arrangements group items with the greatest number of shared features. Single features are neither essential to group membership nor sufficient to allocate an item to a group (Sokal and Sneath 1963: 14). The idea is illustrated in the following much-reproduced form:

	1	2	3	4	5	6	7
x	a	b	c				
y			c	d	e		
z					e	f	g

Polythetic classification has been the subject of recent interest in disciplines other than biology; for example, anthropology (Needham 1975) and philosophy, where it is akin to Wittgenstein's notion of 'family resemblance' in ordinary language. This approach does not necessarily represent objective reality more faithfully, although the maximising of informativeness requires increasing polythetism. Some biologists have seen it as a means of yielding 'natural' taxa, but this only points to a difference between polythetic classification in scientific and folk systems. In the former it is associated with increasing information; in the latter it is a response to too much. Phylogenetic classification is always striving to be less arbitrary, but in folk systems this aim is absent. The notion of adequacy is a different one. Arbitrary polythetic systems are conveniently represented by the kinship categories investigated by Needham (1971), which are not necessarily a reflection of genetic relationships.

The co-ordinates of variation for arbitrariness, as discussed here, might be illustrated in the following way:

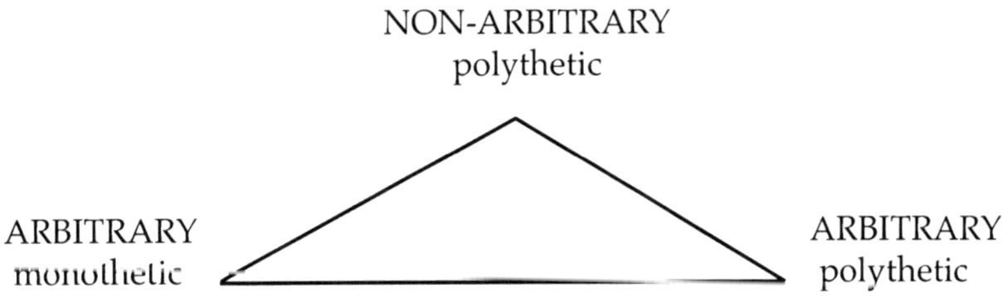

Most classifications are generally mixtures of these different formal models. Although one may be dominant in individual schemes, it would be misleading to see any of them as representing the basic framework for folk systems. It is important to return to the idea that in many classification systems the items are seen as distinct entities rather than the sum of a specified number of distinctive characteristics. This view is by no means confined to students of folk biology. Linnaeus suggested a list of biological families based on an intuitive feeling of affinity. As McLean and Ivimey-Cook (1956: 2121) point out, this is not necessarily a scientifically inferior process, but one which takes into account a large number of 'qualitative sense data', expressed by the term 'facies', many of which are either individually or cumulatively recognised by the observer as a sense-group which, for him/her, seems to entail a very strong presumption of 'natural reality' (cf. Bulmer and Tyler 1968; Ellen 1979). In the sense of matching classificatory representations more closely with what is actually seen, such complex systems are probably less arbitrary than those that are logically consistent.

Expression of Inclusiveness

Inclusiveness in phylogenetic classification is expressed essentially through a hierarchical metaphor involving linked notions of rank, level and contrast. This we know as 'taxonomy', an idea first made explicit in the history of European thought by Aristotle in his *Organon* and *Metaphysics*. The ruling principle is that 'the highest genus is divided by means of differentae into subaltern genera, and each of these is then divided until the ultimate species is reached' (Peck 1965: vii). It was handed down through the Stoics, Porphyry and the Greek commentators to Linnaeus, from whom it passed into modern biological usage. The taxonomic approach gained such wide currency that a great many ethnographers assumed that it must also necessarily order the folk classifications they were beginning to describe and analyse. This assumption gave rise to the complex formal theories referred to in section III above (pp. 42–3).

Some recent work has cast doubt on the general applicability of this approach, gathering evidence to suggest that a taxonomy based on bounded semantic fields ordered exclusively by a hierarchy of inclusion is by no means always appropriate when it comes to the examination of folk systems (Frake 1962; Fox 1975: 118–19; Hunn 1976; Friedberg 1968, 1970). This critique is, in part, a response to the so-called 'special problems' of taxonomies, which are seen in many cases as simply artefacts of the method. Examples of these include multiple and interlocking hierarchies, extra-hierarchic relations, synonymy, homonymy, polysemy, anomaly, covert categories and residual taxa. As a result we are left with inelegant complications of formal models which, additionally, provide no basis for either distinguishing induction from deduction or explaining how taxa are actually generated (Conklin 1962; Hunn 1976: 510–11, 519). Randall (1976) has criticised the model on the grounds that its assumptions about transitivity suggested incorrectly that elicited taxonomies represent structures involved in memory storage. Rather, he suggests, taxonomic trees are the result of classifying behaviour (see also Coxon and Jones 1979).

It appears that many systems can be non-hierarchical while retaining the idea of contrast. An example of this is the scientific logic of the Chinese Mohist philosophers of the fourth and fifth centuries BC. Although later logicians may have been working with an Aristotelian notion, the Mohist metaphor was in terms of 'broad and narrow' (*ta Hsiao*). Everything is classified into broader or narrower groups: the group 'animals of four feet' is 'broader' than 'oxen and horses', while the group of 'things' is broader still. Similarly there is also the idea of 'common point' (*chü*): thus 'oxen' and 'horses' meet at a 'common point' since they both have four feet. An analogy can be made with counting fingers: each hand has five, yet one can take one hand as one thing (Needham 1962: 175–6). Similarly, we are told that the Nuer (being good Durkheimians) classify animals after the fashion of social groups (Evans-Pritchard 1956: 89–90). Friedberg (1979) and Peeters (1979) discuss classifications which they claim can be represented more accurately as 'networks'. In other classifications, or partial classifications, not even the notion of contrast is present. Thus, rather than something being *x* or *y*, it is common for it to be more *x* than *y*, or more *y* than *x*. The idea of gradation eliminates distinct boundaries and has been suitably termed 'fuzziness' (Lakoff 1972). Thus we should speak of 'shrubness' or 'treeness', 'birdness' or 'snakeness' (Randall 1976: 549–51) as well as other phenomena, such as flexibility and consistency. This fits will with a polythetic conception of classification.

Anomaly

Classifications might also be ordered according to the degree to which they generate anomaly. In as much as all classifications are of varying degrees of arbitrariness, so they have a *potential* to create anomaly continually. Dan Sperber (1975: 94) has reminded us that encyclopaedic knowledge is not without its incoherences and contradictions, but that life is concerned with a continuous effort to either avoid or correct them. In this sense anomaly is ubiquitous. However, it is important to distinguish genuine anomalies from those produced by careless use of the taxonomic method. Repeatedly, 'anomalies' have been shown either to be spurious or culturally irrelevant (Hunn 1975a: 310; Sperber 1975a; Willis 1974: 47); rather than falling between taxa they may be separate ones in their own right; rather than being negatively 'anomalous' they may be positively *singular* (e.g. Ellen 1972; Bulmer 1979; Friedberg 1979; and Hunn 1979). We must be careful not to invent anomalies where they do not exist. If we interpret as monothetic classifications those which are polythetic, or employ contrastive logic where concepts are 'fuzzy', all sorts of problems are obviously going to arise. Whereas the inbuilt, rigorous logic of ethnographic method easily gives rise to anomalies, the informal logics of folk systems permit its avoidance.

Nevertheless, even given that the flexibility of folk classifications generally allows for the resistance of many potential anomalies, both in ethnobiological and phylogenetic schemes, the 'higher' the order of categories involved the more likely they are to be evident. Birds fly by folk definition but some that are otherwise perfectly good birds patently do not. For a long time in European biological thought plants were by definition autotrophic, although some are unable to manufacture their own energy. At the same time, though, we also find that anomaly can be more readily erased by sophisticated casuistry at higher rather than lower levels (Bulmer and Tyler 1968).

Clearly there is variation in the appearance of anomaly, both between and within cultures. Nevertheless, everywhere the potential number of anomalies greatly exceeds the number that are recognised, let alone held to be significant and taken up in symbolic communication. Once anomalies have been set in their proper classificatory context we can then focus on their behavioural concomitants and make that all-important 'frontal attack on the question of how thought, words and the real world are related' (Douglas 1972: 29).[4]

Structural Complexity

It is reasonable enough to assume that 'complexity' must be an important variable linking the formal structure of classifications with their social context. But since this is a noun which may easily be applied to ideas that are simply unfamiliar, it must be carefully defined.

Complexity here refers to three dependent subsets of variables:

(a) the number of elements given classificatory recognition (usually by naming), expressed either absolutely or relative to natural species diversity, given some measure of degree of differentiation (Hunn 1975a; Ellen 1978a);
(b) the number of levels in taxonomies, the number of categories at each level of class inclusion, and other related quantifiable characteristics (Berlin et al. 1973). With classifications other than taxonomies *sensu stricto*, or if the taxonomic approach is rejected for folk systems, these characteristics can be described in other ways;
(c) with due regard to the cautionary advice already given concerning 'special problems', complexity also refers to the existence of sub-classifications, keys, alternative schemes and so on.

These matters obviously tie in with the variables discussed already, such as flexibility and the number of features employed in making particular discriminations. Since much has already been written on this subject there appears little sense in repetition. It is clear that the careful delineation of selected semantic fields is a basic ingredient of any research strategy in this area.

Terminology, Nomenclature and Taxonomy

There has been great emphasis in the literature on meticulously dissecting and not confusing these three things, in both biological and folk classification (McLean and Ivimey-Cook 1956; Conklin 1962). However, there is considerable variation in the ways in which they are related in different systems. This has already come in for some discussion, particularly the extent to which terminologies (morphosyntactic features) are a guide to actual classificatory practice. Literacy effectively emphasises the arbitrariness of the relationship between names and signs, so we might reasonably expect the distinction between terms and taxa to be more important in scientific schemes. This is not so true for folk classifications, where naming and the meaning of names is generally more significant in both 'mundane' and ideological classificatory contexts. The extremes of inseparability and total arbitrariness are rare. Much more common is a mixture of the two, and this we would expect since classifications and speech are bound together intricately. So although it may be analytically important to distinguish between these phenomena, it would be misleading to assume that they always serve different purposes.

Integration in Semantic Fields

Finally, classifications might conceivably be ordered in terms of the degree to which semantic fields are autonomous. Although all non-literate classifications of an empirical nature possess contradictions, they are like some other systems in that in the absence of further inputs they tend towards symmetry and economy. This appears to be a cerebral condition for the efficient storage of information. The categorised items tend to be simplified to a cognitively satisfactory form (e.g. Miller 1956); distinctive features are restricted to the minimum necessary, and haphazard assemblages become ordered through binary oppositions (e.g. Lévi-Strauss 1966: 66–8). Thus if particular fields possess such tendencies it is reasonable to expect groups of different fields in the same society, all things being equal, to tend towards a unity. All semantic fields are linked to others in some way, such as in the marginal overlap of content, but the degree to which they are integrated into a single system, through common organising principles, metaphorical and symbolic links, does vary.

Durkheim and Mauss (1963: 81–2) saw primitive societies as representative of ideal classificatory integration, but this specifically related to a symbolic level of experience, which was distinguished from the merely 'technological'. Although they are not entirely clear on this matter, their contention that 'technological' schemes have no relation to 'a first philosophy of nature' or 'the origins of the logical procedure which is the basis of scientific classifications' has been refuted by modern work on folk classification. Rather than contrasting with one another, such classifications seem to merge, but the degree to which this is so varies, perhaps with the elaboration of 'symbolic' schemes themselves. I return to this matter below (pp. 53–6).

V

It would be foolish to think that these variables fit neatly together, thereby allowing the construction of a simple typology. Though certain characteristics may reinforce one another because of their logical dependence, and certain complexes may emerge under particular social circumstances, it is impossible to construct an infallible cross-cultural set of rules. In place of this I would argue the case for what might be called a 'classificatory substantivism'.

I take it as axiomatic that all classifications are discursive practices situated in a given social matrix and general configuration of knowledge and ideas (such as 'epistemes', or ideologies), and that they are products of specific histories (Bourdieu 1977). What we have relatively little systematic information on, and for which an effective framework has yet to be devised, are the various social conditions which determine and correlate with particular articulations of the variables discussed. Like the variables themselves, many of these social conditions are interdependent, but this should only assist us in locating particular classification-context linkages.

It is convenient to recognise two kinds of social condition – situational and structural – although I would shrink from giving this distinction any rigid analytical weight. Situational conditions reflect intracultural variation determined by either the specific social context of classificatory activity, or the material or perceived content of different semantic fields. Different social contexts may give rise to flexibility and differential consistency in the use of classifications which must be considered when eliciting their formal structure. Similarly, there are semantic field-dependent differences related to the phenomena being classified. On these grounds we would expect differences between natural species, cultural artefacts, social groups, abstract concepts and so on; and between analytic (part-whole) and synthetic (class inclusive) fields. This is not to deny that one type of field will influence the structure of another. We also find that particular kinds of natural species, because of either morphological or behavioural characteristics, have the effect of lessening inconsistency and flexibility (Ellen 1979); and that particular objective arrays of species in a local environment will affect patterns observed in the classifications (Hunn 1979).

Structural conditions are those that are predicted by specified social and economic relations, and the functions of those relations. One of the most important of these is the division of labour. The greater the specialisation of work in society, the greater the scope for specialist-specific classificatory knowledge, and the greater the division of knowledge in classifications (see Bousfield 1979). Complex occupational structures often result in the institutionialisation of classification, as in craft guilds and professional associations. Not only does the subject-matter become group- or institution-specific, but so also do the ways of ordering that knowledge and its socialisation. With institutionialisation, too, come more strict beliefs about normal and deviant interpretations.

Although variation demonstrably exists according to particular function, attempts to group specific kinds of classification by gross functional attributes have been less successful. An example is the distinction made by Berlin and his associates (1966) between special-purpose and general-purpose schemes. Many folk classifications are special, determined by specific subsistence and other culturally defined requirements; while scientific classifications are seen as general and logical, derived naturally from a consideration of all other data. Bulmer has argued the opposite (1970), and Berlin (1974: 267) appears to agree that in this sense folk and scientific taxa are fundamentally alike. It is interesting that Berlin should have chosen to use the terms 'special-purpose' and 'general-purpose' in the way that he did, as in another sense they might have been used the other way round. Scientific classifications are developed by specialist groups in society for a highly esoteric purpose – the pursuit of knowledge itself. Folk classifications are generally not the product of groups of specialist minds, and must have general cognitive and social utility.

In Durkheimian theory, changes in the division of labour are linked to changes in the kind of social integration. Douglas (1966: 112) and Lévi-Strauss (1966: 138) have followed this line in attributing to 'primitive society' an all-embracing, dynamic and undifferentiated world-view integrated through symbolic classification, in contrast to the partial, static, differentiated and relatively unintegrated ones of advanced societies. However, they differ from it – knowingly or unknowingly – in not distinguishing 'technological' from 'symbolic' levels of ordering experience (Morris 1976: 543, 553; 1979; Bloch 1977). The distinction does not seem to have been noticed either by some of the formalists; this misunderstanding underlies part of their critique of the sociologists (see Hunn 1979).

There are two points which might be made here. The first is that the Durkheimian model is inadequate in the light of ethnography. Some politically complex societies seem to show a relatively high level of symbolic integration (for example, China, the Incas), even on the admission of Durkheim and Mauss themselves; while some small groups of food collectors show fragmented and apparently unconnected classifications of natural species. Morris (1976: 543–5, 552; 1979) reports that the Hill Pandaram of South India employ classifications highly individualistically and that these are 'largely independent of other aspects' of culture. There are no elaborate schemes of augury, animals and plants do not feature in ritual processes or ceremonial, and there is no totemic system. Not only are Hill Pandaram classifications limited in scope, but they are relatively unconcerned with systematisation. They do not have a systematic knowledge of their natural environment clearly expressed in formal taxonomies. As I interpret it, this does not suggest that their knowledge is limited, that categories cannot be analysed as parts of a rational scheme, or that the *kinds* of categories are radically dissimilar from those found in other societies. These points have been raised seriously as objections to Morris's analysis (Berlin n.d.). Rather than being concerned with abstract and generalised formal classifications, he is concerned with use, degree of sharing and the relationship to a wider realm of ideas and practices.

What seems to be important, then, are the various constraints and degrees of permissiveness associated with different social forms. In simple societies, scale and organisation allow either alternative. But why this should be so–why certain communities have elaborate ideational patterns linking diverse aspects through symbolism into a single totality – is a crucial problem for investigation in its own right (Bloch 1977; Morris 1976: 544). In more complex societies, scale and organisation act as constraints. So whereas we may find surprising instances of symbolic integration, these tend to operate as parts of either subordinate or dominant schemes in ideologically plural societies, are reified in written doctrinal codes or relate to organisationally trivial levels of experience.

Societies of widely differing types often have a number of different classification schemes operating at both technological and ideological levels, but the range of variation is large. Although Durkheim and Mauss distinguished 'technological' from 'symbolic' classifications and report the Chinese system itself as being composed of 'a number of intermingled systems', their argument assumes an unjustifiably neat correspondence between a uniform classification and the integration of society (Needham 1963: xviii–xix).

The second point is that the relations of the 'technological' to the 'symbolic' and the 'mundane' to the 'ritual', are genuinely problematic. Clearly, analytical demands enforce what may seem to be empirically distinct, but the total separation made by Durkheim and Mauss, which is supported by Bloch and Morris, is surely unwarranted. All so-called 'mundane' classifications reflect relatively complex semantic fields, involving other fields, metaphorical extensions between them, and so on. Evans-Pritchard's discussion of Nuer colour terms for cattle derived from different animal species is a good example. The degree to which they are integrated will vary of course, but unless the distinctions are made culturally explicit there are no grounds for assuming them to be operationally contrasted. There are several ways in which the character of this interrelationship can be demonstrated.

One way is to emphasise the arbitrary location of boundaries drawn between the 'mundane' and the 'ritual', and the imprecision of the various terms used to designate these as substantively different types of classification. It seems that the distinction was used by Durkheim and Mauss to separate subsistence from non-subsistence spheres of activity, hence the term is not entirely unambiguous, its suggested synonym 'mundane' poses greater difficulties. I understand by this term such classifications that are derived from human practice on nature, whether this be 'naturally' or socially constructed, rather than from the need to legitimise authority. But this world concerns spirits as much as motor cycle spares, kinsmen as much as biota, time as much as topography and anatomy. The Nuaulu of eastern Indonesia recognise numerous spirit categories in much the same way as they recognise categories of animals. The way in which the fields are organised is similar and there is even an area of overlap where objectively invisible forms are grouped with visible ones, and vice versa (cf. Evans-Pritchard 1956: 178; Douglas 1975: 30 on 'spirit animals'). Along with plants and animals, spirits inhabit the Nuaulu universe in every conceivable niche; in the same way that both flora and fauna threaten and help them, so spirits too have this basic ambivalent nature. The essential unity and continuity of supernatural and natural, visible and invisible taxa is also highlighted in the ambivalence shown over the correct classification of the numerous monsters in myths and stories.

Another way in which the interrelations between the 'mundane' and 'ritual' can be shown is that in both there exist essentially similar modes of information organisation (Brown et al. 1976). Although dualism originating in ritual can affect 'mundane' schemes, dichotomous division is always at work in the ordering of categories of perception in both scientific (especially as keys) and folk classification (Bulmer 1970: 1082; Bulmer and Tyler 1968: 375). Such distinctions may form the basis of ideological oppositions. Symbolism can affect 'mundane' categories; labels may evoke symbolic resonances and relations between species may be expressed through myth (Rosaldo and Atkinson 1975: 50), but there is no predictability in such correspondences (Friedberg 1979).

Then again, although the distinction between 'mundane' and 'ritual' fits quite well when dealing with terminal taxa or 'natural kinds' (Bulmer and Tyler 1968), where there is a direct connection with observable reality the arrangement of categories of higher order becomes increasingly prone to ideological invasion.

But to demonstrate empirical connections is not necessarily to undermine the theoretical or methodological significance of the distinction, any more than Weber's demonstration of the specific links between capitalism and protestant religion undermines either the distinction between base and superstructure, or Marx's separation of knowledge from ideology. It is because knowledge and ideology are conceptually different, and because methods have become somewhat confused with data, that there is some mutual enmity between the formalists' and sociologists' approaches to the study of classifications. The former have been concerned with 'mundane', 'technological' knowledge, with a view of culture that does not stress integration; the latter have been concerned explicitly with ideology, with a stress on symbolic integration (Bloch 1977). It is also because there is an empirical overlap between method and data, knowledge and ideology, that Berlin, Bulmer, Douglas and others can present us with such apparently different explanations of the same thing. It is only when these various strands have been unravelled that we can talk legitimately of the logical primacy of knowledge over ideology, and the 'perceptual' and 'mundane' over the 'ritual' and 'symbolic'.

It is reasonable to assume that the classification systems of all societies tend towards integration, economy and structural conformity between historically unique events. This is a feature of most social systems and subsystems about which we are knowledgeable. But equally, no system or subsystem can ever be a single, integrated totality; there will always be behavioural traits that do not 'fit'. This is both because socialisation is never perfect – there is always a large element of individuality – and because societies and their environments change. And so we have the paradox that integration takes time, but time itself disintegrates.

Those social forces which encourage integration include social interaction itself, institutionialisation and the relative importance of social learning. These are all devices which promote consistency, while having the inevitable consequence of promoting deviance and criticism. Although in all societies knowledge is based on personal experiences, its relation with that acquired through social learning varies. In small-scale food-collectors such as the Hill Pandaram the element of social learning is relatively small; in highly centralised state societies it may be paramount and enforced through specialised institutions such as schools. But it also seems to be related to a number of other dependent variables, such as the degree of symbolic integration, division of labour, scale, level of hierarchy and literacy.

Literacy is a key condition permitting greater complexity, quantitative elaboration and the recording of classificatory data for future use. Although these appear to be general properties of human thinking with regard to the number of items that the brain can handle at a given time (see e.g. Miller 1956), there is no similar limit imposed by written systems. In non-literate societies the entire content of cultural tradition, except artefacts, is held in memory. Purely oral discourse tends to emphasise group ideas and attitudes rather than those of the individual (Goody and Watt 1968: 30). Language is learned in intimate association with community experience, individually through face-to-face contact. Information acquired in this way is stored in the brain, though much is generally forgotten. This is so, despite the possible use of mnemonic devices to assist information storage, such as formal speech, ritual recitation, music, professional remembrancers and the like (Goody and Watt 1968: 30–1).

The invention or introduction of writing may be critical in determining classificatory activity. Its potentialities, though, depend very much on the particular constellation of traits in the society concerned, such as the materials available, types of graphic form and means of organising communication. Literacy – whether general or restricted – permits the construction of more elaborate schemes and the manipulation of letters, words and numbers, encouraging new directions in literature, art, mathematics and science; it also has uses in the sphere of social control. Literacy encourages reflective, analytical and sequential thought, the development of syllogisms, rigorous logics and the division of knowledge into autonomous specialist disciplines (Goody 1968: 17–18). In fact the cognitive products of written language are so pervasive that there is a tendency in European culture not to recognise them for what they are. As Whorf pointed out, European thought has been moulded from Aristotle to the present day by a whole series of practices associated with the keeping of written records (Whorf 1956: 153, 238). It is also probable that the notion of taxonomic hierarchy is in part linked to attempts to represent classificatory relationships graphically and in writing.

With the signs of literate communication it is not always clear what is being signified. Meanings are not simply apparent through use, but are collected in dictionaries. Words acquire successive layers of historically validated meanings, whereas in oral communication the meaning of a word is ratified repeatedly in concrete situations, with vocal inflections and physical gestures. These combine to particularise its specific denotation and accepted additional usages. The process operates cumulatively and becomes more deeply socialised.

Literacy also reveals inconsistencies in classification. But the inconsistency of the totality of written material is less remarkable than its size and historical depth. Unlike the mind, it cannot unconsciously adapt and omit, and therefore the information it stores can only grow. Because there is no comparable means of elimination, no 'structural amnesia', individuals cannot take part in a total cultural tradition as is possible in a non-literate society. Reading and writing are normally solitary activities. The degree of 'semantic contact' is reduced. Because of this, culture may be more easily avoided and is also committed willy-nilly to an ever-increasing series of culture lags (Goody and Watt 1968: 57). And because of all these things the ideologies and sets of knowledge of literate societies cannot possibly have, through elementary classifications, the same inter-connection with other aspects of the social structure as is the case in small-scale societies (see Goody 1968: 5). Division of labour is closely linked to social inequality: the two phenomena reinforce each other and the first is a necessary historical condition for the latter. There are two aspects of inequality which must be considered here.

The first follows directly from the creation of different groups based on their relationship to the means of production. Classifications, knowledge and attitudes towards them, vary according to sex, age, occupation and class position. In small-scale societies, certain kinds of esoteric information are the property of descent groups or particular individuals of high status. Scientific biological classifications developed very much in the context of bourgeois European culture, where learning itself was an important social marker.

The second is that the types of inequalities and hierarchies present in a society shape wider structures and attitudes to classification, as well as the structure of classifications themselves. To paraphrase Marx, the dominant classifications are generally those of the ruling groups in society. They are part of an ideology with an important social control function. The various means by which classificatory uniformity is imposed therefore become critical: for example, rote-learning, passing examinations and government control of communications and schools.

Inequalities can affect all social knowledge and often even the identification of natural species may be arrived at by deferring to the knowledge of a person of higher status, rather than of proven greater knowledge.

The extent to which a hierarchical notion of classification is itself a function of hierarchical systems of social order is still highly problematic. In some cases 'taxonomy' fits well with hierarchical ideologies and in such a way that we might reasonably expect them to be related. I think it is not too fanciful to imagine this to be the case for Aristotelian Greece and post-Linnaean systematics. It may also be the case in some folk systems, such as Tzeltal. On the other hand, hierarchical social systems may have non-hierarchical classifications, as in Mohist China. What may be important, however, is the existence or otherwise of *any* hierarchical model as an idiom to express 'natural' relationships, kinship, historical time and biota. This kind of argument would explain certain features in the schemes of the Hill Pandaram and other immediate-return food-collecting societies, where group structure is highly flexible and genealogical organisation shallow, bound only by a few rules.

It is this kind of argument that Bloch has suggested specifically for 'ritual' classifications, but it might well apply to 'mundane' ones as well. In the realm of ritual classification, correspondences with social hierarchies are much more obvious and predictable. It has been suggested that binary opposition must be the correlate of hierarchy in any semantic theory (Fox 1975: 118), but there is a danger here of confusing social inequality with metaphorical usages of 'hierarchy', which, as we have seen, may be replaced by other means of expressing inclusivity. This is not to deny, though, that both may be intensified and elaborated through the development of particular kinds of hierarchy (insiders:outsiders; royalty:commoners; bourgeois:proletariat, and so on).

Finally, there is utility. At a general, common sense level it is easy to see a relationship between certain aspects of classification systems and the patterns of use. But while it is undeniable that such relationships exist, the extent to which they do so is highly variable, both in terms of the Nida-Conklin hypothesis, the idea that the vocabulary of particular fields expands in proportion to their social importance (see Hunn 1975a; Chapter 4, below) and the relationship between structure and social use (Bulmer 1979; Friedberg 1979).

VI

The mix of variables in any given society will affect the structure, content and function of classification systems in terms of the variables listed in section IV above. But this does not say a great deal. To what extent is it justified to expect to find a series of correspondences in various aspects of a given ideology which include the classification systems of a society? How far can we really predict that particular kinds of societies and ideologies will give us particular kinds of classification systems?

Through cross-cultural analysis it is possible to demonstrate correlations between pairs of variables: between complexity and division of labour, literacy and arbitrariness, semantic field integration and social integration, and so on, linking the formal properties of particular classifications (section IV) with the substantive ones of the societies in which they are found (section V). If we could eliminate all other variables we might reasonably expect such horizontal pairs to show a regular correlation. The problem for the anthropologist, and one reason why I am suspicious of attempts to seek constant macro-relations between classifications and types of society defined in terms of vague and general criteria, is that it is not always possible to find predictable regularities in the vertical relations between variables. For example, literacy does not always accompany hierarchy, social learning is important in many oral cultures and not in others, and the same is true of literate cultures. Rigorous expression of inclusiveness may eliminate anomaly as well as generate it. The pattern observed and the extent to which particular pairs of correlations are evident depend upon the entire nexus of variables.

Having understood this, it is then possible to proceed to analyse the organisation of classifications in particular cases and, for particular semantic fields, how these might affect discontinuities in the structures of different kinds of field and how we might distinguish these objectively in the first place. Thus there is still much to be discovered about the structural and sociological differences between classifications of living species compared with physical objects, abstract concepts and systems of signs. In such investigations it is not always helpful if we are tied to ideological distinctions a priori, such as those between 'scientific' and 'folk'.[5] Inevitably, such an enterprise also involves an investigation into methods of demarcating boundaries of semantic fields, areas of overlap and fuzziness. Then there is the question of the logical and historical primacy of different fields, and the processes which create new ones. There is the issue of variation, both in the ultimate sense of the number of different constructions that can be put on any one field (see Douglas 1975: 10), what determines this and what the limits (if any) are; and also variation in the sense of how this is defined by any one society. The degree of ambiguity of cognitive norms and the extent to which they are endorsed for a particular semantic field vary over time and from one field to another. New information will be accepted more easily the more it accords with current cognitive and technical norms and the more widespread the agreement as to what those norms are (Mulkay 1972: 16–17).

This chapter has been concerned, then, with the social nature of classification, though not the simple social determination of cognition espoused by either Durkheim or (in his very different way) Whorf. Neither is it an apology for the despair of historical particularism. In fact, I have suggested a marriage between the formal and the sociological approaches. This does not involve a denial of the validity of research and speculation on the cerebral aspects of classifying, the seeking of pan-human invariants and evolutionary generalities (e.g. Berlin 1970): it simply emphasises the complexity of the social variables and the subtle relationships between them and the genetic predisposition of the brain. The rigid dichotomy between mind and material world, between mode of representation and represented, breaks down at this point, and it is no good seeking solace in a hopeless and fallacious social relativism (Macrae 1976; Bloch 1977: 282). Our categories may will be socially constructed and yet still refer to the real word (Engels 1934). Perhaps part of the difficulty is that classifications are not, in the last instance, 'things' at all (Bourdieu 1977), but are simply the objectification of a process: classifying. However, in so much as we treat them as things, and I think this is unavoidable, it is the examination of less ideologically complex systems (those we describe as either 'mundane' or 'technological') that can be among the most helpful processes used to reveal that 'hidden architecture' of subtleties, asymmetries and indeterminacies in structure, dynamics and operation (Lehrer 1974: 325) which is characteristic of all semantic fields. It follows that these also provide a convenient focus for the investigation of more fundamental philosophical issues.

Empirical generalisations and phenomenological descriptions of the association between classification and social form in different societies are undoubtedly useful, but the resulting typologies are inevitably superficial. It is insufficient and misleading to embark upon intellectual paperchases to reveal 'inner essences' through their reflection in classifications. The possible outcomes, like those for certain kinds of structuralist analysis, are as numerous as the anthropologists on the job. They should certainly not pass for causal explanation, which can only be found in specific studies of the mechanisms operating in empirically observable schemes.

Notes

1. Foucault (1972) has objected to being bracketed with structuralists and those of a structuralist persuasion, and in a sense he is correct. In so far as he is a substantivist he could never be a Lévi-Straussian, but in so much as he seeks to unearth the 'structure' of an episteme which is internally consistent and has a logical structure related to language form, it is understandable that Leach (1976) should mistake him for one. After all, Foucault himself has remarked that 'structuralism is not a new method; it is the awakened and troubled consciousness of modern thought' (1970: 268); a characterisation that might well be applied to his own oeuvre.
2. Some of the obvious objections to Durkheim and Mauss are given by Rodney Needham (1963). Bloch (1977) has recently taken up the subject again, but is surely mistaken in believing that there has been no theoretical challenge before his own (see also Hunn 1976, 1979; Worsley 1956).
3. Within ethnobiology, Bulmer (1974: 79–81) has identified a number of fairly distinct orientations – lexicographic, formal, social, biological and natural – historical. With typical modesty he places himself in this latter category. While amateur natural history may have been his initial motivation, he is really more of a vigorous hybrid, confirming his own remarks on the overlap between these areas.
4. Despite a great deal of attention in the literature, there is still much to be discovered about anomalies. Most work has so far been on morphological and behavioural anomalies, as represented by Douglas's pangolin, Bulmer's cassowary and Borge's *Imaginary Beings*. But there are also those created by the use of language. Among such semantic anomalies are the paradoxes of Hui Shih in *Chuang Tzu*, such as the propositions 'the tortoise may be longer than a snake' (longevity) and 'white dogs may be black' (eyes) (Needham 1962: 197). We might add 'blackbirds may be white' (albino) or metaphors such as 'The White House is Red' (politically) (see also Sperber 1975a).

5. This is not to deny differences between 'folk' and scientific classifications, for a denial would undermine the possibility of an anthropology of knowledge. But stark oppositions generally contrive to obscure the historical and structural continuity between the two. Dissimilarities tend to be substantive rather than formal: a technical concern about objectivity and utility. For example, folk systems are generally related to a conception that knowledge may accumulate but in the end is finite and cannot change; science is not so strictly bound by this view, although the conceptions of certain kinds of scholar (those we label 'empiricists') may approach it.

There are several good reasons, then, for paying attention to early scientific schemes (see e.g. Peeters 1979), but one of immense importance is precisely their transitional and heterogenous nature: they have not been swallowed up by an all-consuming phylogeneticism. Thus Foucault (1970: 39) tells us that Buffon expressed astonishment on discovering that the work of a naturalist like Aldrovandi contained such as inextricable mixture of exact description, reported quotations, fables without commentary, remarks dealing indifferently with the animal's anatomy, its use in heraldry, its habitat, its mythological value, or the uses to which it could be put in medicine. Such a hotchpotch comes as no surprise to the practical ethnographer of folk biology in contemporary, small-scale, non-literate societies. Schemes such as Aldrovandi's do not represent 'bad science' but parts of rational, ideological constructions of knowledge for the societies that produced them.

CHAPTER 4

Variable Constructs in Nuaulu Zoological Classification (1975)

An analysis of two examples of Nuaulu animal classification (arboreal marsupials and terrestrial cassowaries) which demonstrate the flexible ways in which the same categories can be arranged depending on social and technical context. The paper addresses, in particular, the notion of classificatory anomaly as presented by Mary Douglas.

I

Most published ethnographic studies of particular folk classifications have been concerned with the analysis of the structure (or microstructure) of linguistically defined domains, or fragments of domains, and the enumeration of the constituent taxa at different levels within such structures. A glance at reviews of the literature is sufficient to confirm this fact (see e.g. Sturtevant 1964; Tyler 1969). In this respect the approach has been comparable with any formal analysis of a corpus of linguistic data, and to this extent also the techniques of analysis have had the appearance of being extremely refined, sometimes excruciatingly so. And yet, apart from certain occasional statements in general accounts (see e.g. Tyler 1969a: 4–5; Goodenough 1963: 257–64) and individual papers concerned with context in the use of kin terms, the analysis of social settings, the differential use of particular concepts and with reference to multilingual situations (see e.g. Tyler 1969b: 433–4; 1969c: 487–503; Swartz 1960; Frake 1964; Moerman 1969; Gumperz 1969), there appears to have been little attention paid to the question of variability in folk classification of environmental components. In an openly speculative paper, Berlin (1972) discusses possible temporal variation in ethnobotanical nomenclature, but curiously does not consider that synchronic variation which must be at the root of evolutionary changes in taxonomic structures. In part, I think this can be attributed to the particular approach adopted in the analysis of such systems.[1] In most cases the arrangements involved have been characterised as taxonomies, in which:

> Constituent entities, or taxa, are arranged vertically by nondimensional inclusion ... Hierarchic positions in a taxonomy – biological or otherwise – are not permutable, and so far as folk-taxonomies are concerned, the definition and arrangement of included taxa are non-arbitrary (Conklin 1964: 39–40)

Thus a basic premise is that such systems are inherently hierarchical and contrastive; that categories are ordered by the twin processes of inclusion and contrast (see e.g. Tyler 1969b; Conklin 1962; Frake 1962). Indeed, ever since Conklin first carefully and systematically dissected the features of classificatory systems (1962), these attributes have assumed an almost axiomatic quality. This approach has been very fruitful in that it has presented a convenient framework for the acquisition of data on the subject, and must be regarded as having contributed considerably to lexicography, descriptive linguistics, studies in cognition and the extent of indigenous knowledge in different spheres of environmental interaction. But at the same time, this pursuit of the description of increasingly complex and extensive classificatory domains can be criticised for its single-mindedness and for its failure to include a sufficiently critical assessment of the context and variation of the data elicited. Thus, quite apart from any criticisms of the intrinsic validity of studies of this kind (see e.g. Harris 1969: 568–604), the approach has tended to furnish results which, in some instances, can rightly be accused of spurious uniformity; that is, apparent uniformity where it can be demonstrated or assumed with good reason that, in fact, none exists. Further, while the hierarchical-contrastive approach may be an admirable interpretive classificatory and lexicographical device, it is not necessarily conducive to an accurate assessment of the operational role of taxonomies, that is, how they relate to concrete usage situations. After all, classifications are not ossified rubrics of cerebral apparatus, genetically programmed, although the principles that order them may be; they are culturally determined ordering devices interacting constantly with experience, infinitely variable both over time and between individuals.

In this chapter I want to examine in detail just two aspects of the ethnosystematics of the Nuaulu, a sedentary group of hunters and cultivators of central Seram in the eastern Indonesian province of Maluku.[2] Most of the data were obtained from individual informants and through observation in the coastal village of Rohua; they are supplemented by data obtained in four other Nuaulu local groups: Aihisuru, Watane, Hahuwalan and Bunara (Ellen 1978a: 18, Map 4). Quite apart from any intrinsic interest the examples I discuss may have, I hope to be able to illustrate that the approach characterised above can sometimes obscure the most important aspect of non-written classifications, that is, their adaptability. In practical cognitive terms, in decision-making (as opposed to data-storage and lexicography), it may prove valuable to view taxonomies as being inherently variable constructs.[3] Here I focus on just two Nuaulu taxa: for cuscus and cassowary.

II

In an essay published in 1972 (Ellen 1972) I outlined some major aspects of the symbolic significance of the cuscus, the Phalanger, in Nuaulu thought, and in doing so found it necessary to dwell on the formal properties of classification within the category *marane*.

Following the usage of Bulmer and Tyler (1968: 347), the lexeme *marane* itself appears clear and unambiguous in terms of the morpho-syntactic status of nomenclature, the formal status of categories indicated by it, and the semantic load of the label. Morphologically, behaviourally and ritually it cannot readily be confused with any other animal with which the Nuaulu are familiar. It is a marsupial, but the only other marsupial on Seram is the rare and unmistakable Seram island bandicoot (*Rynochomeles prattorum*). It is arboreal, the only other truly arboreal mammals being the civets *lau*, *kuha* and *tui-tui*. In fact, apart from certain introduced domesticated species not kept by the Nuaulu, dogs, deer, pigs and perhaps civets, *marane* is the largest mammal and quadruped known to the Nuaulu (Ellen 1972: 234), but this does not affect the perception of the content of the category. An animal is clearly and quite unambiguously either *marane* or it is not. There are no practical difficulties in identification such as there are, say, for some Nuaulu plant categories, or as Bulmer and Tyler (1968) have described for some Kalam frog taxa.

Although dividing cuscus from non-cuscus is a simple matter, the internal ordering of the taxon *marane* is not so clear-cut. Table 4.1 lists the four Nuaulu terminal segregates which make up the contents of the category *marane*: two quite distinct sexually dimorphic species (Ellen 1972: 226–7; cf. Bulmer 1970: 1079–80), together with those morphological criteria used in systematic zoology to distinguish between the four phenotypes. Each subcategory has been given a numerical symbol for ease of reference, and this appears as a subscript after a lower-case *m*. Interestingly, the indigenous criteria of distinction correspond quite closely to those listed in the table, although since there is no terminological recognition of the existence of two separate species, each subcategory is distinguished by a combination of species and sexual characteristics. By the examination of caught specimens with informants and in general discus-

Table 4.1 Nuaulu categories for the marsupial cuscus

	Terminal category	Notation adopted in text	Content	Sex	Species characteristics	Sexual characteristics
1.	*mara kokowe*	m_1	*Phalanger orientalis orientalis* (Pallas)	–	Ears almost naked inside; body showing no spotting; dorsal line usually grey, but may vary from dark greyish-brown to nearly white – dorsal line distinct	Variability in length; throat and neck may be suffused yellow or rufous in breeding season
2.	*mara osu*	m_2	–	–	–	Usually darker and smaller than the mle; no rufous suffusion on throat and neck
3.	*mara makinete*	m_3	*Phalanger (Spilocuscus) maculates chrysorrhous* (Desmarest) (spotted cuscus)	–	Ears furred on both sides; body usually spotted; no dorsal line; colour usually white, spotted or blotched, but showing wide variation; larger	Fur thick, soft and woolly; colour typically mottled combinations of black, red and white with white belly; larger
4.	*mara sina*	m_4	–	–	–	General colour grey and black; below white, generally tinged with yellow or rufous, sharply defined from dark-coloured flanks; smaller

A modified version of a table which appeared in Ellen 1972 (p. 226, Table 2). The zoological data are extracted from Le Souef and Burrell (1926: 383, 285, 287).

sion of the question of cuscus classification, the following morphological criteria emerged as being the most important and useful as far as the Nuaulu are concerned.[4] By this, I mean that they are those most consistently adopted and mutually agreed upon.

m_1 black dorsal line present, grey; greyish-brown to white throat to neck suffused rufous *msinae* in breeding season.
m_2 black dorsal line present, smaller and darker than m_1; similar colouring but no rufous suffusion.
m_3 no dorsal line; white body usually spotted but considerable variation in colour; largest cuscus subcategory.
m_4 no dorsal line; darkish body usually spotted; dark flanks in contrast to white belly.

Generally, informants felt that accurate identification and description required the combination of a number of different types of feature. Standards of size and colour were spontaneously offered, but with the caveat that such keys were not a consistently reliable means of identification (cf. Bulmer and Tyler 1968: 354–355). Thus, for colour in order of increasing lightness the subcategories were ordered $m_1 - m_2 - m_3 - m_4$; the series also appearing in the same order in terms of increasing size. The circumspection with which such keys were offered as a means of accurate identification indicates a general sensitivity to variation in the distinctive features of cuscus categories, such that except for distinctions such as dorsal line present/dorsal line absent, male genitalia/female genitalia, it would prove exceedingly difficult to describe the differences between them purely in terms of contrastive features. In particular, it was stressed that *mara makinete* (m_3) above all others varied widely in coloration, ranging through black, grey, reddish brown and white, That such variation is sometimes attributable to age is recognised by Nuaulu informants. This is particularly marked in *mara kokowe* (m_1), where there appears to be a consistent terminological distinction between younger forms (or *mara koko putie*) and older forms (*mara koko msinae*), where the younger are distinguished by their generally much whiter and lighter coloration (*putie*) and the older being indicated by a yellow-brown breast (*msinae* = red, red-brown, brown…). *Mara kokowe* of an intermediate hue are sometimes called *mara makioi,* referring to their mixed (reddish-brown, yellow-brown) coloration. Occasionally also animals of indeterminate status are labelled provisionally as *mara putie* or *mara metene,* referring respectively to specimens of a white or darkish hue, while members of m_1 and m_4 showing a rufous suffusion (typical of the breeding season) are at times termed *mara hehue*. In fact, this list could be extended still further to include other names, but the task would be both unnecessary and tedious. The point that I wish to demonstrate is simply that despite the plethora of terms, there is no question of any of them being considered in themselves as 'natural kinds', so much as descriptions of variant individuals. Predictably, it is the younger immature animals that are the most difficult to readily identify and irrespective of subcategory these are termed *mara porune*, for which restrictions appear not to be so rigidly enforced.[5] In general though, discrimination between adult members of these different subcategories is regarded as being easy and straightforward, and all Nuaulu certainly give the impression of being adept at making rapid visual and, often, auditory discriminations. While outsiders may experience severe problems in identification, the Nuaulu generally find few difficulties.

In Table 4.2 the first column lists the three alternative possibilities for the arrangement of terminal categories within the category *marane* as branching diagrams.[6] The second column gives a linear numerical abbreviation as a convenient means of expressing structural type and for ease of subsequent reference in the text, while column three indicates the number of levels of discrimination for each form. The final column gives the actual alternative possibilities as they were elicited from Nuaulu informants. It should be noted that the single structural arrangement 2:2, in fact, realises two alternative classificatory possibilities as shown in the final column. This point is developed further below. The three structural arrangements represented by the notations 1:1:1:1, 1:3 and 2:2 have been respectively termed 'lexical' (or morpho-syntactic), 'ritual' and 'morphological' classifications for reasons which I hope will soon become evident. Each one is dealt with in turn.

Table 4.2 Possible permutations in the structural arrangements of taxa in the Nuaulu category *marane*

	Structural arrangements represented as branching diagrams	Linear notation for reference in text	Number of levels	Actual Nuaulu structural arrangements identified
1.	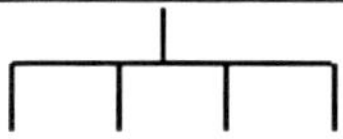	1:1:1:1:	2	$m_1{:}m_2{:}m_3{:}m_4$
2.	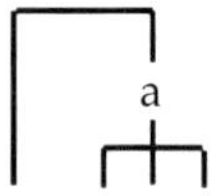 	1:3	3	$m_3 : (m_1{:}m_2{:}m_4)$
3.	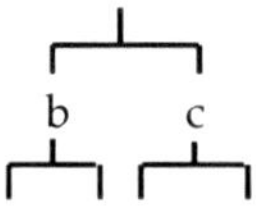 	2:2	3	$(m_1{:}m_3){:}(m_2{:}m_4)$ $(m_1{:}m_2){:}(m_3{:}m_4)$

Lower case letters represent covert mid-level categories. For explanation see text.

The two-level classification of cuscus subcategories is merely an undifferentiated list, in Conklin's (1964: 40) terms an 'index', the contents of which, for the purpose of listing, are taken as having no further criteria of distinction other than their common membership of the category *marane*. This form of primary classification is based on simple class-inclusion and such an undifferentiated form of listing is often the kind of response which ethnographers first elicit. Certainly they cannot afford to assume otherwise at an initial phase in an investigation, although (as has recently been pointed out by Heider) the bias which can follow from assumptions to the contrary is widespread in ethnographic interpretation.[7] At this stage it therefore must simply represent an interim etic assessment of the situation. In such a classification the order in which the terminal categories are given is irrelevant, or must initially be taken as being so. Thus, this was the first arrangement for the *marane* categories which I elicited in the field from informants during formal sessions of questioning. In fact, evidence obtained subsequently suggests that this kind of arrangement is that most commonly used, or rather was that minimally necessary and adequate for most circumstances in which the cuscus is involved. In eliciting, checking and cross-checking the terminal categories for *marane*. I was presented with the items in varying orders. At the time such consistent inconsistency suggested that for the purposes of listing, order was an immaterial consideration. It should be noted that it is only this arrangement which is actually realised in the morpho-syntactic structure of the category (see Table 4.1), and it is for this reason that I have labelled it the 'lexical' classification.

The most common 'contexts of situation'[8] which include physically a cuscus, reference or allusion to it in Nuaulu experience, can be distinguished as follows:

1. occasional chance observations or hearing in the forest while engaged in other activities;
2. confrontation while specifically engaged in hunting cuscus or while consuming its meat;
3. in general conversation;
4. in ritual situations.

I hope to be able to demonstrate that, according to the combination of one of these contexts with different individuals and/or clans, there is variation in the way cuscus classification is envisaged within the category *marane* as revealed through both observation and elicitation of taxonomic information. This is very largely related to the occurrence of one subcategory – *mara makinete* – as a primary totem for three, and a secondary totem for four – giving a total of seven out of the existing ten Nuaulu clans (Ellen 1972: 227, table 3; 1978a: 13, table 4; Chapter 8 in this volume). Thus members of all such clans consider it to be *monne* (sacred), the consumption of its flesh and its slaughter being prohibited. Further, close contact with either a living or dead animal is forbidden, though contact at a distance in the forest, such as near or on a pathway, can be considered auspicious – an omen warning the traveller of danger lying ahead. Violation of such ritual prohibitions is regarded as being followed by supernatural retribution, unless ritual recompense is speedily made. Confrontations with cuscus other than *mara makinete* are generally of no ritual or magical significance whatsoever.

Nuaulu individuals or groups commonly come across single or groups of cuscus when they are engaged in the normal mundane activities which take them outside the village: gardening, hunting large game animals, extracting sago or collecting expeditions of various kinds. Usually identification of variety is adequately achieved by visual means, that is by colour, size and markings (see above). Where greater distances are involved this can be assessed less accurately by size, or more accurately by sound. The Nuaulu are adept at recognising cuscus and its various subtypes by their distinctive calls, and reproduction of these in a village context is a common form of amusement in terms of elaborate play and joking activity. Such sounds and the capacity of the Nuaulu to reproduce them with accuracy becomes particularly important in hunting, when they are used as auditory lures and decoys.

The occasional discovery of a cuscus while taking part in other activities often leads to a chase, either immediately or after the task in hand has been completed. The interval between initial observation, stalking and capture may sometimes be several hours, but this is seldom of any consequence since cuscus are essentially nocturnal and crepuscular creatures, sleeping by day and even when active at night moving only very lethargically. Cuscus hunting may take place as a separate independent activity, but more often it is undertaken in connection with other activities: commonly it is associated with the extraction of wild sago and gardening in distant areas. In the former, the monotonous routine activities of cutting, excavating and processing the sago pith and the extraordinary loneliness and dullness of several days of isolation away from the village are punctuated by the excitement of cuscus hunting. Similarly, the physical exhaustion and drudgery of clearing gardens of primary or secondary growth can be relieved in the same manner. On still other occasions, as I have indicated, a task will be halted while a detected cuscus is pursued, either individually or after seeking cooperation from kinsmen.

Marane is the third most important single animal type in terms of actual gramme-weight and protein consumption in Nuaulu diet; after the pig it is the most important terrestrial source of animal protein. On the basis of dietary records kept over a four-month period it was calculated that some 14.5 were consumed per head per day in the village to Rohua (Table 4.3). However, it has been almost impossible to obtain meaningful figures in

Table 4.3 Catalogue of major sources of animal protein and its consumption, Rohua 1970

Nuaulu category	Content	Mean net weight consumed per head per day over four-month period	Approx. % consumed per head per day over four-month period	Mean number of cals. per head per day over four-month period	Protein by gramme weight per head per day over four-month period
1. *hahu*	wild pig, Sus	22.4	30.5	101.5	2.69
2. *ikae*	all salt and freshwater fish	18.24	25	24.8	3.43
3. *marane*	cuscus, *Phalanger*	14.52	20	19.5	2.9
4. *maianane*	moluccan deer	10.02	12	20.24	1.9
5. *nunu*	all salt and freshwater shellfish	2.5	3.5	1.75	0.25
6. *asuan*	cassowary *Casuarius casuarius*	2.02	3	2.8	0.38
All other species consumed: principally python, civet, crabs, prawns, bats and hornbill		3.56	6	3.71	0.68
TOTALS		74.26	100	174.3	12.23

The figures given in columns 5 and 6 are calculated from constants for the calorific content of foods and the protein percentage of edible portions given in Platt (1962). Kilocalories (calories) are abbreviated to cals.

the field for the amounts of different types consumed. Statements from informants and elementary deduction seem to suggest that in view of the prohibition on the consumption of *mara makinete* for seven Nuaulu clans this cuscus is the least commonly consumed pro rata. There is some evidence to suggest that *mara kokowe* (m_1) and *mara siha* (m_4) are the most frequently eaten, but there are no hard data to substantiate this claim.[9] Thus the cuscus provides an excellent example of an animal which is economically important as a totem, but where hardship is mitigated through the selection of only one terminal type. Its selection involves an element of self-denial, but not so much as to make life difficult.

In the contexts described above the simple two-level lexical mode of classification is adequate for seven of the ten Nuaulu clans, and in formal questioning situations involving members of these clans this was the most common classification elicited, particularly if informants were not questioned further. This is not the case for those three clans for which *mara makinete* is a primary totem where the impression was gained that the reference structure is rather different. Thus in cuscus-hunting contexts and in casual confrontations with the species, it is important for members of these clans to be capable of making rapid and accurate discriminations between prohibited and unprohibited varieties. Again, although it is usually part of the common knowledge of consumers as to what variety of cuscus is being eaten, apart from these clans this is a matter of little moment, except perhaps out of casual interest or in relation to the possibility of eating the genitalia, considered something of a delicacy. For the three clans for which *mara makinete* (m_3) is a primary totem, it is crucial. Thus, in eliciting cuscus categories from such individuals considerable stress was laid on the distinction between the totemic and all other types: the prohibited and the grouped unprohibited. This makes the second or ritual form of classification (1:3) that most appropriate to describe the situation for persons who must consistently differentiate between categories in this manner, regardless of context. It is, of course, realised quite simply by contrasting *mara makinete* (m_3) with all other types subsumed under a single covert category[10] to give m_3: (m_1:m_2:m_4) (Table 4.2). It may well be that here we are simply dealing with a single instance of a general distinction between prohibited and unprohibited animals of all kinds. This is quite likely, but in terms of the internal ordering of the category *marane* it is manifested as a separate method of classifying four grouped terminal types (Figure 4.1).

I now turn to the third or 'morphological' classification of the contents of the category *marane*. It could be argued that the 'ritual' (1:3) classification is in fact based on certain morphological criteria: that *mara makinete* is distinguished by its size and markings. But in this case the features are skewed in such a way as to emphasise the criteria by which one category is differentiated from the other three considered as a group in opposition

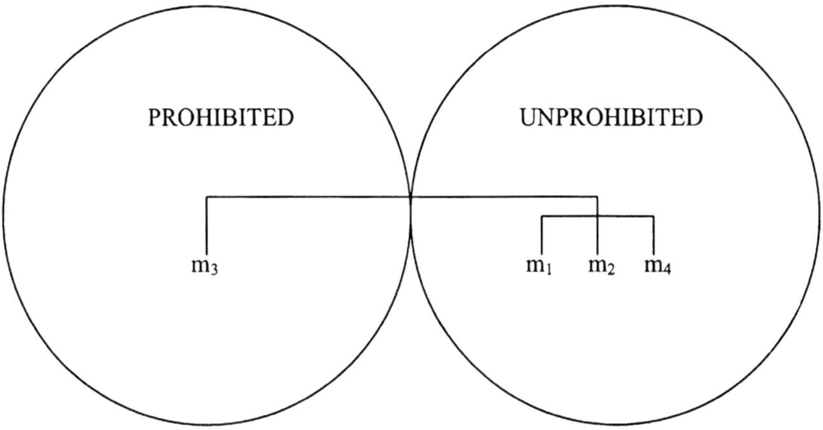

Figure 4.1 The grouping of Nuaulu categories for *marane* (cuscus) in terms of the distinction prohibited:unprohibited

to it. In the third variant of the arrangement of the components of the category marane (2:2), again a three-level structure, observed morphological criteria are important for their own sake and are not skewed to conform with certain ritual attitudes in quite the same way. In fact, there are really two types of morphological classification, one based on the grouping of like sexes and one based on the grouping together of members of the same species or 'natural kinds'. Thus the semantic reference of the covert categories *b* or *c* in Table 4.2 differs in each case. The latter conforms with the phylogenetic arrangement. Diagrammatically, this situation can either be represented as two dendrograms of the formulations (m_1, m_3): (m_2, m_4), or in a single four-celled matrix where sexuality (a) is read horizontally and species (b) vertically (Figure 4.2).

But without careful investigation of the ethnographic contexts in which these different formulations are used, such excessive formalism in expo-

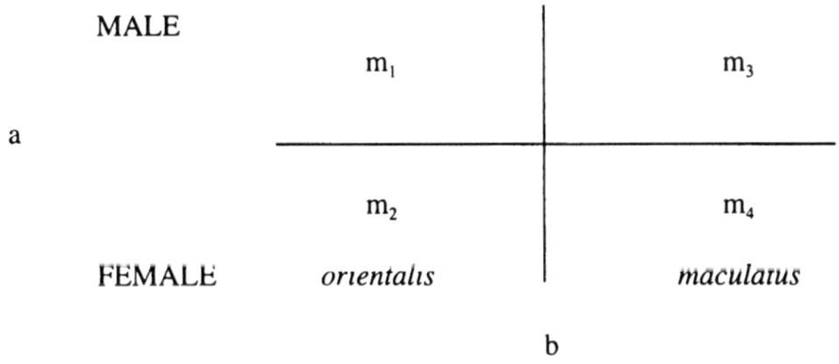

Figure 4.2 Four-cell matrix illustrating the intersection of dimensions of sex and species in classification of Nuaulu categories for *marane* (cuscus)

sition is spurious and misleading. In the first place, this formulation of the arrangement of the categories appears to be the least used by the Nuaulu themselves, as far as observation and formal enquiry can be taken as a reliable indication of this. Ironically, though, it is nonetheless real for all this and is perhaps one of the easiest to pin down, largely because of its conformity in one direction with phylogenetic discriminations. It is a classification which derives either from a need to distinguish between sexes or between mating pairs. These kinds of discrimination, however, are rarely necessary, and this is consistent with the covertness of the mid-level categories.[11] But the formulation is one that is meaningful to the Nuaulu themselves and occurs in certain contexts, not so much as a final and finite categorisation in itself, but as part of a discovery procedure. In practice it appears that differentiation by mating pair or sex is part of the general procedure of identifying *mara makinete*. Thus, distinction simply on the grounds of being male or female (*hanaie* or *pina*) can avoid further lower-level discrimination to verify whether the animal is prohibited or not, since no female cuscus are forbidden as food. But such mid-level covert categories are in practice unimportant since the morphological characteristics which distinguish terminal types from one another are unique (Table 4.1), and therefore more important than distinctions on the basis of sex or biological species. This is of course evident in the absence of Nuaulu terms to gloss the Linnaean categories *Phalanger orientalis* and *P. (Spilocuscus) maculatus*.

III

For the second part of this discussion I want to turn from the cuscus to the Nuaulu category *asuan*, the cassowary. Here the taxonomic problem is of a similar kind, but involves a rather different level of classificatory distinction and a wider morphological range of different animal types. This peculiar flightless bird is a species which has already been the subject of some discussion in the New Guinea ethnography (Bulmer 1967), but in addition to being found in the Papuan ornithological subregion (including the Aru islands) it is also a native of the forests of north Queensland, New Britain and Seram (Rand and Gilliard 1967: 21).

The classification of cassowaries at a species and sub-specific level is still a matter of some controversy and more data and research is necessary. However, on the basis of what knowledge does exist, the Seramese type appears to be of the species *Casuarius casuarius* Linnaeus (van Bemmel 1948: 402), the double-wattled cassowary, the most common and widely distributed species; not *Casuarius bennetti*, the mountain species discussed by Bulmer (1967: 10). Adult birds of both species can be up to 6 ft in height (ranging between 4 and 6 ft), with a blade-like horny casque on the crown, often turned to the left. The wattle tends to vary geographically in shape; the colour of the bare neck and head is mostly blue and red or pink, sometimes with some yellow; young birds have a brown plumage, with much pink and yellow in the skin of the neck; younger birds have the neck feathered; newly hatched chicks are brown, streaked black (Rand and Gilliard 1967: 21–3). The taxonomic and phylogenetic status of the Seramese form is unclear, suggesting (according to Rand and Gilliard 1967: 23) that it has been introduced into Seram, but the evidence either way is slight.

The Nuaulu attitude towards the cassowary is ambiguous and on the basis of what has already been written on the ethnosystematics of the species this is not entirely surprising. However, unlike the situation which Bulmer has described for the Kalam of the Schrader Mountains of New Guinea, this is not a problem which the Nuaulu resolve adequately by assigning the cassowary to a separate and special classificatory status. In fact, the Nuaulu classify the cassowary in two quite different ways, depending on situational context. On the one hand it is unquestionably a member of the higher order category *manue*, together with birds and bats, while on the other it is set within the category *peni*, which also includes the wild pig and the Moluccan deer. In both senses the grouping is 'natural', not biologically (in that it reflects phylogenetic or genetic relations), but logically in that its members possess many attributes in common (see Berlin et al. 1966: 274; Bulmer 1970: 1071). As Bulmer has argued at length (1967; 1970: 1087), higher order groupings, in this case the Nuaulu categories *manue* and *peni*, while natural in the logical sense are understandably not so in a phylogenetic sense. The data which follow illustrate this point, I think, convincingly.

It would have been an interesting and amusing task to have demonstrated that in the Nuaulu case the cassowary *is* a bird, in contrast to the Kalam. However, though it might have been amusing it is certainly not surprising, since it is only to be expected that ritual attitudes to the same species vary between cultures (Bulmer 1967: 10 n. 7; Diamond 1966: 1103). What is much more significant is that at the same time the Nuaulu can maintain in different contexts that it is *not* a bird but a member of a quite separate category, and not think that such flexibility in classification (and there is no question of it not being this) is a matter for comment or correction. The important point to grasp here, of course, is that as with the case of the cuscus just described, it is a demonstration of the simple but much overlooked fact, that classifications of the same species also vary *within* cultures. I first turn to the cassowary as a member of the category *manue*.

The short answer to be obtained in formal elicitory contexts to the open-ended ethnographic question as to what the cassowary *is*, is *asuan* (a cassowary), or when pressed further, *manue* (all boned things which fly), in contrast to being in the residual category, all animals that neither swim nor fly (that is, all terrestrial forms). However, informants found no difficulty in also contrasting the category *manue* in this sense with other 'lower level' categories such as 'snake' (*tekene*) or 'monitor lizard' (*puo*) in order to demonstrate its distinctiveness vis-à-vis other natural kinds. Thus categories at apparently different hierarchical levels, of different orders of classificatory magnitude, are capable of being contrasted with one another (but see Kay 1969: 84–8). The cassowary is regarded as being a member of the class *manue* because the sum total of its morphological attributes (including both minute and gross features of anatomy) and behavioural traits have more in common with the majority of those animals which are capable of flight that it has with any non-*manue* category. The distinctive features of the cassowary in these terms can be rapidly assessed. Among those consistently offered by informants were the following:

1. bipedality;
2. the possession of wings (*man kihena*);[12]
3. the use of plumes and feathers for decorative purposes – arm ornaments and elaborate headdresses;
4. the possession of a bill (*hohe*) and not teeth (*nesiri*), together with the fact that food is swallowed and not chewed;
5. the laying of eggs and not viviparous births.

Some of these points are, of course, not characteristic of bats, which can hardly be said to be bipedal since they do not walk in the conventional sense at all. Class attributes therefore appear, at least sometimes, to be 'statistical' generalisations based on the fact that most, but not all, members possess these traits. There are other examples of this kind of basis for inclusion in Nuaulu animal classification and it is certainly not an uncommon feature of both phylogenetic and European folk classifications. In view of this it might be supposed that the opposition between plumes and fur or hair might serve as a further basis for discrimination. However, in contrast to the situation described by Bulmer for the Kalam (1967: 10), there is no distinctive term for plumes in contrast to the body hair and fur of animals, including man, the root *hunua* simply being altered by the addition of the prefix *man-* (from the root *manu*) to give *man hunua*. From a utilitarian point of view, though, there is a distinction, and one which is fully appreciated. This is that it is only *man hunua* which is used for personal adornment, either for elaborate feather headdresses or as arm ornamentation. In the case of the cassowary it is the plumes of the tail region that are used for the headdresses and to adorn armbands, while the thick quills of the vestigial wings are split and used in the construction of the armbands themselves.

While flightlessness is considered not to be an absolutely crucial determinant of the classificatory status of the cassowary, this fact is not passed over without comment. Its inclusion within the category *manue* is in fact justified in terms of a short but characteristic myth:

> In former times the cassowary had wings and was able to fly as other birds. One day it rested on a fig tree, but it was too heavy and the branch bent over as far as the ground. The cassowary fell off and broke its wings, Now, the hornbill at that time was like the cassowary is now, it was unable to fly. As the branch of the fig tree touched the ground the hornbill jumped upon it. But as the hornbill was lighter than the cassowary the branch soon rose again. Now, the hornbill could not fly – as I told you – so the cassowary offered it its wings. And that is why things are as they are today.[13]

This is a perfect 'Just-So Story'; simply by the power of the myth is the status of the cassowary as *manue* confirmed. But should the problem of flightlessness still leave further ambiguity, the category *manue* is subdivided into two broad intermediate classes: *manue roi ai atu*, 'birds of the forest canopy', i.e. those that fly, and *manua poituomone* (or *manu nohu*), those that do not fly, or more strictly-speaking, 'those that no longer fly'. In some respects this is regarded as a category with certain sacred features, indicated by the use of the terms *monne* and *nohu*, but this appears to relate more to their intriguing classificatory status than to their role in ritual, which is minimal. This category not only includes cassowaries, but also the Moluccas scrub hen (*Eulipoa wallacei* Gray), the brush turkey (*Megapodius freycinet* Gaimard) and similar wildfowl which the Nuaulu classify as 'flightless'.[14]

Clearly the cassowary possesses features which the Nuaulu do not consider to be the primary characteristics of birds: bone-marrow, heavy bones, fleshy thighs which resemble mammal meat more than that of birds, rapid and efficient terrestrial locomotion, and, of course, flightlessness. It is also virtually wingless. The casque (*pipane*) does not appear to present an enormous or fundamental classificatory problem, since the hornbill (*Aceros plicatus* Forster) which, as the myth quoted illustrates, is a perfectly 'good' bird, also possesses a casque. However, it is, I think, of some significance that the only two casqued (as opposed to combed) birds known to the Nuaulu, the cassowary and the hornbill, should be related in such a way mythically. It may be concluded then that in many formal and mundane contexts the Nuaulu find no difficulty in assigning the cassowary to the category *manue*.

In addition to the picture just described, the cassowary is sometimes singled out and classified with *hahu* (domesticated and wild pigs: *Sus scrofa* Linn. and – possibly *S. verrucosus* Miller and Schlegel) and *maianane* (the Moluccan deer: *Cervus timorensis moluccensis* Quoy and Gaimard) in the category *peni*,[15] ritual game animals. At a rather superficial level this term is glossed for outsiders as 'meat', or the local Malay dialect equivalent. If this were really the case it could be argued that we are not dealing here with a genuine ethnozoological category at all, but a term for food or some other specific usage, such as the way in which, in field sport parlance, rabbits and pheasants are both classified as 'game'. However, there is no question that in terms of Nuaulu usage (and as was made quite explicit by informants in appropriate contexts) the category *peni* can be considered contrastable with, and of the same order as, categories such as *manue, marane tekene* and so on, in a way that 'game' is not contrastable with 'bird' or 'mammal'.

There appears to be justification for considering the category *peni* as a valid multi-purpose animal category in terms of six classes of evidence: linguistic, morphological, ecological, behavioural, utilitarian and ritual.

1. In the field I was able to satisfy myself that the term *peni* was being used in the same way as other animal categories, and could be contrasted with them. By applying short elicitory exercises in which the term *peni* occurred alongside terms for other zoological categories, and by observing how the term was used, it was possible to draw certain conclusions which supported this view. Such informal tests, made in food collecting contexts and in connexion with acquiring data on consumption, were supplemented by the collection of brief texts which illustrated the same pattern of usage, with the term *peni* being contrasted with other categories without much difficulty.[16] Thus the morphosyntactic status of the term *peni* is consistent with normal Nuaulu usage in other respects. Although the terms *asuan, hahu* and *maianane* are commonly – perhaps most frequently – referred to simply as 'unitary lexemes' (Conklin 1962: 122), in some contexts of uncertainty or emphasis, a 'bi-segmental composite lexeme' is used, giving *peni asuan, peni hahu* and *peni maianane*. Similarly, in terms of Nuaulu expression of ethnozoological status with reference to categories as members of higher order groupings, it is as appropriate when *peni* is the category concerned as it is for any other. Thus asuan is spoken of as *asuan nai peni*, 'the cassowary of the NATURAL KIND *peni*', in the same way as the formula *nai tekene* and so on are used.

2. From a morphological point of view there are, once it is pointed out, some very obvious reasons for classifying cassowary, pig and deer together, quite apart from those features mentioned above which appear to make it an incongruous member of the category *manue*. Certainly association of the three species is related to their size, being the three largest wild animals known to the Nuaulu and indigenous to Seram. Their bulk is probably matched by their weight, although the reticulated python must be considered a contender in this respect. There are the strong and heavy leg bones in common as well as an overall robustness in the skeletal structure, including the skull. Droppings are all characteristically large – a point which is not without its significance in hunting contexts. Finally,

cassowaries (unlike most birds, but like mammals) possess marrow in their long bones. Bone marrow is considered a great delicacy by the Nuaulu, and that it may be obtained from cassowaries is not without significance.

3. The morphological criteria for inclusion within the category *peni* are, in themselves, hardly sufficiently distinctive. The Nuaulu classificatory logic begins to make more sense when ecological criteria are considered. Broadly speaking, the three species occupy the same habitat, the vast middle and lower altitude zones of primary forest. All dwell on the forest floor. Their food sources are also very similar. All are herbivorous, though pigs and even cassowaries tend to be omnivorous on occasions when opportunities allow. In a domesticated context pigs and small cassowaries will eat discarded flesh, while wild pigs even consume flesh from human corpses in Nuaulu cemeteries. The implication that informants were therefore indirectly eating their ancestors is usually met with a mixture of disgust and amusement. However, the principal food of both pigs and cassowaries is fallen fruit and forest litter in general. Cassowaries, according to informants, tend to be somewhat selective in their eating habits and I was furnished with a list of fruits and seeds considered as typical cassowary fodder. Such knowledge of cassowary diet is employed in hunting and hunting magic. Pigs have the reputation among the Nuaulu, as among others, of being universal scavengers. The eating habits of deer differ somewhat from the pig and cassowary, eating fresh leaves. This means that they are more commonly associated with riverine and more open areas, where shrubby trees and plants are more plentiful. All three species are commonly found in garden areas and are considered pests, despite the fact that the amount of damage each species may cause is by no means equal. Measures taken to dissuade them – particularly pigs – are never entirely effective. Although none is considered to be by nature capable of domestication, occasionally pigs and cassowaries are tamed and fatted. Rarely, though, are these animals allowed to reach full maturity. All three species have no other predators apart from the reticulated python and humans.

4. From a behavioural standpoint there are also important similarities between the three species. The haunts are all characterised by similar traces: pig-wallows in muddy depressions in level ground which retain water, leafy cassowary nests in depressions of the forest floor and deer haunts in comparable but open spots. All animals are extremely mobile. All (including – surprisingly – cassowaries) will swim when compelled to do so. All have characteristic and deadly weapons: pigs their teeth, deer their legs and antlers, and cassowaries their kick. The notorious kick of the cassowary is enshrined in many Nuaulu myths, stories and reminiscences.

5. The size of *peni* animals immediately suggests their significance as important sources of animal protein, and certainly all three are very important in nutritional terms (see Table 4.3). Pork and venison rate first and fourth respectively in terms of consumption; cassowary appears to rate about sixth in importance. Thus although *peni* species provide half of all protein derived from all animal sources and the same in terms of weight, protein is not equally distributed between the three species. The small contribution made by cassowary meat appears to be partly related to its relative rarity compared with other species, although there is no evidence that the cassowary is any rarer on Seram than it is elsewhere. Certainly it has never been the subject of ritual conservation measures (*sasi*) or governmental control, which has been the case for the deer in the recent colonial past. This may be related to the fact that it is only the mountain and interior peoples of Seram who hunt and consume it with any regularity. The low figures for consumption must also be related to the fact that the proportion by weight and mass of the cassowary that is edible is considerably smaller than that for the other two *peni* species.

As well as being important sources of food, *peni* species are also significant providers of other animal-derived products. In fact, apart from *manue* (which provide bird feathers and plumes, and the hollow forelimb bones of bats which are used as pipes for smoking locally grown tobacco), lime and scrapers provided by molluscs and occasionally snakeskin, no other fauna are regarded as useful in these respects. This would not include, though, hunting trophies kept as status symbols and to secure fortune in future hunting. On the other hand, pig and deer provided skins and bone tools and ornaments. Similarly, the cassowary provides feathers and wing quills and claws (sometimes used as lime containers) for the purpose of ornamentation, and leg bone used for making bradawls for use in various kinds of craftwork.

6. The meat of all members of the category *peni* is subject to a prescribed ritual distribution among clansmen and affines, and an offering must be made to clan ancestors on each occasion a *peni* animal is killed. The lower jawbones of pig and deer and, in the case of the cassowary, the breastbone, is then kept in the roof-space of the house, ideally strung up on rattan, though commonly stored in large quantities in baskets to await removal to completed clan ritual houses. This is believed to preserve hunting fortune. It is forbidden to dispose of *penesite* (literally, 'the mandibles of *peni* animals') obtained in this manner, under any circumstances.

The cassowary is clearly quite unlike both the pig and deer in many respects – morphological and behavioural – and there is no question of the Nuaulu being blind to such differences. These are continually appar-

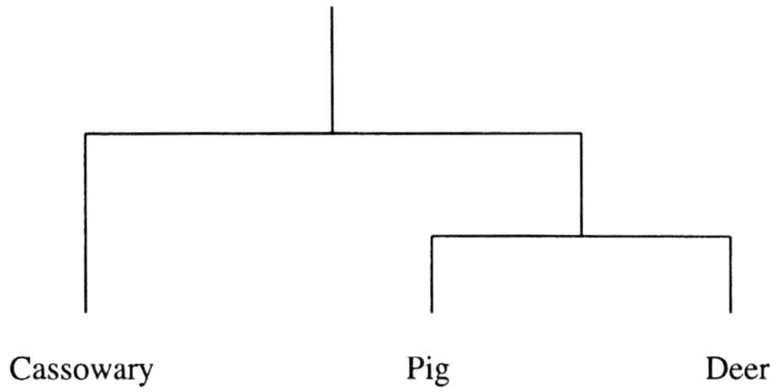

Figure 4.3 Representation of the internal structure of the Nuaulu category *peni* (cassowary, pig and deer) as a dendrogram

ent from even the most cursory inspection: bipedelism as opposed to quadrupedalism, the fact that only leg meat is eaten, and so on. Similarly, the resemblances between pig and deer are obvious: the cuts of meat are alike, as is their internal anatomy and external morphology, they are both hooved, quadrupeds, furred and not feathered, and so on. In fact the Nuaulu recognise that in terms of features which they themselves consider diagnostically significant the deer and the pig are related covertly within the category *peni,* in opposition to the cassowary. Thus it is possible to represent the internal structure of the category *peni* in terms of a simple 1:2 construct (Figure 4.3).

Again, as with the ritual classification of cuscus, we may very well be dealing here with an overarching distinction between the semi-covert category of terrestrial animal and labelled category *manue.* While this may illustrate the considerable taxonomic difficulties that the Nuaulu experience in allocating a niche for the cassowary, it is, in hunting and domestic contexts, an unquestioned and unambiguous member of the zoological category *peni.* Indeed, there is even further evidence in support of this embodied in Nuaulu myths. Thus those explaining the origin of cassowary, pig and deer all have a striking similarity in structure and all are narratives involving the inversion of the properties of autochthonous species in order to account for the present salient features of the animals. For the cassowary, as I have illustrated, this involves the dog. As to whether the category *peni* is essentially a ritual one or a utilitarian one is not important. It is rationalised in terms of the morphological, ecological and behavioural criteria which are characteristic of Nuaulu animal classification in general, and as a zoological category is considered in this respect no different from any other.

IV

It appears most unlikely that the variation described above is simply to be explained in terms of classificatory confusion or the error of an inattentive informant (cf. Heider 1972: 463), or even muddled ethnographic interpretation. As most ethnographers must be aware, sometimes even actual variation can be hidden by mutual agreement between informants, or through the dialectics of disagreement between individuals, who in the end give the impression of uniformity where it does not exist, out of courtesy, to avoid conflict or to save time.

I have tried to be as thorough and accurate as possible given the data at my disposal. But if all arrangements given are valid ones then the implications seem to be substantial, in that taxonomic procedures are perhaps not necessarily so rigid as has been supposed, but admit a degree of variability. If so, what kinds of variability emerge?

I have found it useful to recognise two broad dimensions of variation: (a) variation in usage by the same individual according to different contexts, and (b) variation in usage between different individuals. The types of variation, as illustrated in my data, and which occur along either or both of these axes are as follows:

1. variation of classificatory arrangement according to context within a given category;
2. variation as to the allocation of a labelled category according to context;
3. variation in the distinctive features emphasised as being minimally necessary for class inclusion.

The first type is best exemplified by variation between individuals and by the same individuals in different contexts for the internal structure attributed to the category *marane*. The second is exemplified by the alternative classification of cassowary as *manue* or *peni* by the same individuals on different occasions, while the third and final form is apparent to varying degrees along both axes and for both examples, but is perhaps clearer in the case of the cassowary. Here, since the distinctive features emphasised vary according to classificatory context, it appears that distinctive feature analysis, as a central part of the methodology of ethnosystematics must be used with great caution. At least this must be so insofar as such features are considered absolute and immutable. In particular it points to some very profound difficulties in assessing the validity of the selection of features used for the construction of what are purported to be singular and definitive classificatory domains.

It has become almost a cliché to maintain that synchronic variation does not begin at the boundary of any given culture, and that rather the border represents a threshold where variability is at its greatest. Some authors (e.g. Lienhardt 1961) have made this precise point in relation to cosmologies. Indeed, variation and differences between informants of this and related kinds are universally experienced by ethnographers in the field, but by and large it is not evident in published reports, which tend rather to be composed primarily of 'general statements' (cf. Heider 1972: 448). While the literature abounds in confident discussion of conflict between cosmology and practice, there is relatively little discussion of the contradictions and correspondences between different versions of cosmologies, or sections of them, and of the possibility that perhaps in some cases no single well-defined and consistent cosmological position exists.

The situation described for cosmology applies equally to systems of classification. Among workers in the ethnozoological field, Bulmer has been most candid in pointing out inter-individual variation, in connection with divergent opinions over the identification of individual specimens of live or preserved animals (see Bulmer 1968: 621–3; Bulmer and Tyler 1968: 336, 347, 351, 360). The publication of a verbatim text on the classification of Kalam frogs in particular illustrates this (Bulmer and Tyler 382–3). I myself have collected several similar texts and taped conversations which show the same thing for Nuaulu ethnozoology. In a paper published in 1972, Eleanor Rosch Heider attempted to demonstrate quantitatively such variation, in this case for Dani colour terms, and was able to illustrate some of the problems which emerge from an unsystematic intake of information of this kind. Here there has been no possibility of meeting the sort of experimental criteria discussed by her. The classification of animals presents problems much more considerable than those met with in the analysis of Dani colour names – not least in the greater number of dimensions of variation. For the purposes of this paper the degree of variation is, however, not the point at issue; rather, I am interested simply in its very existence and the way in which this is reflected in formal taxonomic structures elicited from informants.

Variation between individuals in the use of particular taxonomic devices must clearly be related to some extent to individual knowledge of fauna, which is quite unlikely to be completely identical. Although all individuals in a community use some particular form of taxonomic ideas to order knowledge and experience of the animal species with which they come into contact, the extent of that knowledge and the degree to which it is reflected upon, i.e. intellectualised, must be subject to considerable variation. This, of course, is relevant to a consideration of the division of labour, in that particular individuals are singled out as experts. Sometimes knowledge in the field of biological identification is regarded as a branch of expertise appropriate to persons of authority in other spheres, and may be a skill necessary for aspirants to positions of power. Persons of ascribed status, usually on account of age but also headman of formal groupings, may also be acknowledged experts. In such cases it may be possible to identify orthodoxies perpetuated because they have the support of ascribed authority. Among the Nuaulu, although ethnozoological knowledge is equally accessible to all, experts are recognised simply on the acknowledged merit of their past performances. Often these are male elders who have obtained knowledge through experience, while sometimes they are males in defined positions of ritual and political authority, although this is by no means entirely the case. Experts of this kind, especially when they are adept at communicating their knowledge and capable of reproducing it in an abstract fashion, are usually recognised as the real experts in a consultative sense. They also make the best informants!

On both the synchronic and diachronic axes, classifications can be generated in various ways according to context, and to a very considerable extent, semantic usage varies in connection with the demands of particular situations. In this sense classification is like historiography, in that it is possible for at least two quite different versions to coexist. We might, for example, distinguish between classifications which maintain certain ideational subsystems and those which do not. While in some contexts a vertical classification of Nuaulu domestic space is appropriate, on other occasions, in other contexts, a horizontal classification is invoked that is not entirely consistent with the former. Sometimes it is sufficient to classify terrain in terms of a limited set of topographic categories; in other contexts fine discrimination of vegetative cover necessitates the employment of a quite different and cross-cutting set of categories. Thus the 1:3 classification for the cuscus among the Nuaulu perpetuates the ritual properties in terms of the separation of *mara makinete* from all other cuscus categories; but in other contexts such a classification would not affirm certain other significant properties. Likewise, the classification of the cassowary as *peni* draws attention to its utilitarian and ritual features, while neglecting some other more formal morphological properties which assign it to the category *manue*. Species which are often singled out by investigators as being anomalous creatures are frequently only anomalous or marginal in a restricted sense, in terms of one particular form which a classification can take. For the Nuaulu the anomalous character of the cassowary varies according to the paradigm which is being operated. Thus what is functional in terms of one subsystem is not necessarily so in terms of another. There exist inherent contradictions between classifications established with respect to different functional subsystems.

It is also important to bear in mind that the most fundamental (and least changeable) categories in Nuaulu animal classifications are those found at the level where the degree of correspondence between phylogenetic and folk classification is at its greatest; nomenclaturally normally represented by uninominals, and biologically generally equivalent to species or genera. In evolutionary terms also, these might be characterised as possessing some degree of priority, other levels (terminal or higher order groupings) being essentially secondary and derivative (see Berlin 1972). Often, the employment of higher order groupings involves the adoption of a common lower-order lexeme, resulting in a polysemous situation. Thus when the Nuaulu label *manue* at one level it refers to all things that fly, but it is also a generic term referring specifically to the domesticated and certain other types of wild fowl (*Gallus* spp.). Thus the term *manue* is homonymous and consequently ambiguous.[17] This should caution analytical emphasis on the major significance of higher order categories and make understandable some of the apparent 'confusion' I have been discussing. In fact, I would tentatively suggest that the greater the classificatory distance from the level of 'natural kind', the greater the degree of ambiguity we should expect to find.

There is a danger in investigations in this field of treating formal analyses of 'taxonomic' structures as 'things in themselves'; of reifying them when in fact they are intricately related to the practical problems of environmental interaction, extracting and control in the widest sense. Accepting the distinction made by Berlin, Breedlove and Raven (1966: 274–5) between general systems of classification and special systems based on a few attributes relevant for a particular purpose, I am suggesting that sometimes the degree of specificity of so-called 'general' systems may be overlooked. As these scholars have pointed out, 'a general classification can never be perfect for all purposes'. Further, the 'necessity' for specificity can lead to the types of variation in classification I have indicated. I think it is evident from the kind of illustrations given, that they relate to immediate working models which assist in the operation of Nuaulu processes of decision-making, varying according to context of production or man-environment interaction. We are dealing here not with collectors (like biological taxonomists) but users. Indeed, to treat classifications as isolated and abstract engenders and perpetuates the worst kind of anthropological lepidoptery, the accumulation of isolated 'systems of classification' for their own sake and an ossified and not dynamic view of classificatory processes. Although, as Bulmer and Tyler (1968: 334) have pointed out, knowledge, formal taxonomy and nomenclatural syntax must be examined in their own right, they are all closely related and can only be fully understood in terms of the contexts in which they are used. Since Durkheim and Mauss published their *De quelques formes primitives de classification* (1901–2), it has been realised that categories are not neutral but have attachments of an extra-classificatory kind. They do not exist in a void.

Since productive processes and human-environment relations are never completely static, so classification of that environment must be assumed to be in a continual state of flux, having to accommodate new needs and new responses to environmental, economic and, for that matter, ideational constraints. In fact, once genuine intracultural variation of this kind is admitted it cannot logically be assumed that the system is one in equilibrium (cf. Heider 1972: 464). Some ordering devices become increasingly acceptable, others lose their relevance and disappear. This, of course, cannot be demonstrated empirically with the material available, but to consider classifications with reference to a temporal dimension can appreciably affect analysis at any given point in time. Although it is conceivable that a statistically predominant classification for any given domain might be shown to exist, in the same way as it might be possible to isolate a predominant ideology, this does not invalidate any other versions which may exist.

In this chapter I have chosen to illustrate my argument with reference to detailed problems surrounding two primary categories in Nuaulu classification of animals. Other domains and other problems could have been selected to illustrate the same or similar points. For example, the environmental classification of land types represents an area where, much more than in the classification of natural species, this kind of variation is apparent. Indeed, at this level new kinds of variability are encountered: the absence of static boundaries to categories, continua between polar types and so on. Part of the reason is that while natural species – plant, animal and mineral types – are elemental or primary categories (that is, they cannot be reduced any further in terms of component organisms), categories of land forms are composite or secondary, being composed in part of categories of the former kind, and therefore reducible. However, in dealing with a domain where variation is much more limited, I hope to have demonstrated that the points made must necessarily apply to more complicated systems. The corollary, therefore, is that an ethnographer must apply considerable caution before assuming that the structure of a particular classificatory domain has been elicited and suspicious of unsubstantiated claims in the literature to have done so. It should also make us wary of similar statements to the effect that one classification is real and the others simply keys to aid identification or to draw attention to particular utilitarian or other features of a category. Perhaps it should encourage the systematic exploration of variation within such 'systems' which are often somewhat less rigid than might have been supposed (or than we might care to readily admit), and where the dimensions of such variation are not always easily apparent. It must then surely follow that in any examination of such 'inherent variability' for secondary composite categories, and in the ambitious formal cross-cultural comparison of semantic categories and structures, even more caution is required.

Notes

1. Although this chapter, in part, embodies a criticism of the way in which methodology has influenced results in this field, the argument is not constructed around this important issue. See, however, Friedberg (1968).
2. The field research on which this paper is based was undertaken from December 1969 to May 1971 under the auspices of Lembaga Ilmu Pengetahuan Indonesia (the Indonesian Academy of Sciences) in Jakarta. During this period I was supported by grants in aid from the Social Science Research Council, the London-Cornell Project for East and Southeast Asian Studies and the Central Research Fund of the University of London. To all these bodies I am most grateful. I am also indebted to the Department of Zoology, British Museum (Natural History) for assistance. Various versions of this paper have been read to audiences at the University of Leiden, the London School of Economics and Political Science and the Paris conference on *Méthodes enquête ethnologiques sur la conceptualisation et la classification des objects et phénomènes naturels*, and I would like to thank all those persons who have made valuable comments on the manuscript. In particular, I would like to mention Rita Hayes, the late Professor G.B. Milner, Dr D.W. Snow, David Lee and Jacqueline Hill who helped with problems of transcription, and above all, Professor Ralph Bulmer, whose model and pioneer work I admire greatly and to whose criticisms and support I owe much in developing these ideas.
3. I am not suggesting here that the basic units of any classification are therefore simply the arbitrary end-product of ordering systems which reduce the universe to manageable units through standardised processes. I acknowledge that in a very real sense minimal 'natural' units exist, are perceived to exist and are commonly labelled items (see Bulmer 1970: 78–9: Bulmer and Tyler 1968: 349–51, 375–80). Rather, I am concerned with how (given such units) taxonomies can be arranged and rearranged in different circumstances. The problems discussed stem directly from difficulties which emerged during and subsequent to fieldwork in Seram, when in the course of the analysis of decision-making processes resulting in the observed Nuaulu pattern of settlement it became clear that a great deal of attention should be paid to indigenous perception of environmental relations and categories. Inevitably, in retrospect, the data obtained which relate to the discussion at hand are not as detailed or as satisfactory in other respects as I would wish.
4. In the field specimens were examined both alive and dead, in the course of hunting expeditions, prior to preparation for eating in the village and in the ritual context of male initiation ceremonies. It is difficult to estimate accurately how many separate specimens were examined during the course of eighteen months' fieldwork, but judging from records kept for household consumption of cuscus it must have been in the region of sixty-five animals. For a period of four months I kept a male *Phalanger orientalis* in captivity, which gave me an opportunity to observe some of its habits at close quarters and served as a useful aid in discussing cuscus natural history with informants. Unfortunately, due to bulk and difficulties in transportation, only one specimen (from the period 1970–5) was subsequently examined by the Mammal Section of the British Museum (Natural History), a young male *P. orientalis orientalis* (field catalogue number 102: *mara kokowe*). I owe this identification to the assistance of Mr. J.R. Edwards Hill.
5. *Mara porune* was contrasted by some Nuaulu informants with *mara onate*, and this usage appears to apply to all four terminal adult categories. Although

onate can accurately be glossed as 'large, big', *porune* cannot be glossed simply as 'little, small' (*ikine*), despite the fact that, in contrast to *onate*, this must naturally be one of its semantic referents. It is a genus-specific term, used for no other animal, and is therefore similar to such English folk usages as 'cygnet' or 'lamb'. However, in certain contexts the term was used to differentiate an individual from any one of the four adult forms. The reason for this appears simply to be that the characteristics (which as Table 4.1 illustrates are basically in terms of size and fur coloration) are not always visible in the morphology of the younger members of the genus.

6. There are, in fact, five logical possibilities in the arrangement of branching diagrams. Adopting the conventions used in Table 4.2, the remaining two alternatives can be represented as 1:1:2 and (2:1):1. These five alternatives represent the logical possibilities for *any* taxon divided into four distinctive terminal taxa. However the last two types need not concern us, since no Nuaulu informant spontaneously proffered a classification which could be set out in such a fashion, while other circumstantial ethnographic and zoological evidence suggests that in themselves they make little taxonomic or ideological sense.
7. Heider writes: 'No anthropological disease appears more rampant than "Baysian ethnocentrism". That is, an ethnographer uncovers a not easily obtained fact about his field culture which he believes to be of general theoretical significance and which, for his "people", is associated with some more obvious phenotypic trait. Thereafter, his subjective a priori probability for that fact (his conditional probability that the fact will be present in any other culture, given that the phenotypic trait is present) is so high that no negative evidence about another culture will make him reject the hypothesis that the fact is present there too' (1972: 465 n. 1).
8. I use this term in the knowledge of the criticisms levelled against it. It is simply used here in the absence of any other suitable alternative (Robins 1971; Whitely 1966: 144). In terms of Whitely's variables (1966: 141–4), I am concerned with variation in classes to which concepts belong, depending on social group and social context. The term 'social context', however, appears inappropriate for my purpose, since the contexts in which taxonomies are utilised are not always social. They may be more strictly-speaking 'cultural', 'technical' or 'environmental'. When 'context' alone appears in what follows it refers to both social group and other kinds of context.
9. This picture seems also to be reflected in the cuscus types used for male puberty ceremonies (Ellen 1972: 230–1). Although theoretically *mara makinete* can be used for those clans for which it is not totemically prohibited, this seldom happens at the present time on account of the practice of (a) grouping clans in pairs or groups of more than two for initiation ceremonies, and (b) the officiation of elders from other clans for which it may be prohibited. On the two occasions that I attended these rituals in 1971 and 1972, of the total of twelve cuscus involved, four were *mara kokowe* and eight *mara siha*.
10. This term was introduced into the literature on folk taxonomies by Berlin, Breedlove and Raven (1968). The case in point, as with the other examples cited below, demonstrates conveniently the necessity to separate cognitive categories from their labels (see e.g. Kay 1969: 85). There are many taxonomic distinctions which are either normally not verbalised at all or not labelled with a simple and consistent lexeme (Berlin 1972: 73).
11. It might be thought that in discriminations based on sexuality, the terms for male (*hanaie*) and female (*pina*) might be applied. During fieldwork I never came across this usage in general speech. The term *mara hanaie* is, however,

substituted for *mara kokowe* in the presence of members of the opposite sex, as it is used metaphorically to refer to the penis (Ellen 1972: 220 n. 17).

12. The generic term *kihena* also includes the lateral fins of fish and the forelimbs of sea-mammals.
13. A free translation from the original Nuaulu text, obtained from Komisi Soumori, Rohua, 4 May 1970.
14. Strictly speaking, these megapodes are capable of flight, though the adult forms seldom do so (see Frith, e.g. 1962).
15. I have dealt cursorily with the term *peni* elsewhere (Ellen 1972: 228). [For a fuller account of this category in Nuaulu see Ellen 1996].
16. For example, the following is an extract from a text listing different kinds of curing apparatus (*hotune*) used for meat and other foods:

hotu tau muehu marane re	there is a curer for preparing cuscus
hotu-marane hotu-peni	a cuscus curer, a *peni* curer,
hotu-tekene, hotu-ikae	a snake curer, a fish curer…

Informants: Wasale Neipane – tomoien with the assistance of Teliam Matoke, Rohua, 24 January 1971.

17. George Milner has pointed out to me that something similar to this is to be found in the English usage of the words 'fowl' and 'bird'. The latter formerly had a much more restricted meaning than at present, but gradually became cognate with the biological class of *Aves*, while the former from being the more general classificatory term became the more restricted. This development has been accompanied by an appropriate degree of ambiguity (see Leach 1966: 557–8).

CHAPTER 5

Anatomical Classification and the Semiotics of the Body (1977)

Introduces the concepts of synthetic (kind of) and analytic (part of) classification. The chapter examines some cross-cultural examples of body partonymy and shows how these relate to the semiotic use of anatomical parts.

It is now generally accepted that in order to understand symbolic and more general semiotic systems it is necessary to go beyond them and investigate the classificatory structures in which they are set. In some cases the relationship between symbol and category has been worked out in detail, as exemplified in the now considerable literature on classificatory anomalies (Douglas 1966; 1973: 113–67). In others the relationship is less well understood and systematic analysis is still in its infancy. In this chapter I discuss the classificatory basis and some aspects of the semiotic use of that common source of potent symbols – the human body. The first two sections examine the classification of body parts in general, while the remaining sections are an attempt to relate such classifications to some consideration of their cognitive and cultural uses.

Analytical and Synthetic Classifications

In comparison with other fields in ethnoscience, the subject of anatomical classification has been neglected. Sturtevant (1964) makes no mention of it, and the exhaustive bibliography compiled by Conklin (1972) and his associates provides only a handful of items of direct relevance (Franklin 1963; Friedrich 1969; Lenormand 1950; Mahr 1960; Stark 1969; Werner and Begishe 1970). In fact, with a few interesting exceptions, the situation is much as Marsh and Laughlin described it almost two decades ago (1956:

56), useful data being either scarce or non-existent. Considering the distinctiveness of such classifications when compared with those which have been subject to more extensive examination, and their relevance to the study of body symbolism, this is rather surprising. Papers by Lewis (1974) and Perey (1975) are recent exceptions to the general lack of interest.

Those classificatory systems which have been subjected to the most intensive investigation are largely ethnobiological, and can be characterised as being composed of units arranged by a process of aggregation into units with still greater extension: categories are constructed and elements sorted into categories (Cole et al. 1971: 59–91). Examples include systems based on a variety of classificatory principles: index, paradigms, trees, keys, typologies and taxonomies (Conklin 1964: 39–40), and combinations of two or more of such. Studies that ostensibly concern the analysis of classificatory systems in general have tended to refer predominantly, if not exclusively, to classification of this kind, particularly taxonomies (Perchonak and Werner 1969: 229–37; Werner and Fenton 1973: 543, 561). However, some classifications are not adequately described in such terms, either entirely or in part. Instead, the classificatory process commonly proceeds in an opposite fashion, through the separation of parts of a natural totality, or the decomposition into constituent parts of a system at a given level. This sort of operation, which Stark (1969: 1) has termed 'partiality', is evident in human and non-human anatomical classification of parts of cultural artefacts. Thus relevant segregates might be 'human-arm-hand' rather than, say, 'human-mammal-vertebrate'.

This fundamental distinction between two classificatory procedures has not gone unrecognised, but its implications have been followed up with only the most desultory empirical research. Conklin (1962: 131–2) phrased the difference as one between 'part of' (part-whole) classifications and those based on 'kind of' (class inclusion) relations, and following Nagel (1961: 381–3) appreciated the kinds of ambiguities to which the latter can give rise (cf. Frake 1961; Berlin, quoted in Werner and Begishe 1970: 250–5; Werner and Fenton 1973: 561–2). A comparable distinction is made in structuralist theory between structures and aggregates, the former conferring on the whole overall properties distinct from those of the elements, and the latter being composed of elements that are independent of the complexes into which they enter (Piaget 1971a: 6–10; cf. 1971b: 169). All these dualistic distinctions indicate certain qualities of the classifications to which they refer. However, none of these terms conveys adequately and unambiguously the senses required.

Consequently, rather than choose any one pair, I propose to call them 'analytic' and 'synthetic' classifications respectively, placing emphasis on process: on the one hand analysis (separation), on the other synthesis (aggregation). Among its several advantages, the emphasis on process avoids the misconception that the two types are quite independent. In fact, as is the case for the body, both may be present in the same arrangement. To summarise, the following pairs of terms emphasise different aspects of the same basic distinction:

Part of	:	Kind of
Structure	:	Aggregate
Concrete	:	Abstract
Analytical	:	Synthetic

While it is inappropriate to explore these distinctions in any detail here, even less to discuss the range of other semantic relations which can be seen as derivatives (Casagrande and Hale 1967), it is useful to make a few points and map out some of the most significant co-ordinates of each column:

1. Conventionally, synthetic classifications are a means of distinguishing degrees of similarity and difference in natural species and other elements, the point of departure being plural, clearly bounded natural units. Analytical classifications are associated with the categorising of items which are dependently (typically spatially) related, where the point of departure is a whole single natural element.
2. Synthetic classification proceeds through a process of aggregation (grouping together) of lower-order elements on the basis of the distinctive features of each. Analytical classification proceeds through a process of separation of parts of a single unit, primarily determined by their spatially one-to-one dependent relationships.
3. In synthetic classification the basic units are concrete entities, while higher-order categories have no such existence and are artificial constructs. This, in part, accounts for the regularity and intellectual clarity which such classifications often possess. In other words, order can be imposed upon them. The lower-order units of analytical classifications exist only in relation to the whole of which they are part and usually have no existence by themselves; or their existence apart from the whole is of a different order altogether. However, unlike their synthetic counterparts, all levels and elements in analytical hierarchies frequently have a concrete existence.
4. The depth of synthetic classifications tend to be relatively shallow, but with considerable horizontal expansion. In analytical classifications, both vertical and horizontal expansion depends on concrete possibilities. Overall dimensions, therefore, tend to be more variable.
5. In synthetic classifications there appear to be certain restrictions on the number of unitary lexemes strung together in terminologically meaningful chains, whereas in analytical classifications it is possible to string together longer chains (Berlin in Werner and Begishe 1970: 250).

6. In synthetic classifications, contrast between elements at any one level is both essential and emphasised, though it may give rise to ambiguities. In analytical classifications, contrast at any one level exists but is often poor; in part due to the ambiguous status of link items between principle components, and in part due to the fact that 'levels' themselves are inadequately defined. Contrast operates more after the fashion of 'trees'.
7. Spatial terminology is generally absent in the constitution of most synthetic domains, other than in those specifically concerned with spatial phenomena. In analytical classifications, spatially dependent terminology is important in the construction of all domains.

These points, which relate primarily to folk classifications, go some way to indicate the crucial importance of the constraints of material structure on the perception of forms classified analytically. Specifically, anatomical classification is structured through the geometry of the body: the constraints are somatic. A 'hand' does not have a separate existence from the 'body', whereas a 'cackatua' can easily and in a very real sense have a separate existence from the artificial category 'bird', or some differently defined more inclusive category. Moreover, a 'cackatua' can be placed in a slightly different category depending on various cultural and contextual criteria. For the Nuaulu of Seram in eastern Indonesia, the category *manue* is not the equivalent of the English 'bird' or the Linnaean *Aves*, since the criteria for its definition are not the same, allowing for the inclusion of bats. Moreover, depending on the context, the cassowary is classified by the Nuaulu either as *manua* or *peni*, a sacred category of game animals (Ellen 1972, Chapter 4 in this volume). The extent to which the cassowary belongs to the category 'bird' and its approximate glosses in other languages is dependent upon the construction of the category and the distinctive features of the cassowary emphasised. The body, however, has its own concrete existence, not just a mental one, and the hand, according to all anatomical logics, is unambiguously classified as part of it.

The body provides the brain with a ready-made classificatory framework for its parts, though the operational image of the body may indeed be modified through the processes of cerebral organisation and socialisation. To this extent we might expect 'natural' analytical classifications to be less malleable than artificial ones, which are, after all, themselves cultural constructs. Some observational measure of this is to be found in Stark's consideration of the Nida-Conklin hypothesis (Conklin 1962: 132; see also Frake 1961: 121): that there is a positive correlation between the lexical elaboration of a classification and its cultural importance. Stark (1969: 12) found that this hypothesis was not borne out in her analysis of Quechua body parts, although the hypothesis would appear to hold for different levels and segregates within the domain (Franklin 1963: 57).

Nevertheless, both natural and artificial analytical classifications contrast with the fundamental mental construction of synthetic ones, however much the latter may be fashioned from distinctive features of species which exist in a concrete world, and however much the classificatory devices owe to the bricolage of cultural existence in nature. A cackatua remains a 'bird' just as long as the definition fits those properties of the cackatua of which the classifier wishes to express. A hand remains a part of the 'body' since any change in the definition of the body is incapable of severing (metaphorically or physically) the association of hand and body. This may explain why isolated artistic representations of body parts sometimes appear odd and generate a certain unease until they become accepted in their new context. The difficulty arises in part from the unusual environment, but also from the fact of their being part of an unrepresented whole. The perception and classification of the physical relations between body parts is something that seems to occur very easily in the development of a child[1] and although synthetic classifications also appear early, they tend to undergo rapid and more substantial cultural modification. Such a gestalt conception of the human body as an integrated whole has important implications for the study of its semiotic use.

The Relationship between Different Classificatory Processes

Despite the differences between the two types of classification briefly outlined, the relationship between them is not always clear at an operational level; both being observed with respect to the same group of elements and being transformable into each other (e.g. Stark 1969: 14, n. 6; Werner and Fenton 1973: 561–2). Once constructed, synthetic structures can easily become reified as Lévi-Strauss has elegantly demonstrated for the category 'totemism' (1962). Such a practice is the source of many apparent anomalies in synthetic classifications. In Piagetian terms, an aggregate may appear to become a structure; the abstract is concretised. Even the very use in synthetic classification of the term 'kind of relation' assumes that abstract categories have some 'concrete' existence, but this kind of reification is particularly apparent when classifications are written down, as in biological taxonomy.

A more relevant consideration here is that the opposite may also occur. Thus an analytic breakdown of the body into its constituent parts can be systematically subjected to recomposition. An important example of this is the process of establishing symmetry, a fundamental feature of body conceptualisation, in both classificatory and symbolic systems, in terms of entire body-halves or lower-level segregates (Needham 1973). Such a process of the analysis of a whole into its constituent parts and the subsequent grouping of like parts together represents the transformation of an analytic into a synthetic classification, from parts of a concrete structure to differently ordered aggregates of those parts. This transformation can be summed up diagrammatically in a simple version of Lévi-Strauss's totemic operator. Figure 5.1 illustrates such a transformation for two sets of binary discriminations, which also represent separate logical operations: the aggregation of elements into either 'feet' or 'hands' and into either 'left' or 'right'. The former operation necessitates only morphological discrimination of the items; the second, while it can strictly be achieved simply on a morphological basis, usually involves some recognition of body symmetry, the relationship of the parts to the whole, and their associated cultural connotations.[2] Thus while the classification of body parts is primarily (and of necessity) analytic, it becomes secondarily synthetic through reclassification of the parts so obtained.

Evidence of synthetic operations in the classification of body parts,

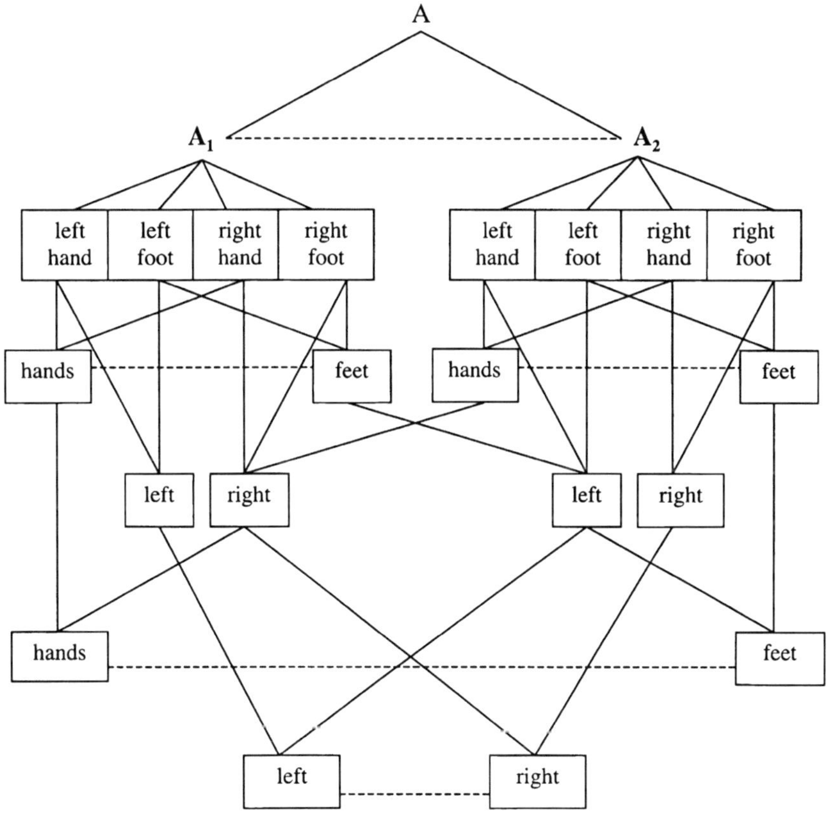

Figure 5.1 How the classification of body parts moves from an analytic to a synthetic mode

however, goes beyond the simple symmetry just described, based on mirror images of body halves. It often involves groupings of a higher order, either as labelled categories ('limbs', 'blood vessels' and so on), or as covert groupings with recognition of symmetry through the use of the same or similar terms for morphologically different parts at different levels of specificity, such as at the level of the entire limb or body half. There is generally a recognition of similarity between the upper and lower parts of the body, reflected in identifiable structural and terminological correspondences between upper and lower limbs. For the Kewa of the New Guinea highlands we get the following terminological equations: 'ankle' = 'elbow', 'heel' = 'elbow' (different term), 'sole' = 'palm', 'toes' = 'fingers' and 'toenails' = 'fingernails' (Franklin 1963: 61–2). Similar terminological parallelism based on the physical (and functional) resemblance of extremities is on record for other languages (Mahr 1960: 29–32; Stark 1969: 8), and indeed appears repeatedly in many anatomical classifications. Additionally, there are instances where the labels for particular anatomical items are dependent on their superficial similarity, but where the resemblance is slight and not part of any general symmetrical pattern. For example, among the Aleut 'uvula' = 'little finger', 'little toe' (Marsh and Laughlin 1956: 51).

All classifications of body parts involve such operations, whether they are clearly related to the constraints imposed by visual perception of the totality, or whether they are not so constrained, as where true taxonomic relations are part of an overall analytic structure (Werner and Begishe 1970: 253–5). Some analytic classifications of body parts presuppose an initial synthetic operation. Thus the statement 'blood vessels are a part of the body', presupposes an operation in which morphologically similar items are identified as *kinds of* blood vessels. Where the members are directly subordinate to the body, such synthetic classifications can be simple (Franklin 1963: 57); alternatively they may be more complex, as in the division of the category 'blood vessel' into 'veins', 'arteries' and capillaries'. Further operations may modify the analytically derived category: thus we have 'pubic hair', 'axillary hair', and so on (Franklin 1963: 57). The extent to which classifications of body parts arrived at by analytic procedures may be so modified varies from one language to another, and often such elements in one language remain unmodified elsewhere. Among the Nuaulu there are separate terms for body hair (*hunue*) and hair on the head (*hua*) (cf. Mahr 1960: 8–9). Here there is no systematic modification of the kind mentioned.

Since anatomical classification proceeds not simply on the basis of a single body (the self or otherwise) but through observations of and interactions with a range of other bodies, the interrelationships can understandably be even more complicated than so far described. Thus from the grouping of like parts of a single body, it is a logical next step to move onto the grouping of similar parts on different, plural bodies. Here the classification of hands of a single or plural body into one class is a procedure of the same kind as grouping cackatuas and cassowaries into the category 'bird': the same synthetic mechanism is at work. However, while particular varieties of the species *Casuarius* may differ so much from a type specimen or the taxonomic definition of the species that they be considered in some way anomalous and uncertain members of the species, this does not happen to the same extent where human bodies are concerned. Genetic variation among *H. sapiens sapiens* may often give rise to symbolic usage's and classificatory difficulties, but this is generally restricted to traits such as skin colour and hair form. In these cases ambiguity does not arise from the classification of various parts of a single whole body, but rather stems from the assignation of a series of individual bodies into classes, the boundaries of which are to a greater or lesser extent (but always to some extent) defined artificially and socially. In this sense, taxa used to classify human beings, such as races (Harris 1970), groups based on intelligence or even sex (Omerod in Douglas 1973: 115–17), are comparable to those employed to classify other natural species.

On the other hand, in analytical classifications the ambiguity arises from the uncertain limits of otherwise unproblematic body parts. Thus areas of transition, usually joints of various kinds, are often seen as links between principle body parts. In his analysis of Kewa anatomical classification, Franklin states that 'neck' and 'stomach area' are perceived as links between the three main divisions of the body, such that the connected series of parts may be written as 'HEAD-neck-UPPER TRUNK-stomach area-BELOW WAIST' (1963: 55–7). The fact that elements at a single level in a classification can have different statuses has important implications for understanding the classification of the body and other analytical structures.

The two types of classification discussed here are closely interrelated, and while the unique features of body-part classification stem from the primarily analytic operation, it is possible to identify readily numerous examples of secondary synthetic operations which have much in common with taxonomies, including the property of reification of abstract categories such that their parts can be reclassified *as if* the categories were concrete totalities. If we now refer back to Figure 5.1, we see that it constitutes a model of conceptual apparatus in which, to paraphrase Lévi-Strauss, multiplicity can be transformed into unity, identity into diversity, and vice versa (Lévi-Strauss 1966: 151–3). But what is important as far as theory of the evolution of classification systems is concerned, is that the perception and classification of the physical relations between body parts appears to occur early in the development of a child (Fantz 1961) such that the establishment of analytic part-whole relations precedes class inclusion, both logically and in terms of socialisation.

Variation in Anatomical Classification

While attributing to the body some kind of primacy, in emphasising its *gestalt* properties and the effect of material constraints (as the assertion of pre-eminence of analytic procedures implies), it is, however, necessary to underscore and map the significance of any intercultural or subcultural variation that may exist. This is in order to avoid both the more crass material reductionism and to emphasise the dimensions of the variation that actually occurs.

Cultural variation in the classification of body parts has already been documented, and it occurs in terms of the structure of classification systems, their lexical elaboration, and the semantics of terminology employed. Variation of one kind is frequently related to variation of another kind. For example, differential lexical elaboration at various levels has certain implications for overall structure. In fact, lexical elaboration is often the root of more readily observable structural variation. Simple and useful indices of variation are understandably difficult to find; but some attempt has been made to calculate the total number of anatomical discriminations made in a particular culture as some reflection of complexity. For example, Marsh and Laughlin (1956: 58–76) have distinguished terms for 330 such items among the Aleut Eskimo. The reasons for such differential elaboration can sometimes be explained in terms of the Nida-Conklin hypothesis, that the elaboration of terminologies (or portions of terminologies) is directly proportional to their cultural importance (but see pp. 94–97 above). Such importance will depend on ritual contexts (oracles, mummification, embalment, cannibalism, head-hunting, dismemberment), economic contexts (knowledge of animal anatomy through hunting, husbandry and butchery practices) and therapeutic practices (knowledge gained through autopsy, dissection, obstetrics, acupuncture, surgery, bodily manipulation and massage). Some workers have put forward some quite specific hypotheses in this area. Thus Marsh and Laughlin suggest that there is a general correlation between therapeutic means that focus on non-corporeal practices (e.g. shamanism) and the underdevelopment of systems of anatomical classification. They attribute Aleut knowledge in this sphere to their attempt at a rational practice of medicine (1956: 39). Even the most superficial studies of this kind indicate that certain anatomical units are not universally singled out for labelling, while other units unfamiliar in terms of our own classification are prominent in those of other cultures. Thus Nuaulu terminologically emphasise anatomical points and units which are not so recognised in English folk classifications, such as the vertex, the highest point of the cranium (*huhui*), and the centre of the chest or xiphisternum (*hikai*). I have already pointed out the differentiation with regard to hair.

Variation can be equally as striking at the level of more inclusive units. This can be illustrated with reference to three arrangements for the classification of the lower limb, although as it happens, it could just as well be the upper limb (cf. Mahr 1960: 31). The first arrangement is where the term for the entire limb is used polysemously to refer also to the vertical portion of the limb in contrast to the horizontal part, as in English usage ('leg' = entire lower limb, but 'leg' contrasts with 'foot'). The second arrangement represents a situation which may be even more common, whereby no term approximately equivalent to the English 'foot' or the French *pied* exists, and where instead this part of the lower limb is included as a verbally unspecific part of a larger unit referring to the entire lower part of the limb from knee downwards. Thus in Nuaulu usage *aini atue* = entire lower limb, and *atori* = lower limb from knee downwards and foot. The latter element is in a rather ambiguous position of contrast with individual items in the upper part of the limb. The final arrangement represents the situation found in some other Malayo-Polynesian languages, where the term for the entire limb is used polysemously to refer to both the limb as a whole and the horizontal portion, which may or may not be in contrast with other elements (e.g. Malay *kaki*). Whether this represents a situation of true polysemy or whether it is simply that the equivalent of foot is not lexically indicated, must be carefully worked out for each case.

At the semantic level variation may occur, for example, in the extent to which terms are descriptive rather than specific. The fact that many folk anatomical classifications contain more descriptive than specific terms is not necessarily of importance. This is true of scientific anatomical terminology, although operationally each term is treated as though it were a specific one, either through ignorance or convenience (Marsh and Laughlin 1956: 50–1). It is also true that often expressions may be specifically invented by language informants, but, as Marsh and Laughlin point out, from the point of view of synchronically studying their anatomical knowledge this does not make any difference, since their ability to generate neologisms may merely indicate their capacity for recognition and the flexibility of their classifying systems. The difference between specificity and simple description is often a question of frequency of use: descriptive terms rapidly assume a specific status if they are used frequently (e.g. 'earlobes', 'eyeball').

Overlap between Corporeal and Non-corporeal Terminologies

The terminology of anatomical description clearly occurs in contexts other than in reference to the human body, and this is an extremely common phenomenon. Correspondences of this kind are well documented with respect to non-human animals, plants and topography, but they are equally common with respect to the form of human artefacts (e.g. ibid., 38).

In all languages terms used for parts of the human body are also used for non-human animals. The similarity in both the structure and terminology of the classifications is obviously related in many cases to morphological similarity. However, the extent to which we may assume that the classifications for other animals are derived from the human model, both terminologically and in terms of the morphological and functional relationships between parts, is more awkward to demonstrate empirically (in either logical, operational or evolutionary terms). Nevertheless, the very fact that human beings perceive and think anthropocentrically in relation to the non-human universe, together with the demonstrable elaboration of human anatomical classification compared with that of other animals, suggests that, generally speaking, the human body is the primary model in both an evolutionary and logico-operational sense. Abstract references to anatomical terms invariably assume reference to the suggested human body part, while the same terms may be used for even the most remotely human forms in zoological terminology, as in the *pseudopodium* of the amoeba, the *cilia* of other protozoa and the 'foot' of the lowly chiton. (It might be noted that this kind of expression of cross-specific identity between body parts and the relations between them generates the problem of the definition of the unit. The use of an anatomical term in more than one species, or even individual, transforms it from an analytic unit to a synthetic category.)

This is not to deny the existence of feedback relationships, which may take several forms. Some anatomical terminology appears to be derived from the cultural function of the parts, as in 'palm' = place of stone flaking (ibid., 50). Perhaps more important, a knowledge of animal anatomy and physiology both in folk and Western sciences, leads to a more sophisticated understanding of the structure and function of the human body: comparative zoology as an aid to human biology (ibid., 40–1, Mahr 1960: 2). Thus while in the last instance the human body is the reference structure for the classification of animal parts, and most terms are exgressive transfers, there is an ongoing dialectical relationship between what is known of animal forms and what is known of humans.

Particular attention has been paid to the animal domain, since here the classification correspondences are so much more direct, but much the same remarks can be made for other domains. Consider, for example, the wide range of anatomical terms used in the English language to express topography, from phrases as simple as 'the foot of the hill' to more colourful expressions of the order, 'Cambridge Gulf is the arsehole of the world and Wyndham is four hundred miles up it'. That such terms are essentially corporeal ones used in a non-corporeal context would, I think, be an uncontroversial conclusion. Exgressive transfers of this kind are found widely and in a variety of domains (Stark 1969: 9). Thus James Fox (1971: 240), in an essay on Rotinese metaphorical language, provides anatomical-botanical equations of the order skin = 'bark', 'teats' = 'sprouts', 'buds'; 'coconut shell' = 'human skull', and suggests a definite tendency towards ingression. Similar examples are not difficult to find. Thus Stark (1969: 9) records the equation 'knee' = 'hill' for the Quechua, stressing the fact that it is the usage for knee which is in fact derivative in this case. The situation may be more complicated than this in that a term may have a primary corporeal referent, a secondary non-corporeal one, and an apparently tertiary referent, which seems to refer to a further body part, or an allusion to a part. This is the case for the term *para* in the Tarascan language of South-western Mexico (Friedrich 1969: 4):

	para	
animal, human back	A → B	outside, exterior of roof
penis shaft, back as in 'behind one's back'	C ← B	

More common than this kind of practice is the use of suffixes in complex and compound lexemes for human body parts as general topographical terminology, as in Quechua *maki-pampa* (hand-field) = palm of hand (Stark 1969: 9). In fact, it is a likely and testable hypothesis that while single lexemes for body parts are transferred exgressively to the topographical domain, suffixes in complex and compound lexemes seem to be ingressive transfers. Much the same can be said for the relationship between anatomical terminology and parts of cultural artefacts.

From the remarks made above it will be clear that there are terminological and classificatory correspondences between a number of domains, all of which can be characterised by their concern with spatial relationships. It is also clear that the relationships, the nature of transferability, and feedback, are complex, such that in logical, operational and evolutionary terms the classificatory structures are, of necessity, closely interrelated. The problem is whether the human body is the primary referential set, other sets of referents simply representing metaphor-like extensions on the basis of underlying similarity; or whether all referential subsets are co-ordinate, all being equally characterised by the underlying abstract definition referring to spatial qualities (exterior/interior, above/below, and so on). In the latter 'theory of co-ordinate referential subsets' only a minority of recognised and labelled body parts actually corresponds to irreducible forms, the majority being morphologically regular derived nouns that are products of a root plus a complex suffix and nominalising suffix (Friedrich 1969: 4, 6–7). Werner and Begishe (1970: 249) stress the importance of spatial addenda in defining foot parts, but here they are qualifiers at a binomial or trinomial level. Such data suggest that none of the body parts are primitive, but are secondary, usually labelled on the basis of their features as products of a root plus a spatial suffix, leading to the conclusion that the body is not the basic figure of orientation. However, as Friedrich points out, it is with the domain of the body that the degree of specificity and of overlap between referents is unquestionably the greatest. Moreover, terminologically non-corporeal elements occur in the suffixes of binomial composite lexemes, and not unitary ones (Werner and Begishe 1970: 248). Friedrich illustrates this point effectively in relation to Tarascan:

> 18 suffixes and 36 other body parts are covered by various extensions and specifications … 195 maximally productive roots which can 'take' all or nearly all the complex suffixes, form far more stems with reference to the body than to any other type of denotation … children apparently learn body-part meanings in a fairly complete way before they learn the other complete sets … the speaker's own body presumably enjoys some sort of real psychological primacy … 14 of 18 more or less corporeal suffixes for various parts of the genitalia is a symbolic condensation of this primacy. (Friedrich 1969: 9)

For Friedrich, then, body parts constitute a sort of *primus inter pares*, a physical model for the classificatory universe, although the lexemes are clearly reinterpreted in terms of their basic common features, being at once physiognomic and geometrical. Typically, it is the body part which motivates most innovation involving the term (ibid., 9), while spatial terminology is important in classification and denotation of anatomical terms (Werner and Begishe 1970: 34). Thus socialisation, logical and operational evidence of the anthropocentric and egocentric nature of classificatory behaviour, argues strongly for some priority of the anatomical domain in both operational and evolutionary terms.

The Body as a Means of Communication

If, as Mauss (1973: 75) remarked, our body is our first and most natural instrument, our first and most natural technical object, and at the same time technical means, it is also our first and most natural classifier and source of symbols, means of verbal and non-verbal communication through its effusions, movements and spatial orientation. The body has always been the subject of investigation and considered an important means of metaphorical expression and symbolic communication, transmitting 'information for and from the social system of which it is part' (Douglas 1971: 387; see also MacRae 1975). Such information may be transferred directly through the physical form of parts, their movement, the solid, liquid or gaseous substances they void, or by transformation and modification through mutilation, ageing, growth, decomposition, concealment, and adjustment. Indeed, the organised experiences associated with the perception and assignation of meaning to one's own body and the idea that a person's body is a psychological object that intrudes into social relationships and cannot be escaped, is an inevitable accompaniment of awareness.

The idea of the crucial pre-eminence of the body is stressed in all disciplines concerned with social communication: for example in philosophy (Spicker 1970) and in psychology in connection with studies of art and perception and the work of the psychoanalytic school. For Jung (1958: 138), 'the symbols of the self arise in the depths of the body and they express its materiality every bit as much as the structure of the perceiving consciousness'. In anthropology the body has, in more recent years, been associated with the work of Mary Douglas (1970: xiii), for whom it is a form for the expression of particular patterns of social relationship. Quite apart from its contemplation in these disciplines and in the arts, it has also been the subject of other studies encompassing a wide range of concerns. The use of the body, corporeal parts and terms in a general metaphorical or metanymic way, as well as for the ultimate life-symbols, has made body symbolism a central theme in the academic discussion of the subject. This is due partly to the ever-present tendency to reduce the social and mental to some kind of physical reality, and partly to its 'autologous' character, that it is the scientific study of ourselves (Firth 1973: 204).

Firth (1973: 226–8) has suggested that we can distinguish at least four kinds of body symbolism: communication through bodily action, the body as a set of abstract constituents, the treatment of social units in bodily terms, and the use of bodies or their parts actually or iconically. Here I shall primarily be concerned with the third of these types. Furthermore, I shall not directly concern myself with the transformation of body symbols into items associated with the body (e.g. clothes), which in themselves represent a rich area of research. Rather, I focus upon the visually perceived and classified parts of the body form: not only the 'flesh, blood, breath and orifices, ingestions and excretions' (ibid., 59), but also its organs, masses and protuberances.

The Metaphorical Use of Body-part Relations

There is no shortage of ethnographic literature demonstrating the metaphorical use of the relations between body parts, but on the whole it has not received the same attention as that paid to 'master symbols'. Here I concentrate on the use of anatomical terms to illustrate social and, sometimes, physical relationships, and vice versa, particularly drawing on the rich material contained in Griaule's *Conversations with Ogotemmêli* (1965) and on some sources from eastern Indonesia. In these cases we are dealing with metaphorical uses of the kind mentioned above, pp. 99–102, although here the term 'symbol' might seem more appropriate, since it stands for a complex non-material set of ideas. In looking at usages of this kind we might recognise a continuum from relational correspondences between different types of material phenomena, where one set of relations can be used to express the other, to complex relational correspondences that are predominantly social and non-material and where individual metaphors or relations between them convey a much greater cognitive load of a more abstract and less concrete kind.

Let us first look at the simple correspondences between body parts and artefacts. Metaphorical correspondences of this kind usually involve some generalised recognition of material similarity. Such usages are found widely in the central Moluccas of Indonesia (e.g. Jansen 1933). Among the Nuaulu, payments for lifting clan-specific dietary taboos on affines involve, for example, the following correspondences:

10 *kondai* (women's hairpins)	=	ribs
kain timor (hand-woven cloth)	=	skin
long machete	=	spine
2 rings	=	eyes
5 bracelets	=	bones of arms and legs
1 *hoho* (large brass bell)	=	heart
1 large red porcelain plate	=	head
1 necklace	=	intestines

A similar set of correspondences exists for homicide payments. In the context of making ritual payments, but not necessarily in any other, the relationship of, say, rings to machete is the same as the relationship of spine to eyes. Although there is a concrete relationship system for body parts, this is not so for artefacts, other than as the result of cultural convention. Consequently, the relational correspondences between the various artefacts is secondary and derivative, unlike the situation where there are two series of material items each with clearly defined and unalterable relationships: one is concrete both in terms and relations, while in the other, though the items are concrete enough, the relations are quite abstract. In Figure 5.2(a), the abstract relations in series B are defined totally in terms of series A. Because $A_1 = B_1$, $A_2 = B_2$ and A_1 is in a material relationship to A_2, therefore B_1 is in a corresponding relationship with B_2.

In the example mentioned in the fourth section of this chapter, both series are composed of concrete relations. This situation is illustrated in Figure 5.2(b) as A_1: A_2, B_1: B_2, and so on. This is well exemplified in the Dogon series relating parts of a granary to parts of a woman, the parts of

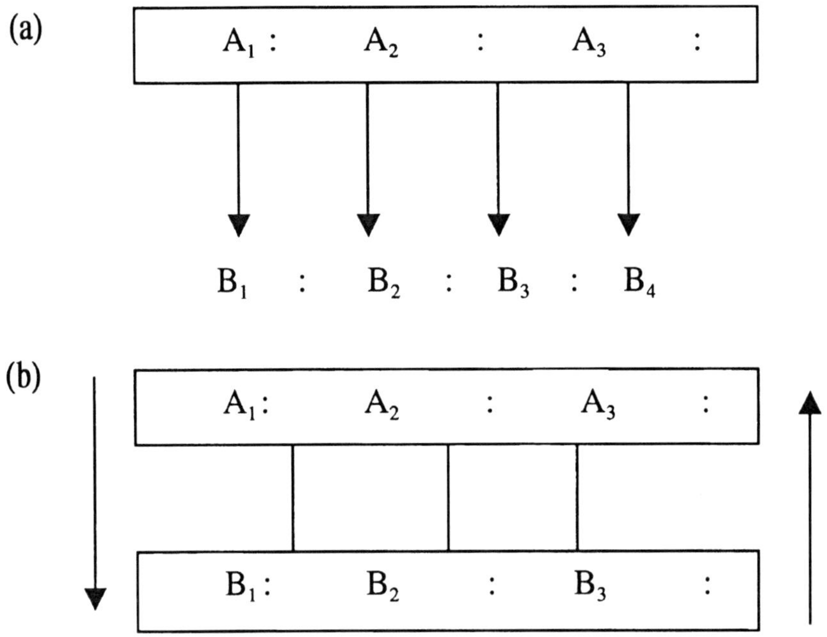

Figure 5.2 Two kinds of analogical relationship

the house compound with parts of the body, and the village explained in terms of an extended anatomical metaphor (Griaule 1965: 94–7). Thus:

> (i) The Dogon granary is interpreted as being:
> like a woman, lying on her back (representing the sun) with her arms and legs raised and supporting the roof (representing the sky). The two legs were on the north side, and the door at the sixth step marked the sexual parts ... The granary and all it contained was therefore a picture of the world system of the new order, and the way in which this system worked was represented by the functioning of the internal organs (Griaule 1965: 37).

Here we see the connection between anatomical classification, the metaphorical use of the relations of body parts to each other, symbolically connected with grain, the most important Dogon food and principle of life-breath.

> (ii) With regard to the house form, Griaule equates the vestibule with the male and the large central room with the female; the outside door represents the male sexual organ. The store rooms on either side are equatable with her arms and the communicating door [p. 96]. A similar theme is further explored in the third example from Griaule.
> (iii) But a house of this sort is only one feature of the village. 'The village', said Ogotemmêli 'should extend from north to south like the body of a man

> lying on his back ... The head is the council house, built on the chief square, which is the symbol of the primal field [p. 96] ... To the east and west are houses for menstruating women; they are round like wombs and represent the hands of the village. The large family houses are its chest and belly; the communal altars at the south of the village are its feet ... The stones on which the fruit of the *Lannea acida* is crushed, placed in the centre of the village, represents its female sexual parts. Beside them should be set the foundation altar, which is its male sex organ; but out of respect for the women this altar is erected outside the walls. (Griaule 1965: 97; see also p. 95 fig. 8)

In these cases, socially important ideas are expressed by relating human anatomical nomenclature to parts of culturally created artefacts. In other instances social relations are not simply implied by two corresponding series of concrete sets of relationships, but are rather expressed directly in terms of the anatomical metaphor. A simple example of this is demonstrated in correspondences drawn by the Nuaulu between digits and relationships between primary kin:

a)	hand:	thumb :	first finger :	second finger :	third finger :	fourth finger
		mother	first son	second son	third son	daughter
b)	foot:	big toe :	first toe :	second toe :	third toe :	fourth toe
		father	first son	second son	third son	daughter

Thus as first finger is to thumb so eldest son is to mother, as fourth toe is to big toe so daughter is to father. It is significant that toes and fingers are used metaphorically in similar ways. As we have seen, they are anatomically and logically similar: as fingers are to the hand so toes are to the foot; there are five fingers and five toes and structurally there are physical resemblances between them – skin surface patterns, joints, nails, bone structure. The same kind of situation has been demonstrated in more complex ways for other cultures. For example, the Dogon use anatomical relations (limb-parts, joints and fingers) to express marriage relations.

In the same category as the Dogon examples must be assigned those instances where local political groups or larger entities are expressed as body parts of a single whole, and related metaphorical usages, such as those evident in terms such as the 'body politic'. Such usages stem directly from the characteristics of the body as a system of part-whole relations, of analytic classification; its properties are such that it is an excellent means by which to express the relation of the individual to the group. If the body is society, then its parts represent the parts of society (Douglas 1971: 387; Lévi-Strauss 1966: 168–9; Perey 1975).[3] Illustrative of these uses is Jansen's description (1933: 457) of the Ambonese conception of local groups (*uli*) as bodies. Here the group that corresponds to the head usually has some kind of political hegemony and historical primacy, other villages both being historically derived from it and defining their relationship to it in anatomical terms. As with the Dogon, anatomical symbolism in general is an important means by which the Nuaulu describe the relations between the elements of their cosmos and social organisation A similar kind of situation is referred to by Steiner (1967 [1956]: 45–6) for parts of Polynesia, where 'parts of the body formed a fixed hierarchy which had some analogy with the rank system'. However, his ethnographic sources are unclear.

Given metaphorical correspondences between two different series, where these may be concrete, abstract, social or combinations of the three, the next logical step is to the expression of each through the mediation or addition of a third. For example, certain Nuaulu familial relations, which may be expressed in terms of the relations between digits, are themselves expressions of items and relations in a third series, this time composed of other body parts. This means that it is possible to construct the following anatomical equations: 'head' = 'thumb', 'first finger' = 'right hand', 'second finger' = 'left hand', 'third finger' = 'right foot', 'fourth finger' = 'left foot'. Although I would not wish to push this form of classificatory cross-referencing too far, its logical consistency in terms of some dominant Nuaulu dualisms can be seen in series read horizontally from the paired items given, such that, for example, 'eldest son' = 'first finger' = 'right hand' = 'male'.

Similar patterns are found in intricate forms in Dogon ideas, involving cross-linkages between different but parallel material and social series. Here body parts of different orders (organs, limbs, digits) may both mediate abstract and social relations, and be mediated themselves by other sets of correspondences, such that there is a complex set of cross-references between things so apparently diverse as granary parts, living beings, constellations, drums, language, techniques, numerals and so on. These associations are illustrated in Figure 5.3, indicating (a) some of the sets in terms of their relation to actual body geometry and (b) an abstracted list of some formal correspondences in sets. Things become more abstract still in, say, a consideration of the metaphorical mathematics of finger symbolism, where the sum of the numerals for each finger (or, in the case of the third and fourth, two fingers) is always nine; a figure equivalent to the head and signifying chieftainship (Griaule 1965: 54).

All the sets of correspondences discussed here are concerned with spatial relationships, since this is the idiom of expression. In some cases the space is abstract, in most it is social. All the abstract relationships are in essence the description of one set of spatial relationships in terms of another. Since at the level of classification there is a close relationship between conceptions of non-corporeal space and parts of the body, this is by no means unexpected. However, while at the level of the model we can say that items and relations in such series have an independent existence, it is possible, even probable, that metaphorical usage leads to some mod-

(a)

	right	left		
	female ancestors	male ancestors		
	even numbers	odd numbers		
upper	4 arm	arm 3		upper
lower	8 forearm	forearm 7		
upper	2 thigh	thigh 1		lower
lower	6 leg	leg		

(b)

laterality	right	left	right	left	right	left	right	left
body-half	below	below	above	above	below	below	above	above
limbs	upper	upper	upper	upper	lower	lower	lower	lower
organ	stomach	gizzard	heart	little liver	spleen	intestine	great liver	bladder
fingers	second	fore	thumb	third	little	thumb	fore	second
sex	male	female	male	female	malke	female	male	female

Figure 5.3 Matrices of analogical linkages between Dogon body parts and general symbolic elements

ification, usually in the more flexible series of a pair. Such changes make the metaphorical relationships involved seem even more appropriate, as for example in the rearrangement of village components to mimic anatomical relations. So the formative processes are two-way: there is cognitive feedback. The body is both symbol source and symbolised, a thing classified and a classifier of things, signifier and signified. In the same way as there is a feedback relationship between the classification of body parts and the use of the body to classify other things, so there is a corresponding relationship between the symbolism of body parts and the use of the body to symbolise other things. There is an indissoluble and dialectical link between the two.

Classification of Body Parts and the Analysis of Symbols

In this chapter I am concerned with the body as a communicative structure, a source of a wide range of semiotic usages other than the specifically symbolic. In many ways the separate analysis of what are sometimes arbitrarily seen as symbols is a false point of departure. In Sapir's terms, condensation symbols should be seen in the context of a large collection of related referential ones, which cognitively operate at a simpler level. The Dogon case is a fine illustration of the arbitrariness of the distinction between sign and symbol and between the levels of classification and symbolism. Here, while body relations are being used as a simple metaphorical device to 'objectify', 'concretise', and discuss social relationships, they frequently transcend the level of the mnemonic and become part of a complex symbolic system in which the relations of body parts are an important mediating feature, conveying information about social relations and ultimately representing the most important material recognition of social reproduction. This process can be represented as a notional evolutionary and logical continuum between a simple pole representing the classification of the concrete and with a single semantic component, and a complex pole representing the classification of the abstract with a multiple semantic component (Figure 5.4). In order to control and handle the latter end of the continuum there is a constant attempt to explain the abstract in concrete terms, to contain and order the non-material in terms of the material.

The properties of symbolic systems are those of classificatory systems. An analysis of body metaphors and symbols conducted in the context of overarching ideas of classification allows for a more systematic and therefore comprehensive approach than the narrow atomistic concentration on particular symbols. It also demonstrates the extent to which classification is both a logically necessary condition for symbol selection and usage and in a dialectical relationship with it, such that one cannot be satisfactorily investigated without the other. Consequently, not only is classification an integral part of the study of symbolic and metaphorical systems, but symbols should be analysed dependently and from the same point of departure.

In their different ways, both Lévi-Strauss and Victor Turner have stressed the importance of looking at the structure of a series of symbols

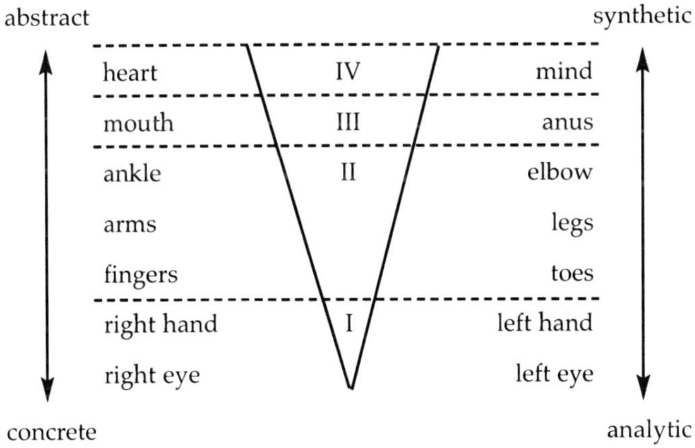

Figure 5.4 Notional evolutionary and logical continuum of bodily polarities on a scale ranging from the simple, concrete and analytical to the complex, abstract and synthetic

as well as individual ones in symbolic systems in general. Yet while the body has been the recognised source of potent individual symbols, and symbols derived from the body have been treated as elements in structural analyses of general symbolic statements and rituals, less attention has been paid to relations between body symbols in terms of their concrete relationship to other body parts and symbols. I am suggesting that the body can be seen as a structured set of symbols or possible symbols and items available for symbolic communication. In the same way that Turner (1966: 295) has insisted that to understand a symbol it is necessary to examine its occurrence in a series of different contexts, or as one in a cluster or *gestalt* of symbols, to investigate its 'positional meaning' so that it is necessary to see the relations of symbols to the classificatory context of the part to the whole and the part to other parts. Thus we are concerned with 'the structural relations and transformations of symbols internally within the system', with the patterned totality of symbolic relations (Piaget 1971a: 8–9).

Body symbols have traditionally been looked at individually, with concentration on single items – the mouth, anus, penis and so on. There is a danger in analysing items of this kind as isolated items at an empirical level, simply on account of their attribution as single potent dominant or master symbols representing key physiological processes with fundamental symbolic qualities. While such items indeed carry a heavy semantic load, which must be investigated systematically, such empirical, functional, physiological approaches tend to ignore the basic context, perception and classification of the body.[4] There has been a tendency to stress the function of individual parts rather than the relationships between them, either anatomically or functionally. The importance of the relational element in the definition of body parts is expressed in much artistic representation of the human body, where different parts are not necessarily indicated by either their form or relative size, but in terms of their relation to other parts. A line represents a penis not because it particularly resembles one but because it is drawn between two other lines representing legs. This is still the case when it comes to body symbolism, although in the general area of classification the emphasis has shifted (Lévi-Strauss 1966: 150–1). To understand the symbolic value of the penis, it is necessary to know something of its anatomical relations (as mediated by a particular form of classification to the rest of the body and to complementary organs of the opposite sex). In the same way that to understand an animal or plant symbol it is important to see it in relation to other categories, so also for body symbols: as eaglehawk is to crow, so penis is to vulva (different sex), or vulva to mouth (same sex).

While the analysis of classificatory context is now accepted as a necessary part of the analysis of symbols derived from different natural species, the same approach, considerations and rigour have not been applied to body symbols. This is as true for symbolic systems associated with analytical classifications as for synthetic ones. However, in the case of the former the validity of the structuralist approach is obvious, since the whole is a concrete entity and the relations of its parts are concrete and materially constrained. Simple one-to-one symbolic associations or contrasts give rise to specific problems if they alone define the co-ordinates of investigation; these are thrown into relief and countered by a more structured and comprehensive approach to the subject.

The importance of relations between different symbols drawn from a single domain is shown at its simplest in the notion of metaphoric and symbolic complementarity, in binary oppositions. The representation of the penis as a symbol implies the existence of something, which is non-penis, generally or specifically. At the general level, penis may contrast with non-penis: in the anatomical domain it is penis and not anus, mouth, ear, and so on. This is evident at a simple semantic and lexical level. Selection of any one body symbol implies that something remains unselected. At the level of anatomical classification, it may be more specific, as in the contrast between penis and vulva. Another example of specific symbolic complementarity is in the contrast between right and left hand. To use one hand as a symbol frequently implies the existence of its complement. Here the complementarity is strikingly more morphological, whereas in the penis-vulva example morphological similarly is less important than functional and behavioural associations. Thus the symbolic use of the body operates on the complementarity of its parts, arrived at through the process of classification, which is at the same time both cerebral and social. Here again synthetic and analytic classifications are identical, for the right hand can only exist in the horizontal dimension in relation to the left, and in the vertical dimension in relation to the arm, finger and so on. In the same way a taxonomic species only exists because it both contrasts horizontally with other species and vertically with higher and lower order groupings, varieties, phyla and so on. But having said this, it should also be remembered that the emphasis of particular pairs is at the expense of de-emphasising other things. To contrast penis with vulva as symbols of masculinity and femininity is to emphasise sexual dissimilarities at the expense of general anatomical similarities, which are, after all, far greater.

The next step from simple complementarity is the recognition of the morphological and/or functional similarity of otherwise different body parts: labia – lips, nose – penis, buttocks – cheeks, and genitals – face (e.g. Hallpike 1969: 257). As Freud (1954: 387 and *passim*) has shown, the secondary items in these pairs may come to represent their primary 'equivalent' in certain circumstances. Such ideas of body part transposition are of great importance in symbolism.

While in both simple complementarity and more complex forms of symbolic association, discrete organs and anatomical parts are usually specified, it is important to recognise that their complementarity or similarity does not rest solely on morphological or functional criteria, but is set in the broad context of body symmetry. The complementarity of left and right hands is structured, in part, in terms of their localisation on opposite body halves. The transpositions cited above are structured in terms of the opposition of the upper and lower halves of the body. Other geometric dimensions may also be relevant. Mouth and anus are not simply opposed in terms of the contrast upper : lower but also in terms of the contrast front : back. This is part of the anatomical classificatory context in which such distinctions are made. Additionally and quite crucially, the opposition is also functional, as in ingestion : exgestion, food : faeces.

It is at this level of abstraction that anomaly begins to become important, but it only does so because synthetic classification replaces analytic. The relationship of mouth to body is unambiguous; but if the mouth is isolated from the body and a class of mouthlike entities constructed, it immediately becomes ambiguous and (most significantly) a potent symbol, having class similarities with other orifices such as vulvas and anuses. It is at this classificatory level (resynthesis) that Freudian notions of symbolism appear to operate. Anomaly is not an inherent property of analytic classifications because items occupy field-dependent spatial positions that cannot be claimed by others. There are boundary problems between items, but here they are not due so much to the intrinsically ambiguous nature of the semantic content as to the need to define the material limits of the spatial area occupied and designated by a lexical item. As I have already mentioned, joints are of particular interest in this respect because they represent the links between parts, which can be areas of classificatory uncertainty. Equally, however, they may become reified and become a relational system in their own right, as in the case of the Dogon, where they may be seen as 'the chief thing in the body of a man' (Griaule 1965: 51, 140). The classificatory advantage of joints is that, in anatomical terms, they tend to be points rather than areas, places rather than spaces, which can be specifically located. In the Dogon example the joints represent different ancestors, and are connected with different colours associated with the celestial granary of Dogon cosmology or those of corresponding seeds.[5]

The relationship between classification and semiotics is two-way. Of equal importance to the matters so far discussed are what symbolic and metaphoric use of the human form can tell about its classification. For example, the dualism of right and left and their pre-eminence in cosmology and ritual tell us something of the fundamental importance of symmetry, asymmetry, and contrast as means of ordering information (Needham 1973), while schematic representations of the body (either 'representational' or symbolic) tell us something of its key distinctive features. The '+' which Jung saw as being related to the human form (Firth 1973:

59) is an indication that relationships between parts are often more important than individual features. In this case the key relations are head : trunk, left arm : right arm, and the relationship between the horizontal and vertical axes represented by these elements. In material figurines, the proportions can be the all important feature: the contrast between breast and buttock, head and trunk. Iconic representations such as these often enable us to arrive at the critical distinctions in body classification.

Classificatory complementarities are useful elements in symbolic systems, since they can at the same time code large quantities of information and yet do so in a simple and accessible form. But because of this it is important not to be misled by their apparent simplicity. Those derived from anatomy may involve minimal cultural modification. The contrast or association of pairs (arms : legs, fingers : toes) which often occur as figures of speech are apparently simple. Their origin in terms of the classification of body parts is obviously related to the parallelism of extremities already discussed. Semantically, however, they may acquire more complicated attributes. Other simple complementarities may involve the identification of functional similarities (eyes and ears). Still others may concern ideational speculation on humanity, and involve the categories that are only in the most abstract sense anatomical (heart and mind, body and soul), at which point they merge with the host of abstract dualities associated with cosmological systems. Thus anatomical complementarities can be ranked on a scale of increasing abstractness. In Figure 5.4 I divided this scale into four basic categories, but the allocations must to some extent be arbitrary. The lowermost category contains pairs of identical organs, or identical in everything except in terms of contraposition or lateral reversal. Category II contains all the obvious unambiguous anatomical parallelisms I have mentioned, which can be classified in anatomical terms alone. Category III contains morphological parallelisms of a more abstract kind, where they entail a high abstract content and reference to functional and behavioural considerations; morphological similarity may be of relative minor importance. Category IV contrasts are almost wholly defined in abstract terms with a superficial allusion to anatomical materiality. While the symbolic potency of pairs in the lower categories may be high, pairs higher up the scale are maintained almost solely because of their symbolic component.

The Materiality of the Body

The materiality of objects, and the analytical process derived from it, is an important determining and organising factor in classification. The importance of material similarity of different parts of the same body has already been mentioned. However, the materiality of body parts is significant also in the extent to which it allows for unambiguous cross-cultural identification, as between, say, the words for 'penis'. Although there may be some semantic confusion stemming from differences in boundaries (such as whether it is the penis specifically or the entire male genitalia which are implied), because of their material referents and the analytical classification of which they are part, cross-cultural identity and consequently explanation of such items is a relatively straightforward business. This is in marked contrast to some symbols not derived from human anatomical classification: the more morphologically vague psychoanalytical notions, and symbols derived from entire representatives of natural species and their groups.

Since Durkheim (1915: 17) the stress has been on the cultural and social character of bodily symbols and the role of the underlying cerebral organisation and physiology has been underestimated or neglected. Such emphasis is usually part of an attempt to demonstrate just how much of our perception of even the most natural and physical of things is reducible to our social organisation of that reality (Berger and Luckmann 1967). The work of Mary Douglas has been essentially concerned with the way in which the 'social body' constrains the way the physical body is perceived. 'Physical nature', she writes, 'is masticated and driven through the cognitive meshes to satisfy social demands for clarity which compete with logical demands for consistency' (Douglas 1973: 113). More specifically, the body as a symbol is more often no more than society reified and sanctified in ideology, mediating the social structure by itself and its images (Douglas 1971: 387; Ellen 1972: 236–7).

It is difficult to deny the importance of cultural ideas in affecting the classification of body parts. For example, culturally attributed functions of an organ may fundamentally affect the most 'primary' of classifications, as in medieval medicine (Singer 1957). But clearly, while this may be generally accepted, it would be wrong to dismiss altogether material influences on perception and classification and submit entirely to the vicissitudes of vacuous sociologism. While not seeing it quite in these terms, Firth (1973: 307) has pointed to the 'great variety of circumstances in which physical structure and powers of the human body are perceived in direct relation to performance, irrespective of the character of the social body'. My contention is simply that the human body forms the concrete basis of a characteristic classificatory apparatus for parts ordered analytically, which acts as a primary constraint in structuring 'cognitive meshes', and that this is not obliterated by the process of cultural reorganisation, since the very mechanism of the process is itself partially constrained by it. It is only by assuming a core of materially constrained behaviour in perception and action that cross-cultural interpretation and recognition make any sense. While a pot may be lifted in a variety of ways, there are a certain number of key actions involved, which are everywhere the same and indicate cross-culturally the nature of the action. Similarly, while the body may be verbally classified in a number of ways, there are always key elements in both verbal and non-verbal classifications which are derived from the structure and function of the body.

In one sense it is true that body classification is not arbitrary: cognitive structures are, indeed, extensions of biological structures, but are at the same time discovered through the process of cultural and social interaction. The process of classification may be visualised as operating at two coexisting and interpenetrating levels, represented by the analytical and the synthetic. At the first level structures may be regarded as 'deep', dominant ones being determined by a combination of material constraints and cerebral apparatus, and influence of the cultural is superficial only in terms of providing lexical labels for culturally defined material parts. At the second level culture is dominant, and the body, for example, is defined largely in cultural terms, although cultural categories are, if many stages removed, tied in various ways to material and cognitive constraints. The relationships between these two levels are subtle and complicated, since operational and observable reality will generally be composed of both in varying proportions, with the cultural component being self-amplifying. While the body, as with all nature, may be redefined and reified in cultural terms, it is not in the first instance of perception defined as such: the classification itself takes on a concretised form. In this it differs from the perception and classification of natural species, both in terms of socialisation and the evolution of classificatory systems. Thus, while with Durkheim and Mauss (1901–2) I would recognise the intrusion of the social on the material, unlike them I argue the necessity to account for the dialectical relationship between the cerebral, the material, and the social, such that classificatory structure and function are virtually inseparable. I am suggesting that we should neither ignore that famous but uninvited guest of Lévi-Strauss (Mendelson 1967) nor ignore his chair.

Notes

1. For Inhelder and Piaget (1964) the earlier process takes the form of seriation. David Reason has suggested to me that in more general terms this might indicate the emergence of topological body space before Euclidean (orientated) space.
2. This does not preclude, however, conflation following from inadequate or erroneous information, sometimes sustained or determined by cultural factors; witness, for example, the cloaca-theory of psychoanalysis, in which the anus is confused with the vulva. The history of anatomy is full of similar if not so obvious confusions (Singer 1957: 66–7, 78).
3. The same kind of notion is found in Scherner's *Das Leben des Traumes*, with its representation of the body in dreams as a house, and the parts of the house representing specific organs. Irrespective of the criticisms of Freud (1954) and

others of his psychology, the use of the metaphorical relation of house parts to body parts illustrates the ubiquitousness of such metaphors.

4. In another paper (Ellen 1972) I have drawn attention to the opposite tendency in the study of anthropomorphic symbols – the neglect of depth-studies of particular items. There too I was stressing, but for different reasons, the necessity of rooting explanation in the analysis of classification and the structure of categories.
5. There may be some relationship here between the classificatory and symbolic connotations of joints and the attention given to them in ethnographic art.

CHAPTER 6

Grass, Grerb or Weed? The Ethnography of a Plant Life-form (1991)

A reflection on the status of the rank 'life-form' through an examination of a Nuaulu category which approximates to 'grass' and 'weed'. The chapter illustrates the difficulty of assigning to life-form categories the status of universal perceptual constructs which cut 'nature at the joints', when many display the features of functional categories which reflect the cultural particularities of a specific situation.

> Weed ... a herbaceous plant not valued for its use or beauty, growing wild and rank, and regarded as cumbering the ground or hindering growth or superior vegetation ... an unprofitable, troublesome, or noxious growth ... any herb or small plant (*Oxford English Dictionary*, vol. 12, 1933: 251)

Introduction

The contribution of Ralph Bulmer to the study of folk biology has been marked by at least four characteristics: a scrupulous attention to ethnographic detail, a respect for the knowledge of individual informants, an insistence on the necessity to embed classificatory abstractions in overall social and cultural contexts, and a scepticism (often witty, though never disrespectful) of the universalist-evolutionist generalisations of others (e.g. Bulmer 1974; 1985).

In my own work on the ethnobiology of the Nuaulu of south central Seram, eastern Indonesia, I have tried to emulate, though not always successfully, Bulmerian standards. As a tribute to those standards, I wish here to take up a particular theme and treat it with as much thoroughness and good sense as I can muster. The theme is the merging of what Brent Berlin has called 'general purpose' and 'special purpose' categories, particularly with respect to the notion of 'life-form'; and I take my cue from Bulmer's repeated observation (e.g. Bulmer 1974a: 23) that categories (and especially more inclusive and 'primary' categories) are defined as much by cultural significata as by their objective biological characteristics. The subject is the Nuaulu plant term *monote* and the categories we may infer from it.[1]

The Category *Monote* in Nuaulu Ethnobotany

Of the one thousand or more labelled Nuaulu categories for plants, about forty-eight (and about the same number of Linnaean species) were recorded in the field as being affiliated in some way to the more inclusive category of *monote* (Table 6.1). This is about 6 percent of all labelled plants. Of those recorded only thirteen or fourteen were habitually prefixed by *mono* in ordinary speech in such a way as to suggest that this was an intrinsic part of the term. In some cases this is clearer than in others: thus *mono nuae* is an obligatory binomial, since *nuae* by itself means only 'sea', serving here as an adjectival qualifier. There are a small number of terms which are optionally binomial and uninominal with respect to the prefix *mono*, such as *(mono) panu-panu*. Some, despite being unequivocally placed in the broader category *monote* are never prefixed by *mono*, mainly I think because the trinomials which would result (some even containing reduplicated elements, such as *soka-sokae msinae*) would be clumsy constructions in everyday communication, or because semantically they would anyway be redundant. There is no reason to believe that because a term is prefixed by *mono* it is therefore a more acceptable member of the category, though for the ethnographer it is perhaps more easily located. Indeed, where terms have been deliberately marked, especially where the second element in the binomial is an adjectival qualifier, we might expect the terms to be recent additions and therefore semantically peripheral. None of this in itself is remarkable, and we have long ago accepted the idea that there is no simple uniform relationship between semantic content and morphosyntactic structure.

The term *monote* is used by the Nuaulu specifically to refer to spontaneously occurring plants of little practical utility found in the village area, in first year swiddens (*nisi honue*), second year swiddens (*nisi monae*) and old swiddens of the first phase of vegetative regeneration (*nisi ahue*). *Monote* grow rapidly in young gardens, some being hardly affected by burning. Little attempt is made to control them, although the presence of some broad-leafed cultigens, such as taro and *Xanthosoma*, inhibit their development. The growth pattern changes as a swidden gets progressively older, and also varies from place to place within and between swiddens. Spatial variation depends on the cultigens grown, the preceding vegetative cover, existing vegetation surrounding the plot, as well as topography and soil. For example, on low land hidden from direct sunlight the growth after two years is dominated by *Euphorbia hirta* and a fern of the genus *Pteris* (*kau-kau*). By contrast, high sloping land and ridges exposed to direct sunlight are dominated by composites, such as *mono manhutanane* and *mono mahusine*. The interstitial growth of groveland is also predominantly pteridophyte (again, a species of *Pteris*), but also notably containing *Cyperus diffuses* and *Selaginella*. Various species of bamboo may appear at an early stage (Ellen 1978a: 177–8). A few of the plants to which the term *monote* is routinely applied are listed in Table 6.1.

What is distinctive about the category in formal botanic terms is its outrageous diversity: at least sixteen families – mainly monocotyledoneae but also dicotyledoneae, largely angiosperms but with a significant (hardly incidental) number of cryptograms (Polypodiaceae and Selaginaceae). In terms of that gross morphology typically reflected in folk-botanical distinctions, it includes grasses (but not all grasses), bamboos (but not all bamboos), ferns (but not all ferns),[2] young tree saplings such as *Homalanthus populifolius* (which in its mature form may reach a height of 12 m), and vines (the bramble *Rubus moluccanus*), as well as herbs. That such physically salient plant types should cut across the boundary of a category is surely significantly diagnostic.

From an ecological and phytogeographical standpoint most *monote* (at least 69 percent) are common pantropical heliophilic weeds[3] introduced accidentally during the historical period, a pedigree reflected in the absence of obviously cognate terms in other genetically related and local languages. Taxonomically, pan-tropical weeds have a pretty clear profile, being well represented in the following families: Amaranthaceae, Leguminosae, Euphorbiaceae, Malvaceae, Labiatae, and most frequently Compositae. Amongst these, perhaps, the most ubiquitous types below the family level in the Indo-Pacific region are *Desmodium* and *Euphorbia hirta*, the latter having been originally disseminated as an ornamental species of American origin (Merrill 1954: 118–31).

However, not all pantropicals are placed by the Nuaulu in *monote*, an example being the musk plant, *Abelmoschus moschatus* Medic. (Malvaceae). Neither is this true of all grasses, such as two varieties of *Miscanthus* (*niune*), a reed used in binding. Of the bamboos, the most surprising omission is *Schizotachyum* (*suenie*). Though not without its applications, in functional terms this is the most intrusive and fast-growing of the lot – in short, the most 'weedy'.

But if what professional botany agrees to describe as 'weeds' are not to be confined to the category *monote*, then by the same token some *monote* are not weeds, in the sense that they are useful. Some serve as important indi-

Table 6.1 Partial Linnaean content of the Nuaulu category *monote*

	Nuaulu term	Phylogenetic content	Botanical family
1.	*kamruku*	*Pseuderanthemum* sp.	Acanthaceae
2.	*kamruku sororione*	*Pseuderanthemum* spp.	Acanthaceae
3.	*kamruku wane*	*Pseuderanthemum* sp.	Acanthaceae
4.	*matapeta onone*	*Asytasisa gangetica* (L.) T. Anders	Acanthaceae
5.	*mono maune*		Acanthaceae
6.	*mo wapane*	*Pseuderanthemum* sp.	Acanthaceae
7.	*ohone*		Acanthaceae
8.	*mono senane*	*Portulaca olearacea* L.	Aizoaceae
9.	*mono tohu*	*Synedrella nodiflora* (L.), Gaertn.	Compositae
10.	*mono une-une taiya*	*Synedrella nodiflora* (L.), Gaertn.	Compositae
11.	*hono-hono*	*Aneilema* spp.	Commalinaceae
12.	*mono manuate*	*Amaranthus viridis* L.	Amaranthaceae
13.	*mono monatohu*	*Cyathula prostrate* (L.) Bl.	Amaranthaceae
14.	*mono marosu*	*Ageratum conyzoides* L.	Compositae
15.	*mono nuetetue*	*Crassocephalum crepidiodes* (Benth.) S. Moore; *Ageratum conyzoides* L., *Synedrella nodiflora* (L.) Gaertn.	Compositae
16.	*nemonone*	*Melanthera biflora* (L.) H. Wild	Compositae
17.	*mono mahusine*		Compositae
18.	*mono man(a) hutanane*	*Amaranthus viridis* L.	Compositae
19.	*monoute*	*Euphorbia hirta* L.	Euphorbiaceae
20.	*hunua*	*Homalanthus populifolius* Graham	Euphorbiaceae
21.	*noha*	*Melanolepis multiglandulosa* (Bl.) Reichb. f. and Zoll	Euphorbiaceae
22.	*anaupua*	*Cyperus compressus* L.	Cyperaceae
23.	*hahusete*	*Cyperus diffuses* Vahl.	Cyperaceae
24.	*ekene*	*Centotheca lappacea* (L.) Desv.	Gramineae
25.	*oni*	*Imperata exaltata* Brongn.	Gramineae
26.	*nesa-nesa hanaie*	*Chloris barbata* Sw.	Gramineae
27.	*nesa-nesa pina*		Gramineae
28.	*uta numa*		Gramineae
29.	*anahuai*	*Leucas zeyanica* R. Br.	Labiatae
30.	*mono nuae*	*Desmodium heterocarpon* (L.) DC, *Desmodium sequax* Wall.	Leguminosae
31.	*(mono) panu-panu*	*Desmodium sequax* Wall.	Leguminosae
32.	*mono nione senene*		Malvaceae
33.	*kauote*	*Urena lobata* L.	Malvaceae
34.	*ahone*	*Microsorium commutatum* (Blume) Copel	Polypodiaceae
35.	*bubu kaiya*	*Nephrolepis hisutula* (Forst.) Presl	Polypodiaceae
36.	*kin'ekane*	*Phymatodes nigrescens* (Bl.) J. Sm.	Polypodiaceae
37.	*ahane*	*Phymatodes scolopendria* (Burm.) Ching.	Polypodiaceae
38.	*bubu onate*	*Pteris ensiformis* Burm.	Polypodiaceae
39.	*sapana*	*Pteris* sp. nr. *vittata* L.	Polypodiaceae
40.	*kau-kau*	*Pteris* sp.	Polypodiaceae
41.	*kopane*	*Pteris* sp.	Polypodiaceae
42.	*soka-sokae msinae*	*Selaginella* sp.	Selaginaceae
43.	*soka-sokae marae*	*Selaginalla* sp.	Selaginaceae

Table 6.1 (continued)

	Nuaulu term	Phylogenetic content	Botanical family
44.	*kupa rosi*	*Rubus moluccanus* L.	Rosaceae
45.	*hahu sina*	*Fleurya interrupta* (L.) R. Wight; *Coleus atrourpurens* Benth.	Urticaceae Labiatae
46.	*sapane*	*Trema orientalis* Blume	Urticaceae
47.	*papate wane*	*Petraeovitex* sp.	Verbenaceae
48.	*mono makae*		

cators of the state of secondary regrowth and the condition of underlying soil. *Trema orientalis, Euphorbia hirta* and *Homalanthus populifolius* are typical of the first phase of secondary regrowth during the first year after cutting and burning a swidden (Ellen 1978: 117), and used by the Nuaulu to assess future planting strategies. Of the more obvious technical applications, the flowers of *Desmodium sequax* are chewed with salt and placed on wounds to afford some degree of protection, while the lignaceous stem of *Petraeovitex* is used for binding and making artefacts such as the *sakainate* device used when climbing coconut palms. Some are occasionally eaten as green vegetables or root shoots, though not of preference. The prefix *uta* in *uta numa* indicates 'greens, vegetables; in Ambonese Malay *sayor*', literally meaning something like 'vegetables of the house'. However, it is difficult to infer from this any culinary use. More likely, we are dealing with a metaphorical extension grounded in the occurrence of this grass in the village area and around the base of house piles. Other plants labelled by the Nuaulu as *monote,* though not with any discovered local use, are employed in various ways elsewhere in archipelagic southeast Asia. One such is *Coleus atropurpurens,* much used medicinally in the Malay peninsula (Burkill 1935: 643–4).

The Semantic Construction of a Category

Given such a complex range of reference in phylogenetic, morphological and utilitarian terms, one might suspect a correspondingly complex Nuaulu semantic landscape. And yet categories – by definition – must be simple, otherwise they cannot function effectively. How do the Nuaulu simplify the category? Let us start by clearing some of the ground, metaphorically speaking.

Although it is true that some species do possess obvious medical, technical and food uses, this is not a characteristic which distinguishes members of the category as a whole. Moreover, it cannot be said that the uses displayed by those *monote* that have them are anything but secondary or even second best. So, since most *monote* are undoubtedly 'spontaneously occurring plants of little practical utility' distributed across both cultivated patches and living spaces, perhaps we should adopt the common sense (if ethnocentric) solution and opt for the common denominator of disutility: in other words, to gloss the category as 'weed'. But although such a solution is probably inescapable if we are compelled to accept a simple dictionary definition, the category is poorly understood as 'weed' alone. I hope to demonstrate why this should be the case in the remainder of this paper.

One reason why it is not enough to adopt the disutilitarian approach is the apparent prominence (though not exclusive presence) of certain 'natural' groupings amongst *monote*, among them grasses and perhaps non-epiphytic ferns, which have no obviously demarcated place in some other category. In this sense, I think *monote* is incipiently 'natural'. Certainly there is evidence that it is conceptualised by the Nuaulu in terms of some overall image, some cognitive prototype: small herbaceous plants or woody shrubs with few uses and some explicitly troublesome. This does not mean that from time to time monothetic definitions are not offered by individual informants, but these seem to range between the natural and disutility models, from the wholly functional and non-morphologic to the wholly morphologic and non-functional. Moreover, in addition to this fundamentally ambiguous semantic core we can recognise a periphery of plants which get into the category on account of their associations (sometimes morphological) with focal members of the category.

So, generalising, we can identify an inner semantic ambiguity in the structure of the category which defies easy cross-cultural translation. If all this sounds suspiciously complex, then it must be remembered that individual language-users rarely articulate the full semantic range of a word which they employ at any one time, even if they *define* the category at all, while different users may not share a completely identical range of reference. The task of the ethnographer is not merely to 'translate' (though given the angst projected in the postmodernist movement this might seem quite enough to be going on with), but also to generalise in ways which are simultaneously culturally faithful and productive for comparative analysis. And what comparative evidence we have (Brown 1984: 133–205) argues strongly for widespread similar ambiguities in the way general plant categories are constituted.

The Factor of Subsistence

Even if we accept the simple gloss of *monote*, or even just the general thrust of dis-utility, we must grapple with one curious and difficult matter, namely that the Nuaulu should have such a highly developed category of 'weed', given their inattention to weeding (*aukani, ahunata*) and the overall historical focus of their subsistence towards non-domesticated resources (Ellen 1988). As an ethnographic query this is sufficiently problematic, but at a comparative level it is decidedly so, especially in the light of otherwise quite plausible assertions made concerning the relationship between ethnobotanical categories and societal scale. Cecil Brown (1984: 70), for example, has argued (admittedly tentatively) that 'it may be that languages usually do not innovate "weed" until their speakers are committed to highly intensive forms of agriculture'. But not only do Nuaulu not engage in anything remotely describable as intensive agriculture, until recently any kind of systematic cultivation was a rather insignificant part of their overall subsistence effort and return.

I do not regard this puzzle as intractable. There is no reason to believe that the terminological recognition of a generic body of pests is conditional on practical steps being taken to eliminate them. Hence, it is possible to have 'weeds' without 'weeding', 'pests' without pest-control, and so on. Moreover, we are rather conditioned to think of vegetable matter being out of place only with respect to plant cultivation – useful or ornamental. In fact, Nuaulu associations of *monote* are as much with the village area as with gardens. In the former, it is expected that all improper vegetation (that is, excluding fruit trees, various sacred bushes and the grass-covered dancing area) be kept clear. Although weeding the village area, or more specifically the area round the house, is regarded as a routine domestic activity, it becomes ritually prominent at the time of the 'washing of the village' ceremony. The weeding of the village is also consistent with the symbolic contrasts between village and forest: the former where humans constantly (and for the most part effectively) impose their cultural will, and the latter where natural forces are oppressively in command. It is likely that to some extent current notions of order, tidiness and cleanliness with respect to the village reflect colonial intrusions – something evident in co-operative path clearing under the direction of the raja of Sepa, the grid-plan of coastal villages (Ellen 1978), and the erection of ornamental openwork bamboo fencing (*pakelo*). However, it seems to me that such changes only serve to reinforce a notion of natural order which was already present.

Of course, as the Nuaulu have been increasingly drawn into systematic cultivation, and especially as they have begun to plant cash crops where protection of young shoots becomes more critical, the notion of 'weed' has been expanded, altered, and become progressively more significant in economic terms (Ellen 1985: 56). Nevertheless, its labelled content must surely still be less than among peoples whose techniques are more intensive, technically elaborated and exclusive as a means of producing food.

General-purpose or Special-purpose Category?

In the light of some detailed botanical ethnography we are now in a position to address the stated theme of the chapter, namely the contrast between special-purpose and general-purpose categories or schemes. This distinction between those categories predicated by logically 'natural' groupings of wide application (e.g. 'vine', 'tree', 'herb'), and those which are characterised as artificial, monothetic or based on a few attributes only, and of narrow utilitarian application (e.g. 'vegetable', 'flower', 'fruit'), is one which we owe to Berlin. It is evident from his earliest writings on folk classification (Berlin et al. 1966) and underpins his general taxonomic approach (Berlin et al. 1974). It has been widely adopted by others. However, a number of authorities have questioned its particular expression and absolute rigidity, noting the intrusion of utilitarian factors into otherwise general-purpose categories (Hays 1982: 90), the conflation of 'general' with 'natural' and 'special' with 'artificial' (Bulmer 1970), the often highly specialised character of so-called 'general' schemes (such as those of botanical taxonomy), the frequent inability of 'general' categories to account for anything but a small fraction of natural discontinuities (Hunn 1982: 834), and the difficulties of disentangling 'special' from 'general' in cross-cultural comparison.

In terms of the original distinction, the analytic category weed is almost certainly intended by those who use it to be represented as a special-purpose category. I am not so sure that we can be equally confident with regard to *monote*. On the one hand *monote* is comparable to, and contrastable with, other Nuaulu inclusive categories for plants where the designation general-purpose would be uncontroversial, such as *ai* (trees and woody shrubs), *rahue* (herbs and shrubby plants) or *wane* (lianas and trailers). These are all life-forms in the slightly differing senses of Berlin or Brown (Berlin et al. 1973; Berlin 1976; Brown 1977, 1984): they are phylogenetically diverse, few in number, include the greater proportion of all plant categories recognised, polytypic, polythetically-defined or identified on the basis of a small number of physical characteristics, labelled by primary lexemes and usually include 'generic' categories as those most immediately subsumed, also labelled by primary lexemes; the only more inclusive category is the unique beginner.[4] The category *monote* is characterised by at least six out of these seven features, and as we have seen, it may be defined optionally in polythetic or monothetic terms. There is no evidence to suggest that in any unprompted division of the domain of plants Nuaulu informants think of *monote* as being qualitatively any different from *ai*, *rahue* or *wane*. Neither is it the case that the intrusion of special-purpose or utilitarian considerations is restricted to *monote*. In some respects *rahue* is complementary to *monote*: it contains broadly the same range of plant types with the same 'natural' focus of small herbaceous plants (though it is much larger), but significantly in functional terms its members are distinguished by their utility rather than their disutility. Intriguingly, the utility of *rahue* is especially clear with respect to non-domesticated species; indeed, informants were hesitant about placing many herbaceous cultigens in the category at all. Such a focus is entirely consistent with what we know of Nuaulu patterns of subsistence as a whole. Functionally neutral or residual plants are to be found in both categories. So, whereas Brown remarks that the general category 'weed' is about as close as we can get to a plant life-form class without actually being a life-form class (Brown 1984: 69), at least as far as *monote* is concerned it is difficult to conclude that we are not dealing with one.

There are two further points which should be made about Nuaulu plant life-forms. Firstly, they do not appear to exclusively partition the domain plant, from which I would anyway exclude algae, fungi, moss and lichens. Palms and ferns, for example, do not fit into any of the four general categories specified so far, and are not collectively distinguished as groups on their own account, even covertly. Secondly, the content of life-forms overlap: some lignaceous plants are *rahue* rather than *ai*, and some seemingly herbaceous plants *ai* rather than *rahue*. *Monote* overlaps with all three, though particularly *rahue*. Moreover, there is uncertainty among informants as to the life-form identity of many plants, which they regard as equally at home in several or in none at all. I have already remarked on the ambiguous status of many herbaceous cultigens with respect to *rahue*.

A Note on Comparison and Life-form Development Sequences

If we now examine categories comparable to *monote* in other northwest Austronesian languages (that is in Philippine, West Indonesian and East Indonesian languages) we discover extensive local variation in content. Thus of the fourteen species listed for the Hanunóo as *?ilamun*, and which Conklin glosses 'grass, weed', only three match those listed in my Table 6.1 for the Nuaulu: *Syndrella nodiflora*, *Imperata exaltata*, and *Centotheca lappacea* (Conklin 1957: 93, 103–4). This may be partly explained by ecological and geographic factors, or through the incompleteness of our respective data. But more significantly, we can separate off those languages whose speakers engage in seed-culture from those who rely on various combinations of vegeculture. Amongst the practitioners of seed-culture, by which in this context we really mean cereal cultivation and in particular that of rice, the 'weed' category is generally strongly associated with grasses. This is the case for the Hanunóo. In such languages it is often labelled by a polysemous term which attracts the glosses 'undesirable non-cultivar' and 'grass'. The Malay word *rumput* and its cognates in other West Indonesian languages is a good case in point (see also e.g. Dove 1985). This accords closely with the definition of weed in botanic-English as 'focally grasses and sedges' (Merrill 1954: 118), and it is perhaps not too fanciful to also see a connection here with cereal cultivation, this time for speakers of European languages. Amongst vegeculturalists in southeast Asia, if there is a category approximating 'weed' at all, I would not expect it to be reflected in a term which can also be glossed as 'grass'. There is no separate Nuaulu 'grass' category, and terminologically the various types of grasses recognised have little to connect them. This may be explained in part by the absence of stable stoloniferous grassland associations dominated by *Imperata* or *Themeda* in the Nuaulu area, these being generally restricted to the more densely populated and deforested western parts of the island of Seram (Ellen 1978: 178); but the major factor seems to be vegeculture itself. Thus in the northwest Austronesian area there appears to be a high degree of correlation between predominant types of cultivar and the semantic parameters of some 'quasi-weed' category.[5]

If we look now at Brown's sequence for the acquisition of botanical life-forms (Brown 1977, 1984), it becomes clear that Nuaulu is a 'stage 5' language in Brown's terms rather than a 'stage 4', and the entry in Brown's *Language and living things* should be revised accordingly. There appear to be four rather than three 'life-forms'. To summarise, the most inclusive categories for plants in Nuaulu thought – their life-forms – are represented by four terms: *ai, wane, rahue* and *monote*. The first two terms may unequivocally be defined as natural groupings, 'tree' and 'vine' respectively; but for the second two terms we can only reconstruct categories which are ambiguously both 'natural' and functional, and in terms of their phylogenetic content and phytomorphology overlapping. Both *monote* and *rahue* focus prototypically on herbaceous forms, but additionally the first is characterised by an overall disutility and the second by an overall utility, at least with respect to non-domesticated plants. *Monote* is definitely not an incipient 'grass' category in Brown's sense, as it cannot be defined attributatively as a special case of 'grerb', that is, small herbaceous plants (green, leafy, non-woody) 'with narrow bladed or spear-shaped leaves and lack of a sturdy stem' (Brown 1984: 13–14). And since grasses are found in both *rahue* and *monote*, and since they are anyway semantically non-salient as a group, 'grerb' would seem to be an inadequate comparative and misleading gloss for just one of these. Similarly, 'weed' is flawed as a gloss for *monote* alone because of its overwhelming 'special-purpose' non-morphopologic connotations.

In phytomorphologic terms *rahue* and *monote* have roughly the same range of reference and presumably a common categorical origin, the one referring to plants which are broadly useful, the other to positively *un*-useful plants. Whether one is the historical residue of the other is difficult to answer, and probably beside the point.[6] In Brown's terms, both might with equal validity be glossed as 'grerb', while both conflate the features through which special-purpose and general-purpose categories have been distinguished.

Notes

1. The data upon which this chapter draws were assembled during the first two periods of my Nuaulu fieldwork, for eighteen months between 1970 and 1971 and again for three months in 1973. The research was conducted under the auspices of Lembaga Ilmu Pengetahuan Indomesia (The Indonesian Academy of Sciences) in Jakarta, and supported by financial grants from the British Social Science Research Council, the London-Cornell Project for East and Southeast Asia, the Hayter Travel Awards Scheme and the Central Research Fund of the University of London. Most of the plant species referred to in the text and listed in Table 6.1 are based on material collected in the field and subsequently identified for me at the Botanic Gardens in Singapore and at the Herbarium of the Royal Botanic Gardens, Kew. I wish to thank Dr Chang Kiaw Lan, Mr L.L. Forman and Dr J. Dransfield for arranging for determinations to be made, and in some cases for undertaking the job themselves.
2. The excluded ferns include epiphytes and species which are saliently designated as food, such as three types of *naine*, focally the polypod *Stenochlaena palustris* Bedd., plus a number of others. What distinguishes these residues may be their strict association with a particular non-domesticated biotope, and their rare or non-appearance in gardens or along their edges. An example of such would be *Colysis macrophylla* (B1.) Presl., known to the Nuaulu as *sabuane*, which grows in clumps on moss-covered rocks along stream banks.
3. So far I have, perhaps coyly but certainly deliberately, avoided glossing the term *monote* as 'weed', on the grounds that I wish to impress the importance of not prejudging what is in fact the central issue of this paper. Having said as much, I hope you will now forgive me if I understandably resort to the term as no more than a convenient and provisional gloss.
4. To contain the present argument I have tried here to project an overall consistency of view. Berlin has shifted his own position on some of the details, and Brown has moved even further away. For some objections to the concept of life-form see Bulmer 1985: 433–5; Ellen 1987: 125–7; Hunn 1982.
5. It is additionally plausible, I suppose, that increasing Nuaulu familiarity with Ambonese Malay *rumput* has influenced their conceptualisation of *monote*.
6. In the Nuaulu case there is therefore no evidence to suggest that 'grerb' originated as a functional 'weed' or 'underbrush' category, as Brown suggests may have happened in Polynesian and Mayan languages (Brown 1982: 220; 1984: 62).

CHAPTER 7

Palms and the Prototypicality of Trees (1998)

As with Chapter 6, this essay raises issues in the construction of a life-form category, this time 'tree'. Palms are often self-evidently assumed to be classified as trees by all people. The data show this not to be the case. What complicates the issue further is the widespread saliency of palms as economically and symbolically important plants.

I wish to open up for discussion the question as to just how universal and prototypical the image and category of tree might be in human psychology and culture, and to explore as a special test case the position of palms in ethnobotanical classifications and symbolic arrays.[1] Palms, as a group of plants (by which I mean here standing palms, not rattans), are of comparative ethnosemantic interest as they are sometimes formally classified as trees in folk and scientific classifications and sometimes not; sometimes labelled as a separate group of plants and sometimes not. Nevertheless, in anthropological studies, in which particular emphasis is placed on their symbolic role, palms appear to function as exemplary members of the category 'tree'. I believe it would be useful to explore whether this is simply a consequence of ethnocentric assumptions on the part of the ethnographer, or whether there is a fundamental and widespread cultural ambiguity in the status of palms as trees.

Palms in European Folk Classifications and in Science

In European languages palms are nowadays unproblematically described as trees (e.g. 'palm trees', *palmier* (*arbre*), *die Palme* (*der Baum*), *palm boom*, etc.), but they are definitely not prototypical cognitively. This is what one would expect in a geographic area where they are non-endemic, infrequent or at the extremes of their range. Nevertheless, it is difficult to place them in any other life-form (or other macro-category) of temperate plants, and so they are, in a sense by default, designated 'trees', though trees, it must be admitted, of a very special kind.

The position in scientific taxonomy and botany broadly reflects what we find in the European folk classifications, and this we would broadly expect given what is known of the history of those classifications. 'Palm' as an ethnobotanical term is derived from Latin *palma*, so-called because of the resemblance of the leaves to the outspan of a human hand (Skeat 1953 [1879–82]: 425). The Latin, but not the Greek *palame*, also signifies 'palm (in the sense of a kind of plant)'. Although distinct types of palm were known from the Roman world, the most likely developmental sequence is that the term (as with its Greek and Phoenician predecessor, 'phoenix') prototypically referred to the the date palm (*Phoenix dactylifera*). It was the date palm which the Greeks had sanctified to Apollo, and which became an emblem of victory or triumph (Corner 1966: 324–5; *Oxford English Dictionary*, vol. 7, 1933: 400–1). Hebrew *tamar* (also 'to be erect') refers to the date palm. It is unclear whether this word was ever extended to include the other endemic palm of west Asia, *Borassus flabellifer* (Hastings 1963: 656–7).

During the early period of European expansion (1450–1650), when many previously unknown species were being reported, introduced and recognised as economically important, palms were neither labelled as a single group, nor were they necessarily considered trees. Perhaps this is not surprising. There is some evidence for the appearance of a tentative and covert collective identity for palms by the end of this period. Thus the pre-Linnaean botanist Rumphius (who had seen many types of palm at first hand in the Moluccas between 1653 and 1702) coined names for some thirteen species. Two of these contained the root 'palm': 'Palma indica nucifera' (*Cocos nucifera* L., the coconut palm), and 'Palma indica vinoria' (*Arenga pinnata* [Wurmb] Merr.); while 'Sagus' (sago: Metroxylon sp.) is included by extension (Peeters 1979: 154–6); we also find the expression 'vinum palmeum', the labelling of rattans by affinity as 'Palmijuncus', and a tree fern (*Cyathea rumphiana* (v. A. v. R.) Merr.) named 'Palmifilix alba'. Linnaeus himself had only seen one living palm at the time of the publication of *Systema Naturae* in 1735, and it was not until 1789 that Antoine de Jussieu (in his *Genera Plantarum*) first designated a single botanical family to encompass all plants we would now describe as palms, the Palmae (Arecaceae).

By the nineteenth century, with the routinisation of the palm category in scientific botanical usage, with the discovery of many hundreds of new species as a consequence of European exploration and imperial consolidation, the presence of more species of living palm in Europe following the development of greenhouses, botanic gardens and the fashion for exotics in gardening (e.g. Jellicoe et al. 1986: 419–20), the status of 'palm' as a distinct type of plant, and as a label delineating many particular kinds, was firmly established. Despite the morphological similarities between different palms (Uhl and Dransfield 1987: 161), their collective identity appears to have had much to do with their tremendous usefulness as a source of food and materials. Rumphius had classified palms on the basis of their respective wine-giving, nut and meal-yielding properties, giving coconut pride of place, 'the captain of the Ambonese herbal' (van Slooten 1959: 333–6, citing Rumphius, Liber 1, *Herbarium Amboinense*). This emphasis on economics in the definition of palms is interesting in the context of debates about the role of utility versus morphology in plant classification (Hunn 1982; Randall and Hunn 1984), and it links up with what I wish to say below about palms in the folk classifications of tropical subsistence cultivators.

The acceptance of palms as trees in European folk classifications appears to have accompanied their recognition as a distinct type of plant. Modern botanical illustrations of the different habits of standing palms (Figure 7.1) indicate the wide range of types, extending from the undeniably treelike to something altogether more shrubby in appearance. If we look at early European representations of palms (Figure 7.2, a–b), here also their treelike qualities are not immediately apparent, indeed they are distinctly suspect. By the nineteenth century, however, representations had definitely become more treelike (Figure 7.2, c). The transition could never be complete as the key defining features of palms in relation to other trees are distinctly ambiguous. Of course, 'tree' is not, anyway, a proper phylogenetic category, though there are botanists who are inclined to give it some weight in classification. Generally speaking, there exists a common-sense botanical definition of palms as something like 'evergreen trees, unbranched (or dichotomously branched), usually erect ....'. However, botanists persuaded more by formal syllogistic logic and a sense of consistency, object that since palms are monocotyledonous and without regular secondary thickening they cannot be trees. They will point to the fact that, instead, the stem or trunk produces from its apex successive leaves one at a time with the leaf base entirely sheathing the stem, that branching is uncommon, that there is no cambium, and that root systems bear little resemblance to those of other trees. In between, we find taxonomists who will only designate as trees the monocotyledons palms and that group which was once accepted as being most closely related to palms taxonomically, the pandans (Mabberley 1987: 635). Those who specialise in palms seem more broad-minded in their definition of trees. So, for example, Corner (1966: 7) is quite emphatic in placing palms, along with screwpines, traveller's palms, tree-lilies, grass-trees and bamboos, along with various bromeliads, aroids, orchids, sedges and rushes,

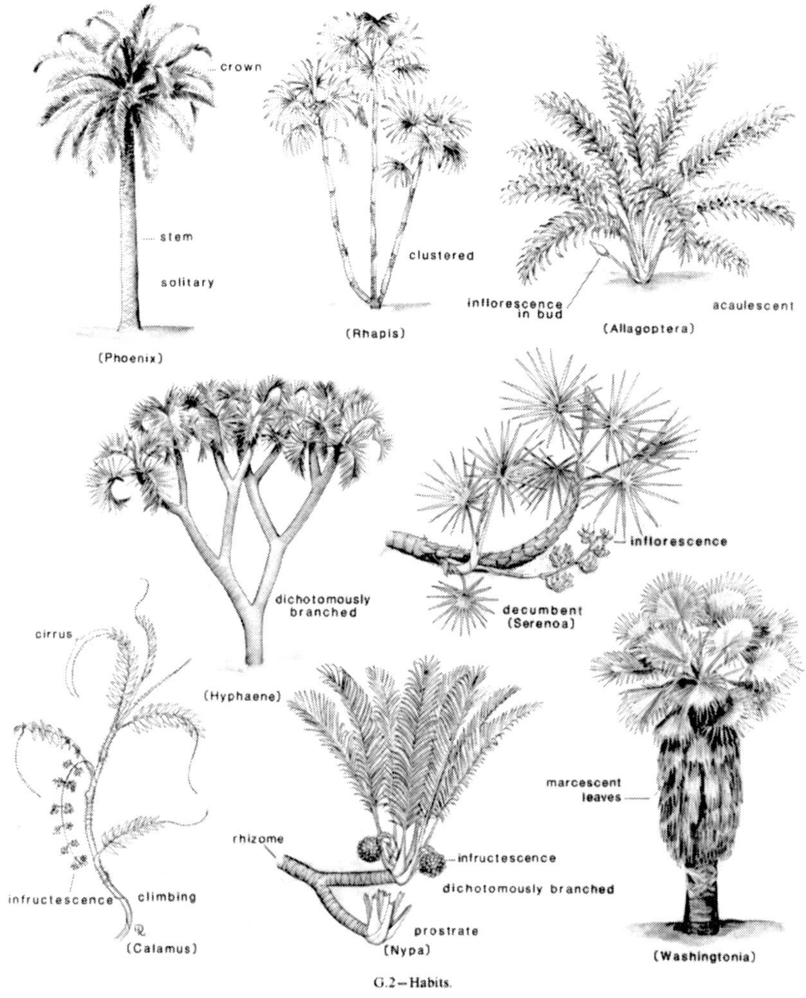

Figure 7.1 Habits of various standing palms (modified from Uhl and Dransfield, *Genera Palmarum* [1987: 556], with permission)

in a category of 'monocotyledonous trees without a unifying and familiar designation', which he describes collectively as 'sword trees'.

Palms in Tropical and Subtropical Folk Classifications

In the tropics (and to a lesser extent in the subtropics) the situation in which potential human classifiers of palms find themselves is different.

Figure 7.2 European representations of palms: (a, top) The coconut palm (*Cocos nucifera*) and (b, left) the talipot (*Corypha umbraculifera*), both from Rheede's *Hortus Indicus Malabaricus* (1968–1703); (c, opposite) Fontes fluvii Paraguay with *Mauritia* palms, from Martius' *Flora Brasiliensis* (1829–33) (all reproduced from Corner 1966, with permission)

As we move from the poles to the Equator so the number of palm species increases dramatically (Henderson et al. 1989), with only two genera reaching Europe compared with thirty-nine in Brazil (139 species). Such abundance might be thought to translate into perceptual salience and thence collective categorisation and labelling, and to more obvious incorporation into the life-form 'tree'. However, on both counts we find the opposite to be the case.

Palms are rarely classified or labelled by folk biologists in the tropics as trees in explicit formal terms. In the cases listed in Table 7.1, selected it is true on the basis of the clarity of the data rather than statistical typicality, there are only six examples of explicit inclusion, as opposed to sixteen of explicit exclusion or ambiguity in status. In some languages, some palms are included and others excluded, in others the term for tree may be applied to individual stands, but there is a distinction between 'stand' and 'wood' (where 'wood' is also polysemously 'tree'), as in Malay or standard Indonesian *pohon* versus *kayu*. Thus the term *pohon kelapa* (coconut tree) is frequently encountered while *kayu kelapa* is rare. Claudine Friedberg (1990: 213–18) reports that in Bunaq (a Papuan language from Timor) there is a term for tree (*hotel*) which includes palms, collectively termed *lepu pol* (and where *lepu pol* in turn is part of *hotel upan guha*), and which are together close to pandans and bananas in their classification. But in addition there is a current Austronesian term *ai*, which never refers to palms.

It is also the case that palms are rarely grouped under a single collective term (Table 7.2), though the supporting data here are more restricted.

Table 7.1 The status of palms as trees in selected languages of tropical and subtropical peoples

Population	Location	Trerm for tree	Notes	Status of palms	Source
Agta	Luzon, Philippines	+		excluded	Brown 1984: 153
Akawio	Guyana	+		excluded	Brown 1984: 181
Alune	Seram, Indonesia	+		excluded	Florey, pers. comm.
Bunaq	Timor, Indonesia	+		ambiguous	Friedberg 1990: 213–18
Carapana	Colombia	+		excluded	Brown 1984: 183
Dusun	Brunei, Borneo	+	large woody plants	excluded	Bernstein 1996: 442–4
Hanunóo	Mindoro, Philippines	+	wood, shrub	included	Conklin 1954: 260–3 and *passim*
Isirawa	Irian Jaya, Indonesia	+	= wood	excluded	Brown 1984: 177
Kalam	highlands, New Guinea	+	= wood	excluded	Bulmer 1974
Koiwai	Irian Jaya, Indonesia	+	large plant, vines	included	Brown 1984: 160
Lotuho	southern Sudan	+		included	Brown 1984: 198
Mokilese	Carolines, Micronesia	+	= wood	included	Brown 1984: 186
Nimboran	Irian Jaya, Indonesia	+	= wood	included	Brown 1984: 179
Nuaulu	Seram, Indonesia	+		excluded	Ellen, field data
Semelai	Malaysian peninsula	+	includes coconut, excludes *Licuala*	ambiguous	Gianno 1990: 54–5
Spanish	Puerto Rico	+		excluded	Brown 1984: 174–5
Sri Aman Iban	Sarawak, Malaysia	+		excluded	Christensen, unpubl.
Tequistlatec	Oaxaca, Mexico	+	= wood, includes coconut	ambiguous	Brown 1984: 184
Tobelo	Halmahera, Indonesia	+		excluded	Taylor 1990: 87–119
Waodani	eastern Ecuador	+	includes banana, yucca, bush	ambiguous	Brown 1984: 167
Wola	New Guinea highlands	+	woody plants	excluded	Sillitoe 1995: 204, 208
Yopno	Huon peninsula,	+	excludes cultivated trees	excluded	Kocher Schmid 1991: 187
Zapotec	Oaxaca, Mexico	+	includes erect cactus	included	Brown 1984: 158

Note: I include here only sources that make explicit reference to the categorical relationship of palms to trees. Reference to Brown 1984 as a source indicates his own field materials plus data acquired through personal communication and access to unpublished sources.

Table 7.2 Presence or absence of generic terms for standing palms in selected languages

Population	Location	Overarching term for standing palms	Total number of locally named palms[a]	Source
Alune	Seram, Indonesia	–	8	Florey, pers. comm.
Dusun	Brunei, Borneo	–	8	Bernstein 1996: 442–4; Bernstein and Ellen, forthcoming
Hanunóo	Mindoro, Philippines	–		Conklin 1954
Nuaulu	Seram, Indonesia	–	14	Ellen, unpubl. field data
Palawan	Palawan, Philippines	–	6	Revel 1990: 146
Tzeltal	Chiapas, Mexico	–	4–5	Berlin et al. 1974: 161–411
Tobelo	Halmahera, Indonesia	–	15	Taylor 1990: 156–7
Wola	New Guinea highlands	±[b]	9	Sillitoe 1995: 204, 208
Yopno	Huon peninsula, New Guinea	+	9	Kocher Schmid 1991: 176–86, 316

[a] At basic (generic) level; does not include rattans.
[b] Optional

However, the family resemblances between different kinds of palm may be acknowledged through overlapping polythetic groupings, which receive varying degrees and types of lexical recognition. Thus amongst the Brunei Dusun (Bernstein and Ellen, forthcoming) *benjiru* (k. o. *Licuala*) is a kind of *pinang* (*Areca catechu*), or *Licuala* is likened to *piasau* (*Cocos nucifera* L). For the Tasek Merimbun Dusun, *Licuala* palms form a covert grouping, and perceived resemblances between a broader range of palms may mean that in some cases we might speak of palms more generally forming a covert category. Among the Palawan of the Philippines (Revel 1990: 146) palms appear to be grouped into sago-producing plants (*Arenga, Caryota, Metroxylon*) and cabbage and fruit palms (*Areca, Pinanga* and *Veitchia*). The coconut is classified quite separately. This would appear to reflect a more widespread contrast between soft-centred and hard-centred palms. More unusually, Yopno in the Huon peninsula area of Papua New Guinea (Kocher Schmid 1991: 176–86) label all palms collectively as *dsopang silep* and pandans as *kiyang silep* (*silep* = family, household; *dsopang* = *Heterospathe* sp. and *kiyang* = *Pandanus brosimos, P. julianettii*). In other words, both palms and pandans collectively are labelled with respect to their most prototypical and salient member. Among the Alune in west Seram (M. Florey, pers. comm.) palms are not clearly grouped as an overt category, and probably not as a single covert category either. 'Moreover, the lexemes for palm morphology (most importantly the terms for infloresence) differ between kinds of palm.' Subtropical Tzeltal in the Chiapas province of Mexico (Berlin et al. 1974: 161, 419) variously classify palms amongst trees or as unaffiliated covert plants (e.g. *Chamaedorea*), but have neither a general overarching term nor a covert category. Overall, whether palms are considered trees, and the extent to which they are given distinct categorical recognition, appears to transcend any broadly-based genetic classification of languages, or classification by geographic region or habitat.

Although palms are rarely labelled as a group of plants separate from any other group in ethnobotanical classifications (though they may exhibit degrees of covert recognition), they do appear to have a utilitarian and symbolic status which exceeds that of the average dicotyledonous timber or fruit-producing tree. Thus there is a very strong link between classificatory status and function. Most prototypical trees do not provide a basic source of carbohydrate or food, though it is always possible to list important exceptions, such as *Canarium*, breadfruit, *Ricinodendron* (Harris 1977). By contrast, palms commonly provide a major starch staple (Ruddle et al. 1978), nourishing fruits (Rival 1993: 638–9), edible apical 'cabbage', alcoholic beverages, stimulants such as betel (Ellen 1991), and may have a wide variety of multiple uses as construction materials, to the extent that they may become culturally dominant in particular economies and life-ways. For the Nuaulu of Seram (Ellen 1977b: 110; 1988) sago palms (*Metroxylon sagu*) are not only the most important source of edible starch, eaten at every meal, but also a source of proteinaceous grubs of the weevil *Rhynchophorus bilineatus*, which are extracted from rotting stumps, and of thatch (leaves), walling (woody leafstalks) and an adaptable manufacturing material (woody leaf sheaths) for the making of containers and other utensils.[2] Fox (1977: 26) provides a similar exhaustive list for the role of *Borassus* among the Rotinese. No wonder then that palms should also have an important symbolic role. Examples of palm symbolism are provided by Bonnemère (1998), Giambelli (1998) and Howell (1998), but the literature on the material and symbolic role of palms is substantial.

Are Palms Symbolic Trees?

Not only are palms economically and symbolically important for many tropical peoples, they somehow appear to become exemplary trees in ritual discourse and practice, even though they may not be formally classified as such. We can summarise this paradox in a simple diagram. Figure 7.3a summarises the conceptualisation of palms as an exemplary kind of tree in symbolic schemes; Figure 7.3b illustrates the conceptualisation of palms as peripheral in ethnobiological classifications based predominantly on plant morphology.

Bonnemère (1998), Giambelli (1998) and Howell (1998) all understand the connection between palms and trees on the basis of metaphoric and symbolic evidence rather than on the basis of language or ethnobiological classification in the conventional sense. In the case of both the Lio of Flores, discussed by Howell, and the Balinese, discussed by Giambelli, there exists a metaphorical repertoire which unites palms and trees generally. This is something which is well documented for eastern Indonesia, especially the imagery of trunk (base, source, origin, beginning, cause) and tip (treetop, shoot, buds) (e.g. Traube 1986: 14–15). Thus, for the Rotinese (Fox 1975: 119) *tuu* (lontar palm) appears to function as a tree in symbolic terms. But this function is not necessarily restricted to a single symbolically dominant palm. In his account of Umeda symbolic life in the Sepik, Alfred Gell (1975: 123–33) shows how *Areca*, coconut, sago and Caryota are all important, with coconut as a kind of symbolic *primus inter pares* (cf. the 'Palmyra indicum' of Rumphius, and also the ethnobiological status of the coconut among the Palawan, discussed on pp. 58 and 62). But Gell (1975: 237) is also very clearly suggesting that all these palms are somehow standing in for some unspoken abstract image of 'treeness', especially when we are invited to see clear meta-linkages between trees as symbols and humans as symbolic vehicles. In Bonnemère's account of the Ankave-Anga in the New Guinea highlands, not only is *Areca* (a palm) treated as an exemplary tree but so are pandans, *Cordyline* (a shrub) and

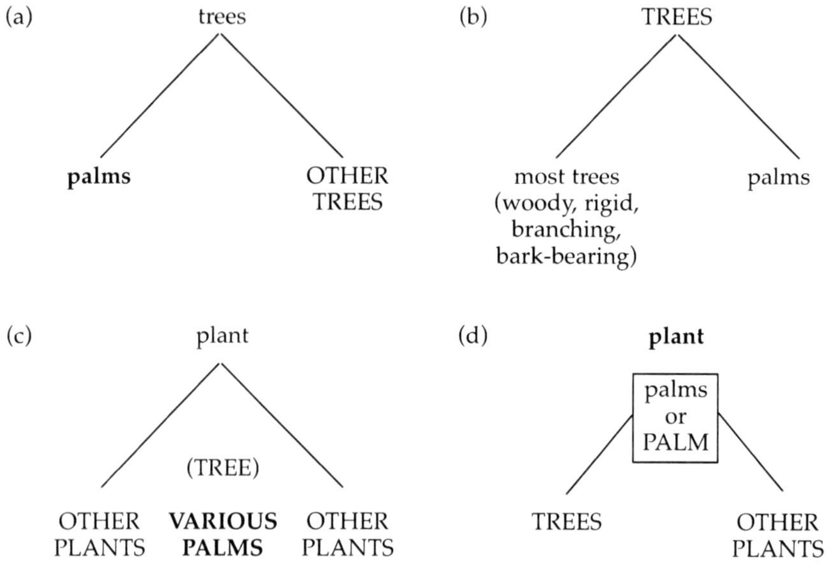

Figure 7.3 Relationship between palms and the category 'tree' in (a) symbolic and (b) morphological classifications. In the first, palms are conceptualised as an exemplary kind of tree; in the second they are peripheral. (c) illustrates the relationship between 'palms', 'trees' and 'plant' in terms of lexical and ethnobiological salience for a hypothetical palm society. (d) illustrates the relationship between 'palm', 'tree' and 'plant' in terms of symbolic focus for a hypothetical palm society. In the diagrams, UPPER CASE lettering indicates lexically expressed categories, **bold type** indicates conceptual salience and lower case covertness.

Ficus (a strangling fig), all of which are problematically peripheral in most definitions of the tree category.

This is all very puzzling and confusing. Why should palms – and other doubtful tree types – rarely be labelled as a separate group in the classifications of tropical and subtropical peoples; why are they are seldom explicitly classified as trees, and yet at the same time classified as honorary trees in symbolic terms? Is there a connection between these three observations? Certainly palms appear to have an intermediate status between trees and other plants. This can plausibly be explained partly in terms of general vegetational diversity, and partly in terms of the diversity of palms in particular. Thus in the tropics the distribution of plant types is more continuous than in temperate areas, at least as far as the minds of ordinary humans are concerned. Botanists may be different. There are various intermediate and ambiguous groups (tree-ferns, pandans, rattans), while the number of kinds of palm is greater, and they are distributed more widely. In some areas palms may be dominant (as in sago swamp, *Nypa* coastal fringes, and plantations), while a greater proportion of all palms are domesticated or semi-domesticated compared with other forest trees. Palms themselves also vary in their properties and potential, although their overall morphology is the same. Some are soft-centred, some are hard. Soft-centred palms are often sources of food (sago flour, lontar syrup); hard-centred ones can be used for wood (*Oncosperma*). Both kinds provide cabbage and fruits.

In short, the argument favouring palms as 'prototypical examples' (Rosch 1977) of the category 'tree' is weak; neither are they an immediately recognisable *gestalt* (Atran 1985: 309). Where they obtain a collective categorical status this appears to be almost in opposition to prototypical trees, and through culturally enhanced salience as a special-purpose grouping. In this respect the category 'palm' is a bit like the animal life-form 'mammal'. Both, in effect, are only unambiguously labelled in scientific classifications, though incipiently exist to varying degrees in different folk schemes. Both comprise a number of highly salient and functionally important species, which in the case of mammals in European societies has made them exemplary animals. Their common distinctive features stem not so much from simple exterior morphology as from an aggregate of anatomical and growth features which rarely become indicators for folk-biologists. As a group, palms do not possess all of the key qualities which make trees good symbols: they certainly produce food (and in abundance) but they do not usually have the branches, timber-producing woody trunks or roots which match the imagery widely associated with prototypical trees. Thus the category 'palm' and the various covert and labelled groups which subdivide and cut across it, are excellent examples (depending on your theoretical predisposition) of either the intersection of mundane and symbolic classifications or the difficulty of finding operative ethnobiological classifications for particular peoples which exclude significant cultural criteria.

'Tree' as Label, Cognitive Prototype and Symbol

Our discussion of the classificatory status of palms would be almost complete at this point were the classificatory status of trees as a whole to be more straightforward. What I wish to demonstrate in the final section of this chapter is that our understanding of palms as objects in classifications and as symbols cannot be separated from a fundamental paradox in the classificatory status of trees. Thus, according to Wilkowski, Brown and Chase (1981), following Berlin (1972: 66–9), a general term for tree is a recent addition to languages – recent, that is, in terms of the evolution of language. On the other hand, if tree is an historically recent term it confounds other evidence from cognitive and developmental psychology that 'tree' is a basic image prototype (e.g. Boster 1996), together with the implicit evidence of much ethnography that it is what Fox (1975) has called a 'primary symbol'.

For Witkowski, Brown and Chase the appearance of a discrete tree life-form is a response to a corresponding decline in what Bousfield (1979: 203–4) has called 'semantic contact'. By this is meant that as people are removed from the world of plants, as societies become larger and more complex, with greater division of labour reflected in functional access to living and growing organisms, so the need for general life-form terms increases and the need for specific terms decreases. Occasionally tree terms may only refer to a specific type of tree, as in the much-cited case of 'cottonwood tree' = 'tree' (Trager 1939) in the native languages of the American southwest. Indeed, Brown and his associates argue that several thousand years ago, terms for 'tree' were either absent or encoded only as 'a low salience category'. Where a tree concept is recognised, suggests Brown (1977), this necessarily implies a second life-form, that is 'herb', where the main discriminating dimension is size rather than ligneousness. Indeed, there is complementary evidence from child language acquisition studies that the first distinction to emerge is between large and small plants (Dougherty 1979). This orthodoxy appears now to have superseded earlier assumptions of distinctive feature analysis employed classically by Charles Frake (1980 [1962]: 12) in his description of Subunan botanical life-forms, where categories are determined by the presence or absence of just two features in a contrast set: woodiness (W) and rigidity (R), so that *gayu* 'woody plants' = W,R; *sigbet* 'herbaceous plants' = $\overline{W}R$, and *belagen* 'vines' = --$\overline{R}$.

The late acquisition of a 'tree' term is consistent with other evidence regarding the difficulty of isolating a natural cognitive prototype in the visual landscape (Hunn 1987: 148; Brown 1990: 31–2). Thus Figure 7.4 illustrates in outline the form of twelve species selected for the range of habits which they display, but these in turn are drawings of ideal trees standing in isolation. Although tree germplasm is genetically programmed to generate a phenotypically particular structure (with its distinctive branching pattern, erectness of growth, consistency of trunk thickness, form of canopy, overall symmetry and so on), this is seldom achieved due to environmental constraints. Although they conform to precise architectural principles and provide models which have taxonomic integrity, trees growing in clumps or in a forest rarely have the same appearance as those growing individually in the culturally modified spaces of settlements, tree-lined avenues or botanic gardens.

Similarly, it is difficult to establish a clear boundary between trees and non-trees in the visual landscape (Figure 7.5): trees, bushes and shrubs all merging imperceptibly, displaying varying degrees of size and woodiness and multiplicity of stem. What we describe as a tree is not 'due to phylo-

Figure 7.4 Tree forms, selected to indicate range of types (based on original illustrations by John White in Phillips 1978; not drawn to scale)

genetic relatedness but to evolutionary convergence in response to common adaptive challenges constrained by laws of form' (Hunn 1987: 148). At the same time, trees as individuals elide with trees as a collectivity; individual 'stands' (to take a British English example) becoming 'clumps', clumps becoming 'copses' (coppices), copses becoming 'woods', and woods becoming 'forest'. Indeed, in some languages the word for 'tree' is the same as that for 'forest' (e.g. see Morris 1976). Forest trees are, therefore, simultaneously singular and part of a group, while trees as things are not completely separate from the environment in which they exist. Unlike animals, which are visually autonomous and can wander around as individuals, trees are like rocks and hills, not simply in the landscape but of it as well. Their literal rootedness and groupiness only highlight this. No wonder we cannot see the wood for the trees.

Figure 7.5 Plant morphotypes, selected to indicate continuity between recognisable tree forms and shrubby herbs (based on original illustrations by Jan Masek in Lawrence 1985; not drawn to scale)

And when Brown suggests that early tree terms were encoded as 'a low salience category', he also proposes that this was through semantic extension from 'wood'. This is why wood/tree polysemy is so widespread. Indeed, some wood terms do appear to have emerged before tree terms (e.g. Blust 1974: 5, 11–12). Such polysemy disappears as societies become more complex. Thus the less inclusive item, the reference of which appears to have been extended, is that which acquires its salience from cultural use rather than from intrinsic perceptual qualities: wood as a material with many technological applications exemplifying trees in general; or (as in Austronesian bird/chicken polysemy) chickens as domesticates which have coevolved closely with human populations and which provide food and sacrificial items exemplifying birds as a whole (Ellen 1993: 81). In either case, the conceptual identity is expressed by using the same word.

All this brings us back to some well-worn utilitarianist versus universalist arguments (Hunn 1982; Randall and Hunn 1984). We need not go over old theoretical ground here, but of particular relevance is the claim by Atran (1985: 306) that there is an inconsistency between Brown's claim for the definition of tree in terms of size, and his functional definition in terms of wood. Atran continues (p. 307):

> it will not do to argue that referential expansion simply consists in relaxing the functional component of the definition and stressing only the perceptual component. ... The perceptual features attaching to the artifact 'timber' and the living kind 'tree' are quite different in nature: those that attach to 'tree' are virtual properties that include phenomenally typical attributes of trees, whereas the only perceptually logical characteristic of 'timber' relates to being wooden and cut.

Despite the persistent controversies surrounding formal distinctive feature analysis, the continuous character of vegetative morphs in the landscape, the implication that wherever wood / tree polysemy occurs 'tree' has a low saliency, and the heat generated by the functionalist arguments, 'tree' is always the first botanical life-form to be encoded, judging from evidence of cross-language comparisons (Brown 1977). This in turn suggests that its psychological saliency might be qualitatively different from botanical life-forms such as 'vine', 'grass' or 'bush'. If, indeed, some life-forms are more natural than others, then 'tree' is a prime example. Some promising experimental cross-species evidence for this contention is found in the observations that pigeons discriminate trees from other objects in their field of vision (Hernnstein et al. 1976), though presumably do not contrast them with other botanical life-forms. However, the extent to which this implies conceptual thought rather that vague 'imaginal' codes, or innate perceptual distinctions rather than learned behaviour, has been questioned. Certainly, the picture becomes more complex if we examine recent work on primates, where phylogenetic similarities with humans are closer (Cheney and Seyfarth 1990: 86–91). What evidence we do have points to visual environmental stimuli being organised more according to function (food sources, potential predators, nesting sites, toolmaking materials) than in terms of abstract proto-lifeforms. Nevertheless, there are at least some data to support the theoretically plausible view (Boster 1996: 276–80) that a number of features of 'natural' classification might be a consequence of co-evolution and natural selection, though the evidence does not extend to the lexical tagging of such apparently universal images.

There is also an additional body of evidence, a set of compelling theoretical propositions, as well as some strong intuitive reasons, for supposing that 'tree' must have been from a very early time a major metaphoric vehicle for the classification of other kinds of more abstract relations, as evident in kinship discourse and the widespread use of the tree partonyms 'root', 'branch' and 'trunk' in everyday as well as symbolic language. In his work on Rotinese ritual language, Fox (1975: 113–15) locates seven linkages between 'tree' (*ai*) and other primary symbols, making it the most connected and, presumably, the most salient Rotinese symbol. In addition, 'tree' (*ai*), 'fruit' (*boa*), 'leaf' (*dok*), and 'trunk' (*huk*) all occur in an inner core of symbols. And that such usages need not be tied to words rather than to unlabelled culturally informed images is supported by increasing evidence which downplays the linguistic model of culture (Bloch 1992, 1993). Cultural variation, nevertheless, must have a considerable impact on the form of 'tree' metaphors. Analogical correspondence or consubstantiality between tree (or plant) and human development, reproduction, longevity and relatedness (Fox 1971), is more widespread than the occurrence of trees which symbolically mediate between houses and people (as in 'heartwood' = 'bone', or tree/housepost simultaneity) or which express the animate/inert ambiguities of timber. Indeed, it might be tentatively suggested that wood/tree polysemy emerges only where houses are more than temporary shelters and their construction a significant cultural activity. There is some evidence to suggest that non-agricultural nomadic forest-dwelling populations not only recognise fewer basic terms for plants, but especially fewer terms for wood-producing trees (Ellen 1999).

So although not all life-forms are 'natural' in the sense employed by Berlin, Boster and Atran (1985: 311), some are more natural than others (Randall 1987: 143).The obvious configurational qualities of trees make them, at the very least, in Eugene Hunn's apposite phrase, 'perceptually compelling', and 'it is not hard to understand why folk biologists almost everywhere should be motivated to give trees nomenclatural recognition' (Hunn 1987: 148). Even if 'the tree' as an abstract icon – something that bears no particular relation to any one species – is a complex cultural simplification (Ohnuki-Tierney 1981), and there is no 'natural' basis for the *gestalt* property of treeness, such properties need not always be associated with continuities in nature. They might, instead, be associated with deductive discontinuities (Brown 1990), permitting perceptual continuities such as 'tree <> woody shrub <> shrubby herb <> herb' to be effectively subdivided. In this case, a better bet might be a propositional model for prototypic trees (e.g. Wierzbicka 1985: 182–3): trees produce fuel, wood for construction, shade, substances (nuts, fruits, seeds) that can be eaten by humans and others; are taller than people; have trunks; grow for a long time. These specifications need not be equally weighted, and 'when tree categories are consolidating in languages, utilitarian properties of prototypic trees are by far more significant than specifications entailing size, appearance, growth, and so on' (Brown 1990: 31–2). Brown continues:

> Those botanical entities in nature that produce wood which can be used as fuel or in construction, and *also* provide shade for creatures the size of people, and *also* produce substances which can be eaten by people and/or other creatures, tend strongly to include an array of things that happen to share certain perceptual properties: trunks, bark, leaves or needles, branches, large size (bigger than people), and so on. These particular things constitute a segment of a botanical continuity which people focus on because all things associated with that segment have *all* the utilitarian properties listed above. ... This segment is singled out for special attention when a name or label is assigned to all those botanical things having all of the noted utilitarian

> properties. It just so happens that most botanical things so named also share a number of perceptual properties. As a consequence, naming produces or, better, imposes a discontinuity on the world which, in fact, is not naturally there. This, of course, is a deductive discontinuity. The deductive discontinuity relating to 'tree', then, underlies the consolidation of a Gestalt property of 'treeness'. (Brown 1990: 32)

If we now return to Figure 7.3 we can see illustrated in (c) the relationship between 'palm', 'tree' and 'plant' in terms of lexical and ethnobiological salience for a hypothetical society where palms are important economically and ritually. In many societies there is no general term for 'plant' (Berlin 1992), nor for palm (as we have established). The only degree or level of categorical inclusion which is lexically expressed is 'tree'. This would be a perfectly accurate description of, say, the Nuaulu case. However, lexical expression may be a poor guide to symbolic significance, and if we stress general metaphoric and symbolic usages the plant image may be more important than trees in general (d), except when idioms of longevity, durability and hardness exemplified by trunk, and shade by canopy are required. Palms can sometimes fulfil these symbolic requirements, but not always. Compelled by a taxonomic logic of transitivity which is common in the literate cultures of the West, we tend to emphasise a logical-sentential string of the kind: palm is kind of tree, and a tree is a kind of plant. Given what we now know of the ambiguous character of the category 'tree', the middle term in this transitive phrase may be redundant, or at least only relevant in certain places for certain purposes. Thus when it comes to symbolic considerations, what is most important is not that palms are 'trees', exemplary or not, but that they are salient, life-giving 'plants'. In certain cultural settings, anyway, the symbolic force of the 'arborescent' motif may therefore have been overstated (cf. Deleuze and Guattari 1987).

Notes

1. Some of the material discussed in this chapter draws upon two recent projects funded by the British Economic and Social Research Council with which I have been involved: 'The ecology and ethnobiology of human-rainforest interaction in Brunei' (a Dusun case study), R000 23 3088; and 'Deforestation and forest knowledge in south central Seram, eastern Indonesia', R000 23 6082. I would like to thank Margaret Florey for permission to use unpublished material, and John Dransfield of the Royal Botanic Gardens Kew for his helpful suggestions.
2. Some palms even provide fuel and wood for construction, contradicting one of the key features which overall would appear to separate them from dicotyledonous trees. For the Nuaulu, the hard wood of *panuke* (*Oncosperma tigillarium*) was the favoured material for the manufacture of arrow midshafts, door-bolts and longbows. Cf. the role of *Bactris gasipes* amongst the Huaorani of Amazonian Ecuador (Rival 1993: 639–43).

CHAPTER 8

The Inedible and the Uneatable (1998)

Totemism has an historically important place in the anthropological study of symbolic classification. This essay looks at biological species selected for prohibition by Nuaulu, and asks how we might explain the choices which they make with respect to ecological and cultural rationalities, and in relation to whether the prohibitions are social phase dependent or constant over time. It presents further examples of how the way we classify is fundamentally pragmatic and contingent.

Introduction

I want to begin by elaborating what to me seems a basic analytic dichotomy in the study of prohibitions, but which to my knowledge has been the subject of little previous discussion. This is the distinction between those prohibitions which characteristically relate to a limited time-span (such as occur during life-crisis rituals or at menstruation), and those of unlimited duration (such as are typical of what is still conventionally described as 'totemic' classification). The first category I call 'phased', being those prohibitions that apply to all persons in a particular social category, but only at certain moments in their life-cycle or at other moments in cyclically-structured behaviour. The second category I called 'fixed' prohibitions, which apply to members of a particular social category all of the time. The interweaving of the two, when plotted against the empirical discontinuities of physical experience, provide a grid of cultural denial specific to a particular human population, with inevitable (if muted) ecological resonances. The extent to which these resonances serve as the basis for Darwinian selective pressure has been the subject of some debate (see e.g. Laderman 1981: 468–9; Lepowsky 1985), to which I shall return at the end of this chapter.

I shall consider the phased-fixed distinction as it applies to the Nuaulu,[1] a group of intermarrying clans speaking the same language and with a common subsistence focus on sago extraction, hunting, collecting and swidden cultivation, living in and around the lowland rainforest of south central Seram. I concur with Valeri (1992: 150), that prohibitions as a generic focus of analytic scrutiny are too numerous and too varied to make sense of (a prime example of Lévi-Strauss's infinitely self-reproducing polycephalous hydra), that the reasons for particular prohibitions are often contingent, that they are variable in their significance and social distribution, and that identifying discrete prohibitions is often difficult. I note also the awkwardness with which proscriptions are assigned to conventional and convenient analytic categories, whether motivated by imputed social function (as with 'totem') or practical utilitarian considerations (for example, 'poisons'), or some combination of the two, as we find in the concept of 'food taboo'. I argue, however, that it is possible to distinguish in a general way between potential foods which Nuaulu know full well can cause harm *intrinsically*, and are therefore unconsumable, and those which are inedible for all people some of the time or for some people all of the time, for *extrinsic* reasons: the difference, if you will, between the inedible and the uneatable.[2]

Avoidance and Prohibition

There are specific plants which Nuaulu avoid consuming at all costs, and which may indeed be employed as poisons, for example the bark of *hanasane* (*Barringtonia* sp.), used in fishing. In addition there is *munu*: to be precise, the stronger and more effective vine *awane munu tune* (*Garcinia dulcis?*), the weaker *munu rapa, awane minne* (probably the shrub *Derris uliginosa*, with its filementous root-like climbing stems), and *awane munu apane* and *kokune* (*Callicarpa* sp.), which are all widely used as freshwater fish poisons. Also employed for stunning fish is *asaherane* (*Myristica knema*; *M.*sp.prob.*fatua*), the forest nutmeg. Such obvious poisons are grouped with plants and other substances of animal and inorganic origin of varying degrees of toxicity. These range from those species which are really dangerous and life-threatening, such as *Antiaris toxicaria*, through plants which are not technically poisons but are mildly toxic, such as *sinatane urone* (*Procris frutescens*), the fine hairs of which can produce a painful rash, to things which are just unpleasant and unpalatable, such as the fruits of *mataponane* (*Cerbera manghas*; *C.odullum*) or the wild banana, *uri poi* (*Musa* probl. *uranoscopes*). When it comes to fungi (*unate*), Nuaulu apply a general – though by no means infallible – rule: those species which grow on living trees, dead wood or sago palms are regarded as edible – at least in principle – while freestanding mushrooms and toadstools are regarded as inedible, even though many of them are non-toxic. There is also an intermediate group of plants classified as food but which are clearly empirically dangerous in certain states or strengths and not in others. Thus fish which have been stunned with *Garcinia* can be eaten, as the traces are generally sufficiently low not to cause harm to humans, though they must be carefully washed and gutted. The yam *kawasine* (*Dioscorea hispida*), allegedly much used in sorcery, contains the toxic alkaloid dioscorine, and can only be eaten once tubers have been boiled or left soaking in cold water for a period. The so-called 'bitter' varieties of *Manihot esculenta* (in Nuaulu, *kasipi unuhutu* and *kasipi paru*) contain levels of cyanogenetic glucosides which readily yield prussic acid. For this reason they are best prepared as *embal*: that is, shredded, the moisture removed through pressure and then baked as hard biscuits.

All potential foods which are avoided altogether because of their empirically identifiable properties, or which must be eaten with circumspection, or which are plain unpleasant, are described by Nuaulu as *minne*, and are not subject to the phased-fixed convention. However, some plants and animals are avoided as food not because of their intrinsic empirical characteristics but because they have a special relationship with particular socially defined groups, groups constituted either temporally or spatially or in some combination of the two. Such potential foods are included, along with other things, in the category *monne*. There is, I believe, a parallel between the *minne* range of avoidances and the *monne* range of prohibitions. Both invoke rules about what can and cannot be consumed, in both cases there are sanctions manifest in the form of physical discomfort, or worse. Some avoidances are weak and others strong, and this (as we shall see) is also true of prohibitions. But what are for the most part congruent behaviours at times merge into a conceptual grey area where mundane avoidance appears simultaneously as sacred sanction. Such occurrences are logically similar to those situations which I have described where Nuaulu confidently assert that an animal is simultaneously a spirit, or that the characteristic signs of spirit presence really indicate an invisible but quite ordinary animal (Ellen 1993a).

The Nuaulu concept of *monne* is not confined, however, to the sense of prohibition. Indeed, it approaches that constellation of meanings conventionally attached to 'taboo' in anthropological literature, referring to objects, actions, utterances and rules. It is an intimidatingly complex, polyvalent, concept (Steiner 1975 [1956]: 33), implying by turns separateness and sacredness, danger and pollution, both behaviour and words. Some things are *monne* because they are prescribed, some things because they are proscribed, some things because they just are (e.g., mythic narratives). Eating certain *monne* foods is enjoined, eating others is rewarded with ancestral wrath. But what is apparent in Nuaulu experience is the sheer volume of *monne*, the time devoted to attending to them, and the anxiety provoked by a failure to do so. What Nuaulu sometimes say distinguishes them from their Christian and Muslim brethren is the heavy burden of *monne* which they carry around with them.

Phased Prohibitions

Most phased prohibitions are those connected with life-cycle rituals and bodily rhythms. Young men during their initiation ritual should ideally not eat at all, while a girl for the duration of her first menstruation must avoid all foods cooked in the normal way, and must begin by fasting from around three in the morning until the following midnight, when she is ritually fed a little bit of each type of food wrapped in a leaf. During a first menstrual seclusion there can be no speaking except in whispers. The taboos which apply to a first menstruation also apply to all subsequent menstruations. Women in menstrual seclusion are not allowed to eat betel or use coconut oil, nor are they allowed to have a lamp. A woman in seclusion following the birth of a baby is subject to the same dietary taboos as a menstruating woman. Special utensils (such as baskets) are reserved for the menstruation hut, and on no account can opposite sexes come into contact during such periods, for fear of mutual contamination. For the clan Sounaue-ainakahata, between the time when a house is entered after emerging from birthing seclusion and the encircling of the house the following day, fire cannot cross the threshold, and this includes a lighted cigarette. The blood of a cuscus may not be drunk by a woman who has given birth, as this will make her too hot and she will be unable to have further children. Men, by contrast, can drink blood. At male initiations sago porridge cannot be consumed by neophytes who are also not allowed to smoke or chew betel, or eat at all for twenty-four hours prior to the ceremony. Family of the deceased cannot eat coconut or *Canarium* nuts or bathe for four days after a death. Such phased prohibitions are all linked to classic life-cycle rites of passage, but in addition any person who hosts a feast must abstain from all food for the duration of the feast, those travelling or engaged in various productive activities (such as hunting) may be subject to taboos, including dietary taboos, and those who are ill may be required to refrain from eating certain things. Indeed, an entire clan may be subject to a temporary prohibition if there is much sickness around. The sum effect of all these must be significant, both in the sense of the discomfort felt and anxiety provoked, at least if they are all equally and assiduously attended to. And what is additionally strange is that they seem to be invoked when people are least able to cope with them, when they are particularly vulnerable.

Fixed Prohibitions

Fixed prohibitions are those which stay with an individual for the duration of his or her life, though we should perhaps qualify this by adding *adult* life, as some prohibitions are not activated until sexual maturity or marriage. Furthermore, in some circumstances 'fixed' prohibitions can be relaxed or rescinded, as I explain below. The term 'fixed' must, therefore, be understood rather as a convenient analytic device, to permit contrast with those prohibitions which are always associated with rites of passage, that is 'phases' in the life or any other ritual cycle.

Some fixed prohibitions are honoured by all Nuaulu clans. These are what Bulmer (1979: 60) has called 'super-totems'. The trees *kama wae* (*Agathis dammara*) and *kama onie* (*Shorea selanica*) are *monne* for all Nuaulu: the timber may never be used for construction purposes, nor the resin as a means of illumination. This does not prevent, however (at least under present circumstances) their extraction for sale. Similarly, *tonate* (*Intsia bijuga*) and *nunue* (*Ficus* spp.) are prohibited as building materials. The bamboo *tenne* (*Gigantochlea*) is *monne* for all Nuaulu, except the sub-clan Neipane-manunte in the village of Bunara. In terms of food, *tenne* shoots are obviously prohibited, as is the consumption of the banana *uri punau* (*Musa* X *paradisiaca* var.). The grains *hotone* (*Setaria italica*) and *salea* (*Sorghum vulgare*) are also universally proscribed, except that in certain ritual contexts they may be offered to the ancestors.

Most prohibitions are, however, clearly clan-linked. But not only must you honour the *monne* of your natal clan, under certain circumstances you must honour the *monne* of other clans as well, particularly of affinal and maternal clans. When a person marries they must honour the prohibitions of their spouse's clan, but a woman may not relinquish those of her father's clan, nor a husband those of his wife's clan until bridewealth payments have been completed, or appropriate compensation paid, whatever the type of marriage entered into. On marriage, to be released from a prohibition, a girl must pay a fine to her father's clan, often in the form of a large plate.

The extent to which individuals honour the prohibitions of clans other than their own is, therefore, extensive. This outflow of *monne* restrictions from clans of origin has certain practical disadvantages for Nuaulu individuals. It certainly increases, as they see it, possible sources of misfortune, or at least explanations of such. In so far as they apply to food, it would also seem to increase the likelihood of some nutritional impact. But it is also a source of confusion for both students of Nuaulu society and for Nuaulu themselves, particularly younger people and others not well versed in ritual matters. For such individuals it may not always be clear whether a prohibition they are required to respect is historically that of their father's clan, or whether it derives from another through affinity. In such a situation it is tempting to speculate that Nuaulu-wide prohibitions of the kind described above may have historically arisen through the requirement to 'follow' the restrictions of other clans, later becoming incorporated and 'fixed'. In this sense it has been a factor contributing to the process of Nuaulu ethnogenesis, the forging of a common identity over several hundred years among otherwise relatively autonomous and disparate clans living in different areas of central Seram.

Although fixed prohibitions generally relate to clans, some may relate to one of the paired 'houses' which constitute each clan, either a *numa onate* (house of the clan chief) or *numa kapitane* (house of the traditional war leader). For example, the newly-acquired prohibition on the eating of papaya, and respect behaviour towards mice, is restricted to the *numa onate* of the clan Peinisa in the village of Rohua, apparently the result of a visitation from an ancestral spirit during a dream. Similarly, the eating of the bean *kihue manora* is prohibited only to the *numa onate* of Sounaue-ainakahata, and not for ordinary members of this clan. Other fixed prohibitions apply only to one sex, or to one sex in a particular clan. Women as a whole, for example, cannot eat food which has been first presented to ancestors. More specifically, the prohibition on chewing *kanai putie* (white var. of *Areca catechu*), or eating *weni nante* (*Dioscorea alata*) and *uri numanaeta* (k.o. banana) applies only to women in the clan Soumori. Soumori women are additionally subject to a complex array of interconnected prohibitions focused on contact with non-flowing water. Neipane women cannot eat the shoots of the *tomone* bamboo. Still other taboos are only for women who have married into a clan. Thus women marrying into Matoke cannot cross the river Nua, so are unable to move to the new settlements on the Wae Pia or travel north into traditional Matoke territory.

Prohibitions may also relate to individual persons, such as clan chiefs. In Rohua, the government-recognised headman and chief of the clan Soumori has a personal chicken (and egg) prohibition, and is not allowed to cut the nail of his right hand thumb. Similarly, the clan chiefs (*ia onate*) of Peinisa, Sounaue-aipura, Matoke-hanaie and Matoke-pina are not allowed to live near the sea. The *ia onate* Matoke is not allowed to eat snake, although the restriction does not apply to other members of the clan. The *ia onate* Matoke-hanaie cannot eat rice.

Thus fixed prohibitions may operate along several (sometimes intersecting) axes, defining individual identity in different ways and to different degrees of inclusiveness. To summarise, these are: in terms Nuaulu versus non-Nuaulu, one clan versus another, one clan section versus another, members of a ritual house versus others; according to gender within a clan, whether a woman is an affine or a kinsperson, and depending on completion or otherwise of required payments which accompany marital alliances. In addition, particular individuals may have personal *monne* linked to a particular ascribed position. As we move from the most encompassing to the least encompassing, from the collectivity to the individual person, so the volume of restrictions increases: the more your status places you in a mystically dangerous position, the more you are subject to restrictions in behaviour. Moreover, when a husband follows the *monne* of his wife's clan, or a wife the *monne* of her husband's clan, their social position is articulated both through descent and alliance, kinship and affinity. *Monne* moves, in a sense, like other material objects and knowledge which are subject to the rules of exchange and which define social position (Ellen 1996c). Thus although I do not have the data which would permit a cluster analysis (see Aunger 1993), it is quite clear that these rules contribute to a remarkable degree of intracultural variation in the observation of taboos. Moreover, we might well also conclude that the Nuaulu person is significantly constituted in terms of what an individual is *not* permitted to do.

Objects and Phenomena Selected for Prohibition

The easiest prohibitions to identify and make sense of are inevitably those with respect to biological species. Some fixed prohibitions on plants and animals are set out in Tables 8.1 and 8.2. What is perhaps remarkable is that there are no animal foods which all Nuaulu are required to abstain from eating all of the time, with the possible exception of dogs (see Valeri 1992: 151–2) and, of course, humans (Ellen 1996b). The ban on eating dog is clearly related to the commensal relationship established between humans and dogs – we feed them, so we do not eat them (see Ellen 1996b; Valeri 1992) – though the ban on eating self-raised domesticated stock is less categorial than Valeri reports for the Huaulu. Chicken and even cow may be eaten; even dog is now occasionally (though rarely) consumed, though there is still a general aversion and consumption appears to be limited to animals which the Nuaulu themselves neither own nor kill. All other prohibitions are either circumstantial or group-linked.

In the ethnic and religious world of the central Moluccas this immediately and most obviously distinguishes them from Muslims, who are required by the Koran to avoid pork and all meats which have not been ritually slaughtered, and who must not drink alcohol. By extension, most Seramese Muslims will also avoid other wild mammals, reptiles and amphibians not mentioned in the Koran as being edible, and anything which has had contact with pigs or is associated with pig-eating animists. Certain Christian sects, such as Seventh Day Adventists, also prohibit alcohol and other stimulants including tea and coffee. Such permanent and universal prohibitions are noted by the Nuaulu and feature in significant ways in their perception and construction of their own ethnicity.

Table 8.1 Distribution of Nuaulu animal totems according to clan

	Ma-p	Pe	Son-aip	Pi	Hu	Son-ain	Num	Ne-tom	Ne-ne	Ka	Som	Sop
1. *puhaa* *Crocodylus porosus* estuarine crocodile	a		a		b	b						
2. *hahu* *Sus scrofa* pig		b?[1]				b[1]						
3. *asuan* *Casuarius casuarius* cassowary						b2						
4. *enu* all sea turtles		b						a				
5. *peku* *Cuora amboinensis* Amboinan box terrapin		b						a				
6. *puo* *Varanus indicus* monitor lizard		b?										
7. *isa* *Hydrosaurus amboinensis* sail-tail lizard								b				
8. snakes (generally)	b[3]	b						b		a	b	a
9. *teke patona* *Python reticulatus* reticulate python								b			a	a
10. *teke panarine* *Boiga irregularis* banded tree snake								b			a	
11. *mara makinete* male *Phalanger maculatus* spotted cuscus	b	b	a		a	a	a?	b	a		b	b

Table 8.1 (continued)

	Ma-p	Pe	Son-aip	Pi	Hu	Son-ain	Num	Ne-tom	Ne-ne	Ka	Som	Sop
12. *notane* all bats				b								
13. *mara putie* young male *Phalanger orientalis*, cuscus							b					
14. *manue* *Gallus gallus* domesticated fowl	b	b				b	b	b[4]				
15. *Kinoke* *Philemon sub-corniculatus* bald friar bird						b[5]						
16. *Kihoke* *Lorius domicella* purple-naped lory						b		b				
17. *susi onate* imago of Anobid woodworm						b						
18. *nakatua* *Cacatua moluccensis* Moluccan cockatoo						b						
19. *puane* *Macropygia amboinensis* Amboina cuckoo dove						b						
20. *ikae tuyo hutan* unidentified wrass							b					
21. *awane* *Anguilla bicolor* pacific freshwater eel				b								

Key. Clans: Ma = Matoke (Matoke-pina and Matoke hanaie), Pe = Peinisa, Son-aip = Sounaue-aipura, Hu = Huni, Son-ain = Sounaue-ainakahata, Nu = Numanaeta, Ne-tom = Neipane-tomoien, Ne-ne = Neipane-nesinopu, Ka = Kamama, Som = Soumori, Sop = Sopanani.
Totems: a = primary, b = secondary.
Notes: 1. spirit only; can be eaten. 2. spirit only; can be eaten. 3. Only clan head of Matoke forbidden to eat. 4. Includes eggs. 5. Feathers only?

Table 8.2 Distribution of some Nuaulu plant totems according to clan

	Ma	Pe	Pi	Hu	Son-ain	Num	Ne-tom	Som
1. *(ai) rapa* k.o. tree					a		?	
2. *ai suto* *Premna integrifolia* k.o. firewood	b							
3. *ani ate* *Canarium* sp. k.o. hardwood	b							
4. *ana kinanoine* *Oryza sativa* local red var. of rice		b						
5. *ana* *Oryza sativa* store rice	a							
6. *akioae* *Premna serratifolia* k.o. tree		b					b	
7. *kaiohite* *Ficus conora* k.o. strangling fig							b	
8. *kanai putie* *Areca catechu* var. k.o. areca fruit								b(f)
9. *katoe* *Saurauia* sp.					b			
10. *kihue manora* k.o. bean (Leguminosae)					b[2]			
11. *kikun* *Hornstedtia* sp. k.o. ginger					b[1]		b	
12. *labusina* *Curcubita* sp. prob. *pepo* k.o. gourd								
13. *makanotue* (Marantaceae) k.o. large-leafed herb			b				b(f)	
14. *meu hehue* k.o. rattan							b	
15. *mukune* *Cyathea* spp. k.o. tree-fern					b			
16. *naine tinse* *Stenochlaena palustris* k.o. climbing epiphyte		b			b		b	
17. *naka (-naka)* k.o. leaf used medicinally		b						

Table 8.2 (continued)

	Ma	Pe	Pi	Hu	Son-ain	Num	Ne-tom	Som
18. *nana* *Pterocarpus indicus* Ambonese mahogany							b	
19. *napu* *Curcubita* sp. prob. *moschata* k.o. gourd			a					
20. *nihasa* prob. *Spondias* sp. k.o. tree					b			
21. *nusi huni* *Citrus aurantifolia* lime				b		b		
22. *nusi mananai* *Citrus hystrix* var. lemon		b						
23. *nusi ramatae* *Citrus hystrix* var. lemon		b					b	
24. *oune* *Microsorium commutatum* k.o. fern							b	
25. *pate* *Ficus* sp. k.o. tree							b	
26. *rorong* *Benincasa hisipida* k.o. curcubit		b			b			
27. *soi mutune* *Zingiber* sp. k.o. ginger							b	
28. *tenne* *Gigantochlea* sp. k.o. bamboo	b	b	b	b	b		b	b
29. *tomone* k.o. bamboo		b(f)					b(f)	
30. *tone* *Solanum melongena* aubergine	b	b					b	
31. *unuhutu (msinae)* *Clerodendron* sp. k.o. wood								b
32. *uri kasupa* *Musa X paradisiaca* k.o. banana		a						
33. *uri manane* *Musa X paradisiaca* k.o. banana					b			

Table 8.2 (continued)

	Ma	Pe	Pi	Hu	Son-ain	Num	Ne-tom	Som
34. *uri numanaeta* *Musa X paradisiaca* k.o. banana						b		b(f)
35. *wainite* (Marantaceae) k.o. large-leafed herb		a						
36. *weni nante* *Dioscorea alata* k.o. yam								b(f)
37. *wan apone* k.o. bamboo	b							

Key: See Table 8.1.
Notes: 1. *Kikun hua naue* only. 2. *Nuna onate* only. (f) = females only, or females marrying into a clan

My concentration so far on animal and plant foods is arguably artificial. There is no special labelled category or domain of food taboos, or indeed taboos related to natural species. These are categories which I have chosen to impose. If we inspect the array of prohibitions in Tables 8.1 and 8.2, many concern inedible materials such as various species of rattan, bamboo and timber used in construction and as fuel. The feathers of some prohibited birds are used in curing. Moreover, these tables have quite deliberately been designed to exclude prohibitions other than those based on natural kinds. Much clan-specific *monne* relates to behaviour with respect to other natural phenomena. Thus some clans are not permitted to drink or swim in seawater (Peinisa, Sounaue-ainakahata). General contact with rainwater is prohibited only for females of the Soumori clan, though the rule that women should at all times wear a head-covering outside the house, to keep their hair out of sight of males, never to wash the hair with water or to get it wet is observed by Matoke-hanaie and Soumori. Prohibitions relating to rain-related phenomena, thunder and rainbows, are, however, more widely observed.

The Intensity of Observence

Prohibitions vary in the intensity of their observance, both in terms of shared rules relating to the agreed importance of the prohibition and in terms of what people actually do. When referring to prohibitions of particular salience, Nuaulu speak of *monne mainae* (lit. 'huge *monne*'). *Monne mainae* relate to all major life-crisis rituals, rituals involving allusion to head-hunting, respect for what I have called 'primary' clan totems, and possibly (according to one informant) those prohibitions to which Nuaulu are collectively subject. Beyond this the rest are just *monne*: but even those that are not adjectivally qualified are differentiated. For example, there is variation in intensity between clans. Thus the banana *uri bunau*, which is sacred for all Nuaulu, is especially so for Matoke, from whose ancestors it is believed to be derived. Matoke wives must wear a hat until after the birth of the first child, but touching of the head by rain is not taboo. Also, when prohibitions seem to be for all intents and purposes fixed, there may still be specific exceptions. The wood *unuhutu* may not be cut by Soumori except when required for male initiation ceremonies. The tree-fern *mukune* (*Cyathea* spp.) is *monne* only for Sounaue-ainakahata, only with respect to the building of ordinary dwellings. Not only is it permitted to be used for ritual houses (*numa onate*), its use is positively enjoined. However, the most obvious variation in intensity of observance is in the relationship between different prohibitions honoured by a single clan.

In some cases, that certain clan prohibitions are regarded as more important than others is very clear: this may be reflected in its high profile in conversations with the ethnographer, or in ritual and physical representations. It may also be reflected in the sanctions registered for infringement of particular prohibitions. Thus killing a snake, for the clan Soumori, is the most heinous of *monne* offences. Unless compensation of a large plate and a red cloth is paid to the ancestors there will be continued sickness and ultimately death. However, to completely terminate the taboo (as may happen on a female marrying out of the clan), a more complex payment is necessary, involving a ritual object for each anatomical part (see Chapter 5). By comparison, infringement of the female rain-on-head prohibition commanded in 1970 a payment of one plate and two bracelets, and eating the banana *uri numanaeta* or the yam *weni nante*, one finger-ring each. Thus there is a sense in which an individual can manipulate *monne* restrictions, or at least lessen the burden, through the payment of plates and clothes, as when final payment of bridewealth releases a woman from the restrictions of her natal clan.

So protagonists regard some prohibitions as more important than others, while some are negotiable. Of course, this does not mean that they can always be unequivocally placed in a static and linear rank-order, or that that some can be represented as being of equal significance. I have preferred to represent these as complexes of prohibitions from which varying degrees of ranking might be inferred. Following Frake (1964) it is important to acknowledge that categories of the kind which imply prohibitions are interlinked in various ways. There is no finite number of discrete elements which can be represented as a list or taxonomy; rather, it is best envisaged as an aggregative cluster or network of semantic relations (Fox 1975), complexes of connected behaviour and prohibition. What is striking about the patterns which are revealed is that all clans have one (or occasionally several) natural kinds which stand out markedly from the rest of the prohibitions. It is these that I have in previous publications (Ellen 1972, 1993a, 1993b) called 'primary' totems to distinguish them from the rest, which I have labelled 'secondary'. This is far from being a perfect distinction and has been based on a much more cursory inspection of the relevant data than the present discussion, but it was a helpful and not entirely misleading start. As variation palpably does exist in the intensity of observation and in terms of the respect accorded particular totems, some means must be found to express it.

Implications for the Theory of Totemism

The Nuaulu have no word for totem, which is not in itself surprising. What I have called totems are a special kind of prohibition involving respect behaviour, *monne* typified by an intensity of significance, usually with mythical resonances and evidence of being a prime emblem for a particular social group. No wonder, then, that the things selected are all perceptually salient, and among clan prohibitions more obviously those near the top of the hierarchy. However, there is an ambiguous area between totems and other group-linked prohibitions. Prohibitions which are highly ranked tend to have the classic characteristics of totems, but as we descend the rank order whether or not we are really dealing with totems rather than clan-wide taboos becomes less clear. This is the case for the Soumori relationship with *imasasae*, the gecko. If it is heard when a person is sick, it means that an ancestral spirit has entered the gecko and is guarding the sick person and must not be harmed. There is a similar relationship between Neipane-tomoien and the death adder, *Acanthophis antarcticus* (*nanate*).

Some prohibited items are often part of a complex of related things which only make sense in terms of some accompanying mythical narrative. Thus, according to myth, when the world was still soft Sounaue-ainakahata lived inside the *rapa* tree (= *ai naka*). This is familiar stuff, but we also need to know that they were released from the interior of the *rapa* by the woodworm *susi onate* boring a hole to let them out, which gives this creature its totemic significance. Not all prohibitions have this kind of narrative to underline their totemic status and justify a particular point in the ranking, and as we have seen, some prohibitions have their origin in very recent events.

To some extent the data presented here on Nuaulu prohibitions are consistent with the analysis of totemic phenomena offered by Lévi-Strauss (1962, 1964). Thus totemism as an anlytical scheme emphasises a kind of classificatory logic in which distinctions in the relations between natural kinds are used to express distinctions between categories of people and to establish relations between persons and groups. But the Nuaulu data, in particular, highlight the difficulty in establishing totemism as a discrete phenomenon, concerning the contingent and historical character of particular totemic beliefs. That totemic beliefs are in a state of flux is readily evident from the examples provided of new totemic restrictions coming into play.

One problem with the Lévi-Straussian analysis, however, is the suggestion that totemic species are selected because their ability to be contrasted with other species makes them 'good to think' with. This cannot be consistent with either the large number of totemic species for the same clan, or with the prominence of certain species as totems for two or more clans (Tambiah 1969). Thus six Nuaulu clans have the bamboo *tenne* as a totem, though only one (Pia) has it as a primary totem. In the mythical narrative which legitimates these totems, Pia is said to have first emerged from the topmost node, and Huni, for example, from that nearest the ground. Thus, the totem symbolically links a number of clans in a hierarchical relationship. What is important is commonality and relative status rather than contrast. Like Bulmer (1978, 1979), I believe Radcliffe-Brown was broadly correct in claiming that material conditions impinge on the selection and retention of prohibited species of animal and plant.

However, in one other respect – at least as far as the Nuaulu and some other peoples of Seram are concerned – the Lévi-Straussian view has to be defended. Lévi-Strauss has been criticised for his reification of the opposition between nature and society and his acceptance of this as an objective analytic distinction. The concept of nature, it is argued, is emergent within particular cultures and in some cases is difficult to identify as something in opposition to culture (e.g. MacCormack and Strathern 1980). I have observed elsewhere (Chapter 10 in this volume; cf. Valeri 1990) that we can infer a notion approximating to conventional contemporary Western definitions in Nuaulu ritual practice and symbolism, even though no word for 'nature' exists. Similarly, there are Nuaulu totemic rituals which honour totemic animals and plants but not other totemic-like prohibitions and respects. I have in mind rituals for installing new receptacles for totemic spirits (e.g. snake for Soumori and turtle for Neipanetomoien). I have no evidence of comparable rituals for less tangible, non-organismic totemic phenomena, such as rainbows. In addition, totemic animals and plants are said to possess a special name as well as the common one, for use in invocations. All of this suggests a conceptual distinction between living organisms and other objects of respect and prohibition, together with some kind of complementarity between humans and non-human organisms, and between *monne* and *minne*.

Ecological Impact of Tabooed Foods and Other Materials

Like all social practices, Nuaulu totemic and other prohibitions exist within an ecological context and have some impact upon their material circumstances in terms of energy transfer, nutrition and physical modification. Such physical effects are greater for some clans than for others, for the women of some clans (e.g. Soumori) more than for others, and for women overall more than for men. The questions at issue, though, are whether any of this is measurable; if so, to what extent regular patterns of denial of consumption have a beneficial or detrimental effect: and if beneficial, whether this is in any sense purposeful or latently functional. In other words, to ask, as Laderman does (1981: 469), what the relationship might be between symbolic and empirical logic. This is an issue which clearly connects with older utilitarianist arguments in anthropology (Harris 1975, 1978), as well as with those endorsements of the wisdom embodied in 'indigenous knowledge', both the romantic evocations of green primitivism (Ellen 1986) and the literature which takes a more dispassionate and empirical stance (e.g. Warren et al. 1995; Williams and Baines 1993). In terms of totemism, of course, the echo is in the contrast between Radcliffe-Brown and Lévi-Strauss. The conclusion drawn here is not that food prohibitions do not sometimes have useful ecological effects, but rather that blanket generalisations are evidentially unsustainable.

The impact of Nuaulu prohibitions in terms of energy transfer is minuscule. Of the calorie-rich foods listed in Table 8.3 (rice, the four varieties of banana, one species of yam), all have readily available alternatives, and are anyway not important sources of calories on a day-to-day basis. The same is true of the other nutrients provided by the fruits listed, and also with respect to manufacturing materials.

In terms of the amount of animal protein consumed, the kinds of prohibitions discussed probably count for more, though they are still slight in terms of their nutritional consequences (Ellen 1996c). Totemic restrictions on big game are negligible (Table 8.4): pig is a secondary totem for one (possibly two) clans, and cassowary and bats are both secondary totems for just one clan. Of reptiles, snakes are a primary totem for three clans and a secondary totem for a further three, monitor lizards are a secondary totem for two clans, testudines (turtles and terrapins) a primary totem for one clan and a secondary totem for another, while crocodiles are a primary totem for two clans and a secondary totem for a further two, but are virtually extinct in the Nuaulu area. Given that 'secondary' totems are respected though not necessarily avoided as food, these restrictions are not as limiting as they might first appear, especially when interpreted in relation to the frequency with which particular species are consumed irrespective of clan. The only prohibition of wide significance is that placed on the male spotted cuscus, *mara makinete* (*Spilocuscus [Phalanger] macula-*

Table 8.3 Some prohibited Nuaulu plant categories

	Nuaulu term	Phylogenetic content	Number of terminal categories subsumed	Inclusive number of collateral segregates	Number of clans for which it is prohibited (primary totems in brackets)
1.	*(ai) rapa*	k.o. tree			2 (1)
2.	*ai suto*	*Premna integrifolia*			1
3.	*ana*	*Oryza sativa*	3	–	1
4.	*ana kinanoine*	*Oryza sativa*	1	3	1
5.	*kanai putie*	*Areca catechu* var.	1	6	1 (f)
6.	*kikun*	*Hornstedtia* sp.	3		1
7.	*makanotue*	(Marantaceae)			1
8.	*meu hehue*	k.o. rattan	–	9	1
9.	*naka (-naka)*	k.o. leaf used medicinally	1		1
10.	*napu*	*Curcubita* prob. *moschata*	3	–	1
11.	*nusi huni*	*Citrus aurantifolia*	1	6	1
12.	*nusi mananai*	*Citrus hystrix* var.	1	6	1
13.	*nusi ramatae*	*Citrus hystrix* var.	1	6	1
14.	*tenne*	*Gigantochlea*	1	6	6 (1)
15.	*tomone*	k.o. bamboo	2	6	2 (f)
16.	*tone*	*Solanum melangena*	3	–	2
17.	*unuhutu*	*Clerodendron* sp.	2		1
18.	*uri punau*	*Musa X paradisiaca*	1	30	8?
19.	*uri kasupa*	*Musa X paradisiaca*	1	30	1
20.	*uri manane*	*Musa X paradisiaca*	1	30	1
21.	*uri numanaeta*	*Musa X paradisiaca*	1	30	1, 1 (f)
22.	*wainite*	(Marantaceae)	4		1 (1)
23.	*wan apone*	k.o. bamboo	1	6	1
24.	*weni nante*	*Dioscorea alata*	1	8	1 (f)

tus), and as I first argued some years ago (Ellen 1972), what is interesting about this is that the inconvenience is restricted by confining the prohibition to one sex of the two species found on Seram. Having said as much, the impact on the success of particular hunts may sometimes be dramatic. Consider, for example, the following case:

> Bisara Neipane-tomoien and Natunesi Matoke were hunting cuscus in the Lahati area on the 9 May 1970. At that time both were aged between 15 and 20, and of the two Bisara was generally reckoned to be the better hunter. Indeed, even at that time Natunesi had a reputation as a rather feckless clown, which continued throughout the period I was acquainted with him. On seeing a female *Phalanger orientalis*. Bisara began to pursue his quarry up the tree in which he thought it located, but on getting closer found it to be a

Table 8.4 Some prohibited Nuaulu animal categories

	Nuaulu term	Phylogenetic content	Number of terminal categories subsumed	Inclusive number of collateral segregates	Number of clans for which it is prohibited (primary totems in brackets)
1.	*puhaa*	*Crocodylus porosus*, estuarine crocodile	1	1	4 (2)
2.	*hahu*	*Sus scrofa*, pig	1	(3)	1
3.	*asuan*	*Casuarius casuarius*, cassowary	1	(3)	1
4.	*enu*	all sea turtles	2	2	2 (1)
5.	*peku*	*Cuora amboinensis*, Amboinan box terrapin	1	2	2 (1)
6.	*puo*	*Varanus indicus* monitor lizard	1 (2)	2	2
7.	*isa*	*Hydrosaurus amboinensis*, sail-tail lizard	1 (2)	2	1
8.	*tekene*	snakes (generically)	11	–	5 (1)
9.	*tekene patona*	*Python reticulatus*, Reticulate python	–	11	2 (1)
10.	*teke panarine*	*Boiga irregularis*, banded tree snake	–	11	2 (1)
11.	*mara makinete*	male *Phalanger maculatus*, spotted cuscus	–	4	9 (4–5)
12.	*notane*	all bats	9	–	1
13.	*mara putie*	young male *Phalanger orientalis*, cuscus	–	4	1
14.	*manue*	*Gallus gallus*, domesticated fowl	2	63	5
15.	*kinoke*	*Philemon sub-corniculatus*, bald friar bird	–	63	1
16.	*kihoke*	*Lorius domicella*, purple-naped lory	–	63	2
17.	*susi onate*	imago of Anobid woodworm	–	2	1
18.	*nakatua*	*Cacatua moluccensis*, Moluccan cockatoo	2	63	1
19.	*puane*	*Macropygia amboinensis*, Amboina cuckoo dove	–	53	1
20.	*ikae tuyo hutan*	unidentified wrass	–	73	1
21.	*awane*	*Anguilla bicolor*, pacific freshwater eel	–	73	1

> male *Spilocuscus maculatus*, taboo for Neipane. He therefore asked Natunesi to climb the tree and shoot it with his bow. Unfortunately Latulesi was both a bad climber and a bad shot, and could not get close enough to hit it. The cuscus escaped.

Thus in the consciousness of particular Nuaulu individuals and groups it is widely accepted that totemic prohibitions reduce hunting success.

All the fixed prohibition *monne* items are eminently consumable, they all have uses as food or as materials, but most can be considered token examples of categories of things which are generically consumable and which provide numerous substitutes. Thus *weni nante* (*Dioscorea alata*) is a non-toxic yam, but most people can usually replace this with the equally non-toxic *siahue* (*D. esculenta*) or the generally wild *akae* (*D. pentaphylla*). The growing conditions and qualities are not identical, but in present circumstances they can be considered substitutable. The bean *kikun hua nawe* is restricted for Sounaue-ainakahata, but not other kinds of *kikun*. Only four of the thirty or more cultivars of banana and plantain are prohibited. Similarly, *Premna integrifolia* is a useful firewood but it can be replaced with equally long-burning species. *Wainite* (Marantaceae) leaves, used by some clans as arm ornaments to accompany the *tupu-tupue* barkcloths of ritual elders, are replaced in Peinisa and Soumori with cassowary feathers. Curiously, the inconvenience caused for those clans for whom two or more species of bamboo are prohibited seems to represent the greatest material inconvenience of all, rather than any restrictions on food. Thus while not having access to such things certainly involves self-denial, in most circumstances this rarely amounts to deprivation. Moreover, prohibitions are drawn from virtually the entire range of phylogenetic experience, a few species from each of the main life-forms. If selection were to be operating in a significant fashion we would expect more asymmetry in distribution.

By comparison, phased prohibitions also involve denial, but with few alternatives. Where protein is short, food taboos may be felt much more. For instance, the prohibitions placed on birthing mothers must have some measurable effect on their health, as they are presumably at their most vulnerable and should be building up reserves for lactation.

None of these *monne* prohibitions (phased or fixed, patterned or individual) can be convincingly shown to have an even marginal selective advantage. Indeed, on balance, they amount to a slight ecological disadvantage, and occasionally some not inconsiderable inconvenience in scheduling subsistence arrangements. But when this happens there is always the possibility of at least partial or deferred observence. Despite the rhetoric of *monne*, Nuaulu life is full of compromises, especially the favouring of short-term practical advantage over mid- to long-term cosmological disadvantage, of negotiation and special pleading with the ancestors. Those restrictions which might genuinely confer some selective advantage to Nuaulu individuals or groups have not been discussed in this paper. These are those called *sin wesie* (rather than *sasi*): occasional controls on hunting and harvesting deliberately engineered to conserve some resource which is perceived to be threatened with depletion. Though such bans, instituted by the Lord of the Land and clan chiefs, may have the force of sacred sanction, they are unlike other *monne*. As with Nuaulu attitudes to things in their environment which are testably disadvantageous (*minne*), this suggests that when it comes to things which really can have an effect on their health and well-being, there is no need to rely on serendipity. Judicious flexibility and conscious pragmatism informed by tried-and-tested knowledge is far more effective.

Notes

1. The Nuaulu fieldwork referred to here was undertaken between 1969 and 1971, in 1973, 1975, 1981, 1990 and most recently in 1996, at all times under the auspices of the Lembaga Ilmu Pengetahuan Indonesia, and more recently in association with Universitas Pattimura in Ambon. The work has been variously funded by the British Social Science Research Council, now Economic and Social Research Council (ESRC), the Cornell Scheme for East and Southeast Asia, the British Academy, the Nuffield Foundation and the University of Kent at Canterbury. Completion has been made possible by the award of ESRC grants R00023.3088 and R000.23.6082, an earlier version of which was presented at the American Anthropological Association meeting held in Washington DC, 17–21 November 1993. I am grateful to Robert Aunger who invited me to participate in the session on food avoidances which he organised, and to Rosemary Bolton for willingly sharing her field data. Mark Coode at Kew kindly supervised the identification of most plant specimens referred to here. Authorities consulted in relation to animal species are listed in Ellen 1993a.
2. For a recent useful summary of the literature on food prohibition in relation to diet and nutrition see de Garine 1994.

CHAPTER 9

Fetishism: A Cognitive Approach (1988)

The concept of fetishism in anthropology, Marxism and psychology is examined as a particular case of the interplay between theories of cognition and collective representations. Classificatory end-products to which the word 'fetish' has been applied cannot be understood simply as special kinds of objects, or defined in terms of their generic functional attributes. Neither do they reflect a particular mental condition. Rather, they reveal a variable combination of three universal underlying features of categorisation and representation: concretisation, animation or anthropomorphisation; conflation of signifier with signified; and an ambiguous relationship of control between person and object. All lie on a processual continuum which begins with the identification of categories, relationships and phenomena, and proceeds – via reification and iconification – to their personification.

During the last decade analyses of the various connection between cognition and collective representations, mind and culture, and between 'mundane' and 'symbolic' classifications, have all received a certain degree of prominence in the professional anthropological literature. In contrast to some writers (e.g. Bloch 1977, 1985), my own view is that the interrelationships between these apparent opposites as evident in particular substantive cases are often far from clear (Chapter 3 in this volume; Ellen 1986b; cf. Harris and Heelas 1979). Here I wish to make the point a little more forcefully in relation to the concept of fetishism, and hope to show that this perhaps rather unlikely choice is not as strange as it might at first appear.[1] I begin by discussing the historical origins of the concept and its three principal analytic traditions – anthropological, Marxist and psychological. Although a handful of recent ethnographic studies have used the notion of fetishism (and I shall refer to some of these below), all can be placed in one of the three traditions. Only Pouillon, to my knowledge, has attempted to review the field with the aim of adopting a more synthetic approach (Pouillon 1975 [1970]). There are certain parallels between our positions.

The Intellectual History of a Concept

The Anthropology of Religion

The term 'fetish' is derived, along with its cognates in other European languages (Haddon 1921: 66–7; Tylor 1878: 135), from *facticius*, meaning 'to do' or in the passive 'a thing made by art'. By the late fifteenth century it was being applied widely to charms.[2] The earliest English forms of the word (*Oxford English Dictionary*, vol. 4, 1933: 176) are directly adopted from the Portuguese *fetiço* (used in Portugal itself to refer to amulets and the relics of saints). The Portuguese extended its application to certain objects venerated by inhabitants of the Guinea Coast, and it was through this channel that it entered scholarly dogmatism, probably during the second half of the eighteenth century. In this context its use was popularised by the first president of the Dijon parliament, Charles De Brosses (1972 [1760]: 10, 18; Tylor 1924 [1871]: 144). De Brosses had in mind the worship of stone figures and other material objects – the 'stocks and stones' of a later generation of evolutionists – and believed that the savage mind required some kind of tangible object to focus upon, and that only later could the abstract and animate be comprehended.

De Brosses regarded religion as having originated in fetishism and his views were widely accepted until the mid-nineteenth century. The concept gained even greater currency through Comte's use of it to denote a particular theory of religion, in which human mental qualities were attributed to non-human bodies. For Comte (1893 [1830–2]: 2, 545–8) fetishism constituted the first of three stages in the development of religious ideas: fetishism > polytheism > monotheism. It was the first great epoch in human thought in which 'the primitive assignment of passion and will to the most inert forms of nature led almost spontaneously to the assignment of deities to the inanimate and to the animate', and generally to the development of polytheism and organised religion (Voget 1975: 217). In such a scheme, fetishism represented individualistic rather than organised religion, and to a large extent corresponded to what later writers would describe as magic. The Comtean framework was widely adopted and, in some instances, refined. Lubbock (1870: 119), for example, with the fervour of an evolutionary typologist, placed it as the second in a succession of no fewer than five invented stages which had to be passed through before reaching polytheism: somewhere between atheism and totemism. We hardly need concern ourselves with the definitions of any of these, other than fetishism, which for Lubbock was that stage 'in which man supposed he can force the Deity to comply with his desires'.

Tylor (1924 [1871]: 153) rejected Comte's use, preferring to call the attribution of human mental qualities to the inanimate 'animism', while restricting fetishism to the doctrine of spirits embodied in, attached to or conveying influence through certain material objects. Thus spiritual beings worked through fetish objects and objects were to be distinguished from spirits. His description of the 'maraca' or ceremonial rattle used by certain Brazilian peoples is a good illustration of this. He tells us that the fetish:

> was a calabash with a handle and a hole for a mouth, and stones inside; yet to its votaries it seemed no mere rattle, but the receptacle of a spirit that spoke from it when shaken; therefore the Indians set up these maracas, talked to them, set food and drink and burned incense before them, held annual feasts in their honour, and would even go to ear with their neighbours to satisfy the rattle-spirits' demand for human victims. (Tylor 1924 [1871]: 154)

But even during the latter part of the nineteenth century the concept of fetishism was coming in for criticism, and the reports on which the secondary authorities relied were often of a highly questionable kind. For Robertson-Smith it was 'merely a popular term, which conveys no precise idea, but is vaguely supposed to mean something very savage and contemptible' (1884: 209). Haddon (1921: 64) was derisive of its sloppy application to virtually anything connected with West African religion, and he is particularly critical of the way Mary Kingsley and R.H. Nassau – the chief authorities on the subject in his day – used the term. Nevertheless, he was prepared to justify a more specific definition, namely the worship of 'an intangible power or spirit incorporated in some visible form' (1921: 70), while remaining broadly Tylorian in his use of it for a stage in religious development. Even Frazer (e.g. 1922 [1925]: 234) appears to assign no particularly distinctive role to the notion, using it as a vague synonym for things magical or religious.

With the demise of evolutionism there seemed even less justification for a general concept of fetishism. Evans-Pritchard (1965: 24) is disparaging and dismissive of its employment as an evolutionary stage on the grounds that fetishes are not found everywhere and in particular are not characteristic of very primitive peoples. By this he had in mind food-gatherers. Part of the problem was that particular writers insisted on defining fetishism in terms of particular local manifestations with which they were familiar, but which differed slightly from the usages of other writers. For Nassau, writing in 1904, a fetish is a local residence for a spirit, and can be thrown away afterwards. He advises us that it is 'best to limit the word to the worship of natural objects revered not for their own power, but because they are occupied by a spirit' (1969 [1904]: 81). But although anthropologists spent much effort criticising the misuse of the term 'fetishism' amongst others, they were, all the time, missing one of the main features of objects described in this way, namely that there tends to be an inner ambivalence as to whether it is the objects themselves which effect material changes in some mysterious way, or whether it is some spiritual force which is either represented by or located in (but separate from) those objects. I shall take up this important point later.

With such abundant conceptual confusion, in addition to the indiscriminate application of the term to primitive religion in general, it is no wonder that anthropologists began to avoid using it. Increasingly, if referred to at all, fetishes were bracketed with charms (Lowie 1934: 301; see note 2 below), while the word survives as a designation (usually untheorised) for certain kinds of art-object in catalogues of ethnographica and in museum labels. An exception in this tradition is Robert Brain, who in a recent book on African art uses 'fetish' in a quite specific sense to refer to 'machines':

> fabricated by the diviner or sorcerer of various materials and medicines in order to draw upon the immanent life-force of these substances. The sculpture itself may be of minor significance, the fetish being activated by the diviner or sorcerer by performing appropriate ceremonies and incantations over the symbolic paraphernalia attached to it. (Brain 1980: 208)

Thus among the Bangwa of Cameroon fetishes are objects used as part of a divinatory technique to protect individuals from attacks of witchcraft, objects which receive power from the medication of a ritual expert. Apart from such usages, and the conceptually explicit applications which I shall now go on to discuss, the term is occasionally used in a vague, rather deprecating, sense: as in 'the fetishism of reality'. I find such phrases quite meaningless, and will not consider them further.

Marxism

Marx first introduces the concept of fetishism in a short piece published in the *Rheinische Zeitung* (issue 193) for 1842, having read De Brosses on the subject earlier in the same year.[3] It occurs again in *Economic and Philosophic Manuscripts of 1844* (Marx 1977 [1844]: 89, 116) in a context which very much suggests that it matches, and was reinforced by, the use of the same term by Hegel (1975 [1830]: 180–1, 189, 218–19). However, the notion of 'the fetishism of commodities' – as a specific instance of a more general fetishism of property – was not fully developed until *Das Kapital*, where Marx defines it as where a definite social relation between persons assumes 'the fantastic form of a relation between things'. Here Marx deliberately draws an analogy from religious discourse, in which the 'productions of the human brain appear as independent beings endowed with life, and entering into relations both with one another and the human race'. 'This', he says, 'I call fetishism which attaches itself to the products of labour, so soon as they are produced as commodities, and which is therefore inseparable from the production of commodities' (Marx 1970a [1867]: 72). Thus the appearance of value conceals its real nature, while once a commodity plays the role of value equivalent to any other commodity it immediately seems as though it possesses *in itself* the ability to measure the value of other commodities.

It is hardly surprising that in the neo-Marxist resurgence of the 1970s it was anthropologists in particular who struggled with the notion of fetishism (Friedman 1974; Godelier 1970, 1977), stressing the central place of religious forms of ideology in Marx's conceptualism of history (Godelier 1977: 176). The problem for a Marxist theory of fetishism, however, is that the principal relation of production (capital) might be at the same time an illusion (Friedman 1974: 32–3). For Friedman, the earlier 'idealist' and the later 'materialist' interpretation has led to certain ambiguities in Marxist usages. Following the mature Marx, he claims that 'capital is fetish because its internal properties do not correspond to the function it performs in the material process of reproduction, not because it is a deformed image of that process' (Friedman 1974: 43). Balibar (1973) rejects Marx's concept of fetishism as ideological, and distinguishes commodity fetishism from capital fetishism, in an attempt to expurgate all traces of non-materiality from the relations of production (Friedman 1974: 52). Friedman (ibid., 53) criticises Godelier for displaying the same ambiguity found in the writings of Marx, pointing out that 'the problem with the term is that "a fetish" always seems to be the end product of the process of fetishisation, a misrepresentation of some other object or situation, i.e., a deviation phenomenon'. This is where the problem lies in resolving the contradictions in Marxist concepts of fetish. Friedman himself (1974: 59–60) regards fetishism – or at least did so when he wrote the article – as the dominant structure of social reproduction, inevitably contradicting the biological capacities of the species.

The Marxist concept of fetishism has been little used in the analysis of specific ethnographic materials. Friedman (1974) uses it in his explications of Firth's *Work of the Gods* (1967 [1939]) and Leach's *Political Systems of Highland Burma* (1954) (Friedman 1974, 1979); it is implicit in some of Godelier's work on the Baruya (Godelier 1977). Its most extended and successful application, however, is arguably found in Michael Taussig's *The Devil and Commodity Fetishism in South America*. Taussig looks at the image of the devil among proletarianised rural people in Colombia and

Bolivia, which he claims mediates the conflict between precapitalist and capitalist modes of objectifying the human condition. This image can be interpreted as an indigenous reaction to the supplanting of one form of fetishism by another, and is one which permits envisioning the bonds between persons in their contemporary economic activities for what they really are: asymmetrical, non-reciprocal, exploitative, and destructive of relationships between persons (Taussig 1980: 37–8). One manifestation of this is as follows:

> According to the belief in el bautizo del billete (baptism of the bill) in the southern Cauca valley (Columbia), the god-parent-to-be conceals a peso note in his or her hand during the baptism of the child by the Catholic priest. The peso bill is thus believed to be baptized instead of the child. When this now baptized bill enters into general monetary circulation, it is believed that the bill will continually return to its owner, with interest, … The baptized bill receives the names – the 'Christian name' that the baptismal ritual was meant to bestow on the child. It is not commodity fetishism since these people do not consider it to be a natural property of money to reproduce. Indeed, it is seen as so unnatural that supernatural power has to be invoked by the most devious and destructive means. (Taussig 1980: 126)

Marx had long before noted that the fetish character of money varied with social conditions, distinguishing (for example) the veneration of precious metal coinage from general commodity fetishism (Marx 1977 [1844]: 116). There is an echo of this pluralist view of fetishism in Taussig, for whom:

> the fetishism that is found in the economics of precapitalist societies arises from the sense of organic unity between persons and their products, and this stands in stark contrast to the fetishism of commodities in capitalist societies, which results from the split between persons and the things that they produce and exchange, The result of this split is the subordination of men to the things they produce, which appear to be independent and self-empowered. (Taussig 1980: 37)

Psychology and Psycho-analysis

In the psychological literature fetishism refers to the use of a non-genital object to achieve sexual gratification, or an erotic attachment to inanimate objects or ordinarily asexual parts of the human body.[4] The term was first popularised by Richard von Krafft-Ebing (1894), though it had earlier been employed by Binet (1887: 143). Apparently Binet had in turn picked it up through his reading of Rousseau, Darwin and contemporaneous ethnography. Thus defined, such behaviour usually begins in adolescence, though it may (particularly in Freudian theory) have its origins much earlier in infantile experiences and obsessions. It is generally regarded as normal in heterosexual premarital sex lives, and only when contact with the fetish becomes an end in itself is the condition considered pathological (Anon. 1975: 754). The sexual goal is the body part (a hand, an armpit or a buttock), body products, items of clothing (frequently shoes and items of female underclothing), fabrics (fur, leather, rubber), even inanimate objects such as collar studs and safety-pins (Gosselin and Wilson 1980: 43–4). Fetishes may, therefore, have no direct association at all with the body. In its psychological sense, fetishism is generally thought of as being highly gender-linked and culture-bound. It is rare in females and, although not restricted to European and Euro-American societies as suggested by Gebherd (1976), in its usual sense is not well-documented elsewhere. It has been suggested that the Chinese custom of mutilating the female foot and then revering it exhibits some of these classic features (van Gulik 1974: 216–22, 253, 265).

The Freudian definition and explanation is altogether more specific. In his essay on the subject (Freud 1977: 351–2), Freud describes fetishism as the 'after-effect of some sexual impression, received as a rule in early childhood'. The fetish stands – he argues – for the missing penis of the woman. Thus foot and shoe fetishism reflect the inquisitive desire of young boys to approach a woman's genitals from below – from her feet upwards – whereas fur and velvet fetishism becomes a fixation on pubic hair. By comparison, underclothing crystallises the moment of undressing – the last moment in which a woman can still be regarded as phallic (1977: 355, 357). In later essays on the subject Freud argues that fetishism involves disavowal of sexual difference: the fetishist both acknowledging and not acknowledging this difference by use of the fetish to stand in for the missing penis (Freud 1964 [1940]). Winnicott (1974: chap. 1) subsequently assimilated this idea to that of the 'transitional object'.

Fetishism as a Category and the 'Fetishisation' of Categories

There are, therefore, three main scholarly traditions which employ a concept of fetishism, and – strikingly – these relate respectively to three principal spheres of human activity: religion, economy and sex. They might be characterised individually as follows:

1. Anthropological (specifically intellectualist-evolutionist), in which an object is believed to be a spiritual force in itself: the result of malthought;
2. Marxist, in which an object takes on a fixed quality that conceals its true economic function: the result of mystification;
3. Psychological, in which a part (or an associated artefact) replaces the whole as an object of – usually sexual – desire: the result of repression or 'disavowal'.

Occasionally ethnographers have fused two of the meanings: the erotic and the religious, for example (e.g. Herdt 1982),[5] or the religious and the Marxist (as in the work of Taussig). I know of no analysis which has combined fetishism in its sexual and Marxist senses, though it is what we might expect to find among social Freudians in the tradition of Wilhelm Reich. On the whole there has been a reluctance to go beyond these separate, though overlapping, senses to explore what it is they might have in common.

Of the main differences, apart from the major substantive function of the concept in each case (religion, sex, economy), the only one which need detain us is the extent to which each operates at the individual or social level. The Marxist notion of fetish is unambiguously social – the general and objective result of *collective* experience. The psychological usage is for the most part individualistic, though Reich might have envisaged it operating at a collective level. The anthropological usage is ambiguous, for while for the intellectualist it reflected an aberration in individual thought, and functioned – like magic – essentially as 'individualistic religion', fetishes may have collective devotees or their worship may be socially organised. My particular interest in fetishism arises precisely because it is a concept which enables us to focus our attention on the articulation of individual cognitive process and the structure of collective representations.

Of the similarities, only one, it seems to me, must be rejected: this is the idea that fetishism is intrinsically aberrant or reflective of a primitive mental condition. In all three cases fetishism is regarded not merely as abnormal behaviour, but dysfunctional, pathological and deviant: that is, it is defined partly in moral terms. Early anthropological uses, in the context of evolutionism, inevitably impute inferior mental powers. Karl Marx talks of 'perversion' (Marx 1970 [1867]: (3), 806), and Godelier (1977: 16) echoes the master when he speaks of a 'fetish to exorcise' and a 'myth to destroy'. Binet's construction of the concept in psychology was explicitly as a 'separate perversion', and in Freud its pathology is transparent. I contend that this is a fatally misleading way to approach the more general (or, as I would prefer, partial) phenomenon of what in the past has been designated 'fetishism'. This does not, however, entail any rejection of the possibility that fetishism – as with any mode of apprehending the world – cannot *become* 'pathological', either in the sense that its cultural distribution is statistically limited, non-standard and negatively valorised socially, or in the sense that it may threaten the dominant structures of social reproduction.

I wish here to identify four general underlying cognitive processes at work in the generation of these cultural representations (objects or phenomena) which have been labelled 'fetishes', and which are all present – explicitly or analogously – in the three main historical traditions.[6] These are:

1. a concrete existence or the concretisation of abstractions;
2. the attribution of qualities of living organisms, often (though not exclusively) human;
3. conflation of signifier and signified;
4. an ambiguous relationship between control of object by people and of people by object.

These processes, in whatever combination, are not confined to particular kinds of society, primitive or bourgeois; or to types of theoretical paradigm, or to fields of substantive investigation. Thus, I reject, with Pouillon (1975 [1970]: 115–16), the idea that fetishism represents a distinct mode of thought, and hold with him, and with Evans-Pritchard (1965: 105), who found support for this view in his Nuer fieldwork (Evans-Pritchard 1956), that whatever it is may co-exist with other, different kinds of belief. There is nothing about it which requires that it be treated as a completely separate type; and certainly it does no good to banish it to the realm of the exotic. By including here examples from historical and near-contemporary European sources I hope to emphasise more effectively the universal human character of fetish-like behaviour and avoid its relegation to some primitive ethnic 'other'.

To claim that a term and definition devised during a period of intellectual history whose typologising proclivities have been much discredited should now be rethought is perhaps not very radical. Legitimate comparisons can be made with other attempts to deconstruct analytic categories invented by those convinced of their moral and mental superiority in order to distance the mind of some primitive 'other' from that of a European 'self'. One thinks, for example, of *mana*, taboo and – particularly – totem (Pouillon 1975 [1970]: 105). Fetishism, like totemism, has over the years emerged as a confusing hydra. In order to tame the beast it is necessary to lop off its many heads and begin to reconstitute its conceptuality. It will, therefore, come as no surprise that I should at this point take my inspiration from Lévi-Strauss (1962) and ask 'of what greater whole is fetishism a part?' In such an exercise we must not expect the boundaries of the concept to be drawn in the same way as in its previous incarnation, and indeed we may conclude that no firm boundaries can be drawn at all.

Concretisation

It will be evident from the previous discussion that, in principle, the notion of fetish can refer to almost anything, a characteristic of which the earliest writers were well aware (Lubbock 1870: 196; Tylor 1924 [1871]: 168, 302). It may not be an object at all, but rather an abstraction which is treated as if it were. It may be a culturally unmodified, modified or only minimally modified natural object, including such diverse items as bundles of sticks (as in Nuer *kulangi* [Evans-Pritchard 1956: 100]), the celebrated Kongolese nail fetishes, bodily relics of saints, the icons of eastern orthodox Christianity and the Marian images of the Western Church). But whatever its physical status, concretisation or objectification of representation is an intrinsic quality, and a process which we must now examine in further detail.

It is instructive to approach the idea of concretisation by considering the case of the most elementary categories which we can identify ethnographically. Such elementary representations (not to be confused with Durkheimian elementary forms) consist of those categories least affected by feedback loops from more inclusive and complex levels of cognitive abstraction. They are sometimes called 'percepts' and we can infer their existence from empirically verifiable variation in the semantic and morphological construction of categories in a single culture as revealed through ethnography; from the changing character of categories (often through the accretion or deletion of meanings, and the growth of more complex classificatory and social environments) as shown historically; and also from the development of categorisation in children evident from work in developmental psychology.

Elementary representations and the structures created from the relations between them may be transformed into complex symbolic representations in two ways. The first is by increasing abstraction. An example of a string of increasing abstraction would be in folk biological classification: buttercup > herb > plant; or in the social realm: individual person > family > clan > society > humanity. In the second, elementary representations are transformed by compression or condensation of meaning or cultural value on a single item or relationship. An example of such compression of meaning would be in increasingly abstract ideas being associated with a single object: monarchy represented in the body of an individual person, nationhood expressed in terms of a single animal, saintliness in terms of the dried viscera of a long-deceased holy person, and so on. Abstract symbols (often the most abstract) may be turned into icons (often the most concrete) through a process of objectification, and these end-products may be either physical icons (Ohnuki-Tierney 1981: 458) or 'thingified' verbal signs (cf. Pouillon 1975 [1970]: 119). Thus the concept is no longer simply in the minds of people but exists in the external world, culturally transmitted independently of the existence of individual persons. Such objectified concepts – in which we must include fetishes – are therefore treated like other sense images.

A good illustration of how this process of concretisation may operate at different degrees of categorical inclusiveness is with respect to the concept of natural kind. Ethnobiologists, in their attempts to compare different systems of classification and understand the processes of category formation, acquisition and evolution, have sought a cross-cultural concept of natural kind.[7] It would be highly convenient if all cultures operated with a species concept comparable to that in Linnaean taxonomy, which could serve as the basic building-block of classificatory systems. But although different workers agree that all peoples behave as if they recognised a basic level of categories, this sometimes appears to be at one level and sometimes at another. It is now recognised that basic categories can be utilised at different degrees of inclusiveness, sometimes equivalent to phylogenetic species, sometimes to genera, sometimes to families and sometimes to entire phyla; and this may vary within cultures, within the same domain or between domains, and according to context, as well as between cultures. In small-scale societies, basic categories of, for example, animals are more likely to be *gestalt* clusters of features verging on a general prototype, at the generic-specific level, while in industrialised and literate cultures (which are more detached from the world of plants and animals, and who mediate through abstract secondary representations) they are more likely to be generalised categories, distinguished on the basis of a few distinctive features.

Part of the problem faced by ethnobiologists was that they were narrowly comparing Linnaean taxonomy with particular folk animal domains and not looking at language more broadly. For the concept of natural kind is really no different from categories which we apply to people. Both conceptualise groups of generically related objects as thing and that 'thinginess' must be understood as an acceptance that, at least for some purposes, they should be regarded as having a kind of objective existence, like individual unique objects (this stone, this individual bird and so on). It is not so much that such master concepts as species, genus or phylum are an 'internal transformation from human social relations' (Durkheim and Mauss 1963 [1901–2]; Dwyer 1976: 434), which they may sometimes be in terms of the imagery of representation, but that there is a generalised propensity in all human classifying behaviour to reify through concretisation, to treat the most complex of abstractions as things. Even entire classifications – the word 'classification' itself deceptively conveys somewhat more than just a penumbrum of 'thinginess' – acquire a false objectiveness through our insistence on a model of two-dimensional multi-levelled hierarchies. Moreover, by turning abstractions into things we compound the illusion that categories (natural kinds of cultural entities) exist independently of other categories.

Another route to objectification is through our attempts to represent social relationships. Those items which we subject to any kind of exchange, either concrete items (such as food), notional ones (such as credit transfers), or – as in most cases – a mixture of the two, almost always serve to 'thingify' a relationship. A gift given, as Mauss tells us, is inevitably a relationship between persons; a square metre of land owned implies and requires a relationship between owner and non-owner. In contemporary Euro-American culture and its global outliers, this kind of language of things routinely masks the complexity of real-world social relationships, by some sleight of thought making what is sociologically recondite pragmatically pellucid. Consider, for example, the rather special (but nevertheless much discussed) case of the creation of 'fictional' commodities, In Marxist terms, these involve the transformation of production relations into entities, the most familiar of which is money (Marx 1970a [1867], vol. 3: 809–10). Whether interpreted as a logical or historical process, this may be analysed in terms of the five-stage sequence illustrated in Table 9.1.

Money (or capital) qualifies as a fetish in all this because it is seen to 'objectify' transactions and reduce them to a single physical medium. Although it is conventional to exemplify this in terms of the secular economy, it is hardly surprising that once any idea has been in some way objectified it will, under the appropriate economic circumstances, become commoditised. One thinks, for example, of the trade and theft of saints' relics in medieval Europe (Sumption 1975: 31), the purchase of votive offerings for images (Christian 1981: 93), the marketing of *nkisi* figurines among the Kongo (Brain 1980: 210), or *kulangi* among the Nuer (Evans-Pritchard 1956: 100) during the present century. Indeed, in the form of indulgences, consecrated offerings and the like, the payment of money in return for divine help signifies as clearly as anything the transactional character of the relationship.

The turning of ideas into objects inevitably involves an element of separation, decontextualisation or externalisation (Taussig 1980: 460, following A.N. Whitehead). As society finds it necessary to deal with notions of increasing abstractedness by objectification there is a propensity to ignore the wider setting from which they are derived. The creation of a category for a particular animal separates it from other species which are regarded as different though comparable and related species; the recognition of a particular classification cuts off a general representational device of cognitive relations from the particular social contexts from which its existence is inferred. Moreover, fetishes are frequently metonymic, in that one part of something substitutes for the whole. It is significant that it is often 'parts' of saints or holy things that are fetishes, and not totalities: dis-

Table 9.1 The process of de-objectification and re-objectification by which 'fictional' commodities are created

1. objects	C
2. exchange of individual objects	C ↔ C
3. objects come to represent other objects in exchange relations	C ↔ C ↔ C
4. signs are adapted to represent objects in delayed exchanges	C ↔ M ↔ C
5. signs become reified as real things which underpin the economy	M ↔ C ↔ C

membered anatomy and matter indirectly associated with divers sacra, such as pieces of shrouds and tombs, oil from lamps which burned before them, dust from the ground around them (Sumption 1975: 24). Bodies were dismembered in order to establish subsidiary shrines, as 'in the divided body the grace survives undivided' (ibid., 28, quoting Theodoret of Cyprus). Limbs 'were put in separate reliquaries, thus permitting more pilgrims and therefore greater pecuniary reward (Finucane 1977: 29). In my own Cathedral city – Canterbury – though the bones of Thomas Becket were taken upstairs to a new shrine in 1220, pilgrims continued to venerate the empty tomb in the crypt (ibid., 30). Similar processes seem to be at work in the realm of political economy, where the existence of commodities serves to disconnect entities from the social relationships in which they are embedded; and in much the same way sexual fetishes are ultimately a constituent of, and in a sense proxies for, a greater whole – the animated interacting human body.

Attribution of the Properties of Living Organisms

There is a general tendency in human relations with the inanimate world to attribute and represent that world in organic terms, and to attribute to inanimate objects the properties of living things. There is nothing particularly mysterious about this, and it is perhaps the most prominent feature of those things we call fetishes, although by no means only characteristic of them. It happens because we are bound to model our world directly on those experiences which are most immediate, and these are experiences of our own body. Even our conceptions of personhood, and hence personification, are approached through the language of biological individuals and its associated organic metaphors. And we employ that same model as a source of labels and concepts to interpret the world outside the body. The lexicon of animal parts is, after all, for the most part that of human anatomy. Botanical nomenclature is less so, and that of inanimate objects less still, but body terms – or at least terms which appear concurrently in anatomical lexicons – are still crucial (see Chapter 5 in this volume). More than this, if we 'thingify' parts of a living system and then observe that the things move, so to speak, it logically follows that the things may well be regarded as, or spoken of, as if they were real things: they will appear as though they were indeed *animate* things. Thus things which have life (trees, human bodies) are turned into objects (carvings, saints' relics), only to be reanimated – but then usually as autonomous or semi-autonomous parts of some original whole.

The attribution of the properties of living organisms, in the first place, serves as no more that a special case of concretisation. But what it does beyond this, and what concretisation in itself does not do (it may indeed tend to imply the opposite), is to attribute physiological and behavioural characteristics – truly to 'animate' what has first been concretised. Capital, for instance, is often compared to a tree that may bear fruit, or an animal which reproduces after its own kind (Taussig 1980: 131); the thing itself is the source of its own increase: 'Money will breed money'. And these are perhaps among the less exotic expressions of the standard formula for capitalist accumulation. Mauss (1954) is well known for having reported that the Maoris believed that goods transacted were thought to be persons or pertain to a person, and that in exchanging something one was in effect exchanging part of oneself. For Taussig (1980: 36), if the atomistic view prevails, as it does in modern Western culture, then the isolated thing in itself must inevitably tend to appear as animated because in reality it is part of an active process.

Animation of the cosmos is, therefore, omnipresent and pervious. However, the actual organic models used vary along a continuum from general organic analogies (organomorphs), plant analogies (phytomorphs), animal analogies (zoomorphs), general human analogies (anthropomorphs), and the attribution of the qualities of particular personalities (personification). Of these, what Marx called 'the personification of things' (1970 [1887]: 809–10) is the most developed, the most characteristic projection of what we call fetishes. It is so characteristic that it is worth looking in detail at one particular instance – in this case the manufacture of sacred shields by the Nuaulu of the eastern Indonesian island of Seram.[8]

Many Nuaulu clans possess sacred shields, *aniaue monne*, imbued with special powers and subject to veneration. Throughout its manufacture, a new shield is compared in detail with the old one – it must be an exact copy, and is treated and referred to as if it were a person. The shield it replaces is spoken of as 'being close to death … no longer with breath … or strength … too old'. Personification is evident (among other things) from a number of practices:

1. A sacred shield, during its manufacture or at any point thereafter, is never laid directly on the ground, or even on the floor of a ritual house. It is always first placed on a special pandanus mat. Humans, too, must never sleep directly on the ground, only on raised platforms or in traditional-style elevated houses.
2. As the new shield progresses over the months its genesis is likened to pregnancy (*tiai*: pregnant, full).
3. The shield has a proper orientation, the top being referred to as the 'head' and the bottom the 'foot'. It may never be held or placed 'head-down'. And when lying on its 'back' must adopt the setting sun, foot: rising sun, head orientation prescribed for sleeping. The raised strip running along the back is known as the spine (*totu unie*).

4. The head of any shield (sacred or otherwise) is indicated by attaching a charm. These vary from clan to clan, but invariably include ginger and red cloth. In some cases the feathers of totemic birds may be added. The fragments of *Nautilus* shell or porcelain attached to the front of the shield in fixed patterns are compared to the headdress worn by ritual specialists during ceremonies. The headdress too contains *Nautilus* shell, as well as various kinds of feathers and red cloth. All such additive materials are regarded as being functionally equivalent to human bodily adornment.
5. Coconut oil is rubbed over the tips, edges and finally the whole of a new sacred shield before it is considered complete, a process which may be repeated on occasions when the shield is brought out from its place of rest. In the same way humans are smeared in oil or pig grease in preparation for dances and ceremonies. The oil is said to heal the wounds caused by humans during the gouging and cutting involved in its fashioning.
6. The spirit of the old shield is transferred to the new through a final rite of passage conducted on completion. In many respects this rite reflects the structure of those used for male initiation and installation into high office.
7. The first chip to be cut is wrapped in a red cloth and stored in the ritual house of the clan chief. This is functionally equivalent to the placenta and umbilicus in a human birth, which too must be preserved. It contains part of the soul of the wood, as the placenta contains part of the soul of a newborn child. And as with a newborn child in a menstruation house, it may not be removed from the house until complete.
8. All the chippings created in the carving of a sacred shield are collected in a basket and then taken to a spot in the forest where they are buried. Again, there is here a similarity with human personal leavings subject to ritualisation, such as the hair removed at the first hair-cutting ceremony.

None of this is particularly distinctive to shield veneration, though with shields it reaches its peak. We can see many of the same attitudes and practices with respect to Nuaulu ritual houses (Ellen 1986a). Neither are such practices confined to the Nuaulu. Objects from widely separated cultures are frequently represented as if they were human, are involved in processes which are recognisably human, are treated in ways that humans are treated – and in particular are in themselves subject to rites of passage, other rituals and attitudes, which are usually reserved for humans. Of the many descriptions of this kind of practice in the literature, consider, for example, a report of Tylor, that:

> in certain mountain districts of Norway, up to the end of the eighteenth century, the peasants used to preserve round stones, washed them every Thursday evening ... smeared them with butter before the fire, laid them in the seat of honour on fresh straw, and at certain times of the year steeped them in ale, that they might bring luck and comfort to the house. (Tylor 1924 [1871]: 167, following Nilsson 1868)

The additive materials so characteristic of Nuaulu shields are functionally little different from those attached to the divinatory objects described by Brain (1980) for various peoples of West Africa. Fetishes are given gifts, named, massaged and talked to sympathetically and with supplication; follow life-cycles in which they are strongest in their youth and weakest in old age; and after use are frequently laid aside to recuperate their powers. They may or may not be explicitly regarded as persons, but social interactions with them are as behaviour between persons and not that of persons towards objects. Fetishes may sometimes be said to see, hear, understand and act (Tylor 1924 [1871]: 168). They may have the human passions of anger, revenge, generosity, gratitude (Haddon 1921: 83). Nuer make offerings of tobacco and food to their fetishes, and ritually ablute them; but they are also feared and disliked (Evans-Pritchard 1956: 102–3, 158). Elsewhere they may be the subject of contempt and anger (Lubbock 1870: 165). But despite such active personification there is no requirement that fetishes actually take on the physical form of humans, that is, become anthropomorphic figurines.

By using metaphors of embodiment, something that is merely objectified becomes something approaching a fetish. Though to say that non-human objects of all kinds are treated anthropomorphically is not, in itself, to say a lot, since humankind has no option but to apprehend and represent its world in anthropomorphic terms.

Conflation of Signifier and Signified

The relationship between signified and signifier may, as we have learned from Saussure, be either arbitrary or non-arbitrary. Thus the relationship between the word 'dog', the concept of dogginess and the real-world species *Canis familiaris* is quite arbitrary. In much human religious language, however, signifiers do not stand in a non-arbitrary relationship to the signified. The word 'God', for example, is not arbitrary since it is more than a grapheme or lexeme representing the concept 'God', and may itself be treated with respect and reverence.

In many cases of this kind of non-arbitrary usage it is clear from the context of use, or from direct statements about uses, that it is understood that the word is only a signifier, that it stands for something else.

Sometimes the signified is treated as though it were embodied in the signifier. Many of those things which have been conventionally labelled as fetishes are, to a degree, representations which have become signifiers and causative agents in their own right, not merely because they convey or stand for some other meaning. This accords with Tylor's conception of fetish. A similar notion is entailed when a signifier is somehow mystically transformed into the signified, as in the case of the Host in a Catholic mass. In orthodox Catholic theology, the Host does not simply represent the body of Christ, but – miraculously – becomes the body of Christ. The next step in any cognitive (though not necessarily evolutionary) sequence would be for the boundary between signifier and signified to break down altogether. In some cases the boundary between the two may merely become indistinct, though under certain circumstances this may ultimately result in dislocation or disjunction. In this situation the signifier may become more important than what it stands for, and may be venerated for itself. Thus for Pouillon (1975 [1970]: 119), fetish is signification rather than what is signified.

In the Christian Catholic tradition a prime example of the simultaneity of signified and signifier is found in the veneration of the relics of saints, to which the original Portuguese *feitiço* was applied. In other cases the mystical content is different. Nuer fetishes have their own *tie* (soul): it does not stand for anything else. Other mystical objects are inhabited by ancestral ghosts. Nuaulu shields are allocated a soul which in itself passes from one generation of shields to the next through a line of transmission activated in the ritualised replacement of one sacred shield by another. Thus it is also like an ancestral clan spirit (though not one which has ever been a mortal human being). With money, too, the distinction between signified and signifier is blurred: modern coinage and banknotes are no more than promises which indicate suspended transactional relationships. And yet they are treated for most purposes as if they stood only for themselves. This semantic shift has not quite been achieved with cheques or plastic 'credit' cards, though we may surely anticipate it. What is clear from such varied examples is that you cannot define the products of fetishisation in terms of their semantic or mystical content; what is diagnostic is the ambiguity between content and form, between signifier and signified.

Where 'fetishisation' has occurred, therefore, the material object itself may be regarded as an active causative agent as much as anything it might stand for. The evidence of ritual practice proclaims that in many instances it is an image which performs miracles, which is prayed to and to which promises are made (Christian 1981: 93). The ethnography of local religion in Spain is replete with such examples. The Black Madonna, Our Lady of Monserrat, located in a monastery northwest of Barcelona, had been an important centre of Spanish and Catalan pilgrimage for centuries.

The image is nowadays protected by a glass screen, though a hole has been cut to allow physical contact (usually kissing) with the orb which she holds in her left hand. For many supplicants this physical contact is vital, as is the physicality of the spiritual presence. To all intents and purposes it is the image which is being worshipped, as the spiritual essence is intrinsic to this particular object and cannot be said to stand for some disembodied notion which has some temporary incidental association with it.

Theological casuists and diverse varieties of believer will no doubt take issue with such an interpretation, but devotion to objects has long been part of the Christian tradition. Historically, it first took the form of the cult of relics – as early as the second century AD; the worship of images (of saints and the Madonna) followed rather later (Christian 1981: 126; Sumption 1975: 22), though from the earliest period there has been a division of opinion as to its orthodoxy. For divines such as Vigilantius, the cult of relics was a pagan practice. The classic Christian defence is well known: 'we do not worship their relics', protested St Jerome, 'any more than we do the sun or the moon.' Objects were not worshipped in themselves, but merely as aids to the veneration of martyrs of undoubted holiness (Sumption 1975: 22–3), the earthly reminders of holy men. At other times the justification was more subtle, less equivocal – to put it impolitely, more fudged. Thus for Thomas Aquinas relics might enjoy a certain intrinsic merit on account of their holy connections, and by working miracles at their tombs God demonstrated that he wished them to be venerated (Sumption 1975: 23–4). In the Eastern Church, also, the apologetic mobilised against the iconoclasts was that it was not the form which was being worshipped, 'but rather the prototype behind the image manifest through the representation' (Weitzmen 1978: 8). Similarly, with Marian shrines the image is said to *represent* the Madonna, though the specific characteristics of local madonnas sometimes makes this difficult to believe. Such special pleading within the institutional Christian sects is echoed in other religious traditions, and where the explicated practices are not those of the apologists themselves it reflects an aspect of Hume's distinction between 'elite' and 'vulgar' religion (Brown 1981). Tylor (1924 [1871]: 169) had long ago recognised that for any two votaries an image may mean different things: either a symbol or an intelligent and active being. It is precisely this ambiguity, whether reflected in the contrasting attitudes of different supplicants or in the mind of a single person, which is generated by the cognitive processes that combine in 'fetishisation'.

Ambiguous Conceptualisation of Power

Finally we come to power relations between people and objects. By turning ideas or relations into objects you can more easily manipulate and control them, or at least you may believe that you can. The act of animating what has been concretised gives the object a utility over and above its appearance. In this way objects may become – though not inevitably – those 'machines' for divinatory purposes which Brain (1980) describes for the Bangwa. The Nuaulu sacred shield enables people to manipulate the abstract ideas of 'clan-ness'. For Lubbock, a fetish brought a deity within the control of mortals: he reports a West African as saying 'we make and break our gods daily, and consequently are masters and inventors of what we sacrifice to' (Lubbock 1870: 165, 196). In some extreme cases objects described in the literature as fetishes may be reviled, beaten and even discarded if they do not serve a user well (Lubbock 1870: 196; Tylor 1924 [1871]: 158), attitudes which are consistent with, and follow directly from, the conceptualisation of material objects as animate entities. The commoditisation of ideas similarly enhances the degree to which we believe we may control social relationships; for the sexual fetishist the transference of erotic attachment to objects enables a degree of control impossible in terms of conventional relations with sentient and feeling humans.

The ability to manipulate an abstraction because it has in some way been concretised is additionally important if that object itself has the ability to alter the material conditions of life. Those things we call fetishes have this dual quality. As long as figurines or relics are seen merely as passive objects through which the disembodied spirit can work then they do not appear to measure up to one of the more specific definitions of fetishes, that is, objects described as having attained power or which are power in themselves. Nuaulu shields protect not merely physically, but also magically. The Kongolese *nkisi* is regarded as having certain magical effects when properly manipulated. The tenth-century image of St Foy at Conques 'was carried with clashing cymbals through the valleys of the Rouergue whenever the abbey's land was threatened' (Sumption 1975: 52). Similarly some Eastern theologians were inclined to accord intrinsic powers to the relics of saints used in consecrating churches (Sumption 1975: 29). The relic had power, which was activated through ritual manipulation. Contempt for the relics of the saints was regularly visited with dumbness, bodily distortion, disease, madness and death (Sumption 1975: 41), even though supplicants could themselves physically manipulate the objects and seek assistance through them. Failure to care for Nuaulu sacred shields may unleash malign ancestral forces and result in unpredictable events. Money *does* things, apparently on its own (it can be left to accumulate), and yet is obviously also manipulated. The boot fetishist can manipulate the object of his desire, but at the same time he is the victim of his mental condition – and may often indulge his fetish despite his rational feelings. Often he may find it difficult morally to accept his condition given the dominant conformist values of his society.

Thus, 'fetishisation' is characterised by a progressive ambiguity in the conceptualisation of power with regard to objects, and to understand it we must always presuppose a particular ideology of power. The desire to control increases with the intrinsic powers attributed to objects, but as these powers increase so they may counter the power which people have over them. This paradoxical tension is very characteristic of fetishes. The power relations between humans and supernatural beings or objects is always conditional, never absolute. Such an ambiguity derives from the human attribution of power to objects and a desire to control those intrinsic powers. Power is a volatile force, and the more power attributed to objects the more they are likely to be able to control the manipulator.

One of the problems in analysing fetishised objects is that the objective properties of fetishes do not always correspond to their material or cultural effects. Bangwa believe that by manipulating an *nkisi* figurine they can control future events; most anthropologists would claim that they cannot, but seek to explain why – rationally – they think they can. For the Marxist, the active character of money is a figment of a particular cultural imagination: money can never, in itself, *do* what is attributed to it by those involved in a particular economic discourse. Similarly, the boot fetishist is convinced that in venerating boots he can obtain ecstatic sexual pleasure. Though a psychoanalyst may not deny that he does so, the behaviour nevertheless involves a displacement of 'real' sexual gratification. But in all cases what is present is a belief that the manipulation *can* attain particular ends, and that the representation of ordinary experience is sufficient for belief in that ends-means relationship to be maintained.

Conclusion

I began by suggesting that the subject of fetishism provided an appropriate opportunity to explore the articulation of cognition and collective representations. We are now in a position to see more clearly why this should be so. To summarise, my argument is this:

First, the overlapping concepts of fetish used in three historically situated scholarly practices – anthropology, Marxism and psychology – all depend upon the concurrence of four underlying cognitive processes: concretisation, animation, conflation of signifier with signified, and an ambiguous tension between person and object in terms of control. These are all cognitive processes (means, agents, instruments) which help us first comprehend the world and then negotiate our way through it. They do so by acting on and through existing sets of beliefs or representations (the medium) and influencing the generation of new ones; indeed, they are the co-ordinates which determine how much of what comprises belief is expressed and represented.

Second, the processes outlined are apparent in the social construction of categories across the complete range of human experience, 'mundane' no less than 'symbolic'. Thus if we wish to understand the processes which underlie classifying activity in general, and which connect the instruments of cognition with the medium of belief and cultural representations, we would do well to begin with those processes through which are categorised the discontinuities of (as far as this is ever possible) unsocialised nature. Despite feedbacks from pre-existing classifications and representations and their inextricable social contextualisation, animals and plants provide us with some of the simplest possible – in a word 'elementary' – relationships between objects and their representations accessible to ethnographers producing data in natural settings. Categories of natural kinds are about as rooted in the empirical world as categories can ever get, and in a way that those applied to the world of people and social phenomena can never be (see Chapter 3 in this volume; Ellen 1986). So while ethnobiology is in no sense unaffected by cultural relativities, it is sufficiently less so to serve as a benchmark when examining classification more widely.

This latter conclusion implies a distinction grounded in the kinds of 'entities' subjected to classifying activity, though it is sometimes presented as one between specialised theoretical approaches. Emiko Ohnuki-Tierney, for example, has suggested that whereas cognitive anthropology focuses upon the phases in which memory codes are established, symbolic anthropology deals with the phases in which analogy codes are formulated (Ohnuki-Tierney 1981). I cannot agree that such professional distinctions relate to completely separate processes, historically or processually. The model which emerges here, and the evidence which supports it, indicates the mutual embeddedness of instrument and medium, individual perception and collective representation, in terms of linguistic expression, metaphorical penetration and classificatory structures involved. Though cognition and belief are often erroneously conflated, they are intrinsically bound together in particular instances.

Third, the four cognitive processes isolated can be instructively modelled as part of a single logical sequence, by which percepts are progressively transformed into more complex categories. Beginning at the simplest level, we reify what we 'perceive' in terms of our sensory experience of natural and cultural discontinuities; what we reify may in turn be reconstituted as an icon (an abstraction represented as a material thing), and what we iconify animated through conflation of signifier with signified. This is schematically represented in Figure 9.1.

Animation, though an analogy (ultimately with the sentient human body), provides a means for representing, comprehending and evoking; the inevitable consequence of this is the socialisation of the natural, material world. But the socialisation of nature releases ambiguities, most

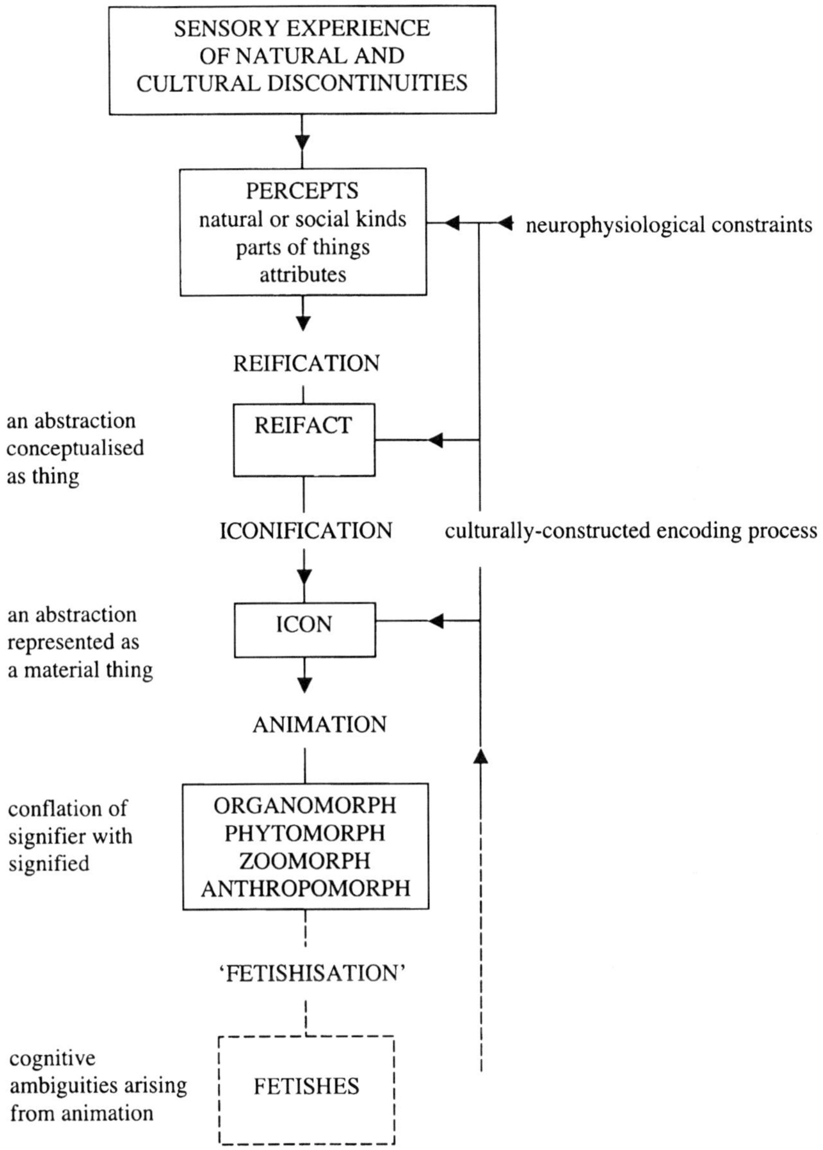

Figure 9.1 Cognitive processes underlying 'fetishisation'

notably in terms of the semiotic status of the objects or categories (their simultaneity as both signified and signifier) and in the perceived power relations between object and person. It seems to me that the best we can do is to see in 'fetishisation' an extension and culmination of this process, differing from iconification in shifting the balance from simultaneity towards 'the thing in itself'. In re-establishing 'things in themselves' as legitimate features of the cognitive landscape (see also Appadurai 1986) we also bring back morphological reality – physically or ideationally construed – as an essential ingredient to understanding, in addition to functionality, iconicity or whatever is 'represented' (Ucko 1969: 28–30). During the last fifty years anthropology has come to place less emphasis on the materiality of cultural phenomena and has become more interested – almost obsessively so – in intricate abstracted systems of belief and webs of significance. Material culture can no longer be treated as though it were somehow outside culture.

Finally, those things to which the word 'fetish' is customarily applied arise from attempts to construct a definite type of belief from a particular combination of cognitive features. The problem is that the same features, in various combinations, are characteristic of an extensive range of particular historically fashioned representations, and it is this array of possibilities which constitutes the 'greater whole' of which that phenomenon labelled 'fetishism' must be considered an empirically ill-defined part. The boundary between fetishes and non-fetishes is consequently vague, admitting such a ludicrously wide area of reference. Fetishes cannot be treated as a special type of object, defined in terms of physical appearance or in terms of generic functional attributes; neither is fetishism a particular kind of mental condition (but rather an aspect of all thought). I have no particular desire to salvage terms once thought obsolete or retain old concepts as they stand, and I think I would actually resist applying the word 'fetish' to ritual objects I might encounter in the course of ethnographic analysis, even if they appeared to satisfy the various conditions listed. I am much more interested in dissecting the cognitive structure of the category implied in its usage, which seems to me to raise issues far too important to be consigned to some cul-de-sac in the history of ideas.

Notes

1. This chapter was originally delivered as the Curl Lecture in 1987. I should like to thank the Librarians of St Augustine's Abbey, Ramsgate, and the Franciscan Study Centre in Canterbury for background assistance in preparing the original lecture, the Royal Anthropological Institute for inviting me to give it and the Department of Anthropology at the University of Manchester for being such perfect hosts. For their comments on a revised written version, or for help in clarifying various points, I am indebted to Josep Llobera, David McLellan and Janet Sayers.
2. It is difficult to make a rigid distinction between fetishes and charms (under which I would include amulets and talismans), though some have attempted to do so. Ruth Benedict (1938: 643–6), for example, suggests that we should use the word 'charm' when material objects are not anthropomorphised, where their mystical power is an attribute of the thing (like colour), and when

they work automatically; when material objects are to varying degrees anthropomorphised, where their mystical power is intrinsic to the entity, and when they have to be ritually activated, then we are dealing with fetishes. A Nuaulu *mauna* is – in this sense – a charm. It is made from a type of croton, leaves of a small tree which the Nuaulu call *akunin* (*Actinodaphne* sp.), and red cloth, the whole tied together with pineapple fibre (see the Museum of Mankind specimen As 1.240). The *mauna* is made by the head of a patriclan section ('house') and given to a newborn child from the opposite section following the birth ritual. It guards a child for a period of three to four months against those evil spirits which are most likely to threaten its life and health during this crucial phase of its development. However, it is not very instructive (and possibly even misleading) to place the *mauna* in a quite separate category to the sacred shields which I discuss below, and to which the term 'fetish' might be more recognisably attached. Such a contrast may have a limited application as an ad hoc working distinction but it will not sustain close scrutiny.

3. 'The leading article in No. 179 of the *Kölnische Zeitung* (1842)', in Marx 1975: 189. He writes: 'the author ... calls fetishism the "crudest" form of religion', and appears to adopt the evolutionist notion – to be later defended by Lubbock – that animal worship is a 'higher form of religion' than fetishism, which is characterised by the attempt of worshippers to seek the compliance of an object in attaining particular ends and the destruction of such objects which fail to do so. Marx had read *Über den Dienst der Fetischgötter* (1785), the posthumous German translation of *Du culte des dieux fétiches* by De Brosses (Marx 1970 [1887]: 115; Rubel and Manale 1975: 23).
4. This latter fixation is sometimes distinguished in the literature as 'partialism' (Gebherd 1971).
5. Consider also the dual fetishistic character of those animated phalli, allegedly used as charms in the Graeco-Roman world. These mainly consist of birds with heads in the form of a phallus, or a phallus with human legs (see e.g., Boardman and Rocca 1978: 157), and originated in the Hellenistic Greek cities of the eastern Mediterranean basin (e.g. Miletus, Smyrna and Alexandria).
6. Haddon (1921: 72–91) offered a 'rag-bag' of no less than eleven 'essential characteristics' of fetishism, an assorted checklist which must have done much to hasten its demise as a useful descriptive term. These were: 1) 'may be any object whatsoever'; 2) 'consists of a symbolic charm with sympathetic properties'; 3) 'may consist of sign or token representing an ideal notion or ideal'; 4) 'credited with mysterious powers owing to its being the habitation, temporary or permanent, of a spiritual being'; 5)'sometimes merely the vehicle or means by which the spirit communicates with his worshippers'; 6)'instrument by which the spirit acts'; 7) 'possesses personality and will'; 8) 'may act by will or force of its own proper spirit, entering or acting on it from without'; 9)'the spirit and the material object can be dissociated'; 10)'worshipped, prayed to, sacrificed and talked with'; 11) 'petted or ill-treated with regard to its past or future behaviour'. This list is so varied and complex that it is of little comparative and analytic use.
7. For a more extended discussion of the concept of 'natural kinds' and 'basic' categories see Ellen 1979, 1986b, 1993.
8. For a more detailed version of this analysis see Ellen 1990.

CHAPTER 10

The Cognitive Geometry of Nature: A Contextual Approach (1996)

This essay was a reaction to the claim that 'nature' is everywhere 'socially constructed'. While acknowledging the multiple ways in which nature may be used in human cultural settings, and the differences between populations in the extent to which there is evidence for a well-formed and labelled concept, it argues that it is cognitively motivated by three dispositions of the mind: to conceptualise organic 'things' (a species-like algorithm), to distinguish self from other and to attribute phenomena with essences.

Introduction

That conceptions of nature vary historically and ethnographically, and are, therefore, themselves intrinsically cultural, is so widely asserted nowadays that it is often assumed to have become a self-evident anthropological truth.[1] Perhaps the best example of this in popular environmentalist discourse, as in some anthropology, is the opposition drawn between the holistic systemic vision of 'traditional', 'tribal' or 'archaic' societies and the dualism of the modern scientific and dominant Judaeo-Christian tradition. How conceptions of nature vary beyond such abstractions is well demonstrated in individual studies, both historical (e.g. Collingwood 1945; Thomas 1983; Horigan 1988; Torrance 1992) and ethnographic. In particular, much attention has been given to how these might arise from particular practices of environmental interaction (e.g. Ingold 1992; Bird-David 1993), and how these in turn might sustain, or be sustained by (e.g. Schefold 1988), particular social ideologies.[2] As Philippe Descola puts it:

> each specific form of cultural conceptualisation also introduces sets of rules

> governing the use and appropriation of nature, evaluations of technical systems, and beliefs about the structure of the cosmos, the hierarchy of being, and the very principles by which living things function. (Descola 1992: 110)

But empirical demonstrations of such relativity – many of which find their origin in the claim by Leach (1964: 34–5) that nature is no more than some topological grid imposed upon a continuous world – have led to an almost indignant rejection of the very idea of nature. Indeed, it has become increasingly awkward and misleading to carve out from these implied 'representations' or 'constructions', a conceptual space which is linguistically, cognitively and symbolically coherent. The new consensus has thus given rise to new problems: that of commensurability between different conceptions of nature (including the assumption that *our* nature always exists as a category comparable to *their* nature); the implication that each culture has a single ruling (and unambiguous) conception of nature, which it is our task to locate, excavate and describe; and the problem as to how those collective notions of nature which we can claim to exist are 'constructed' or negotiated'. I shall argue that we can approach the question of the categorical status of nature in two – superficially antithetical – ways.

The first is a continuation of what the relativists and deconstructionists are arguing; namely that any one population may, depending on the circumstances, generate conceptions of nature which are fuzzy and variable – which may indeed be inconsistent and contradictory – and that such variability may reveal itself at the level of individual praxis and collective representations, or in some combination of the two. Consequently, it is difficult to speak of 'societies' and 'cultures' (that is, second-order constructs) as having a single conception of nature, and an exaggeration to claim that it is even true of empirically identifiable local populations. Indeed, it may be claimed that some peoples have no concepts of nature whatsoever.

The second approach is to buck this trend and identify a minimum number of underlying assumptions upon which pragmatic schemata and symbolic representations are built, and which ultimately constrain human conceptual permutations (cf. Boyer 1993).[3] If I interpret him correctly, this is what Descola (1992: 110) means by 'the social objectification of nature [being] implemented through a limited number of operative schemes', and his acknowledgement that 'modes of representation of relations to nature present certain similar characteristics' (ibid., 123). Such widely observed 'similar characteristics' may be accounted for if we hypothesise that underlying all models of nature are three cognitive axes or dimensions, which will, when the cultural devices they permit are combined in different ways, generate particular representations, all recognisably transformations of some ur- or proto-nature. The first axis is that which allows us to construe nature inductively in terms of the 'things' which people include within it, and the characteristics assigned to such things. The second is that which allows us to define nature spatially, assigning it to some realm outside humans or their immediate living (cultural) space. The third is that which allows us to define nature in essentialist terms, as some force which is exogenous to human will but which can to varying degrees be controlled. To the extent that these three cognitive axes make an equal contribution to representations, they may be predicted to approach that multifaceted ambiguous, but ultimately recognisable idea which we in the West recognise as nature; whereas the more asymmetry is introduced into the model the less familiar the construction becomes. And to the degree that each of these axes dominates a conceptualisation characteristic of a particular context, so it also becomes a 'definition' of nature.

I focus here on examples drawn largely from my own work on the Nuaulu, of Seram in eastern Indonesia. There are no new data, though the way I have used them is different. Thus I start by asking how we might begin to identify cultural phenomena which best approximate each of the three cognitive axes specified above, and by exploring the extent to which they permit us to infer the existence of nature as a domain. I then examine how combining cultural ideas derived from each of the axes generates intrinsic ambiguity, and how this is reflected in the variation accompanying different practical and symbolic contexts.

Nature as kinds of 'thing'

Let us first examine how far the first axis, the inductivist (nature as 'things') model, assists us in generating an approximation, or one dimension, of some hypothetical Nuaulu conceptualisation of nature. In cultural modifications of this model, particular 'things', by virtue of their resemblance to other things, are – once aggregated – seen as part of nature. Thus through induction nature itself becomes a thing which can then be the conceptual starting point of deductive reasoning. It has been suggested (Ingold 1986: 3; 1992: 44) that the fact that we see 'things' at all is what distinguishes *Homo sapiens* from other animals: birds may perceive functional objects such as anvils or missiles, but only humans can perceive something as abstract as 'a stone'. Hence the human environment consists of neutral objects waiting to be ordered, an orientation which is closely linked to the tendency to view animals and plants as physical objects, things of nature. Such a view is – for example – implicit in Lévi-Strauss's theory of totemism (see Chapter 8 above).

If nature is the sum total of its parts then we must begin by examining what these constituents might be, and the most accessible evidence here is ethnobiological. It is now well established that all peoples work with a concept of 'natural kind', whether as a 'common sense kind of phenomenal substance', or as an 'ontological entity with an underlying nature' (Atran 1990: 86, 94). There is some dispute as to whether basic categories always occur at a particular level of abstraction, and concerning the detailed way they map onto phylogenetic templates. The extent to which we can represent and account for more-or-less inclusive categories is contested; but the fact that all human populations engage in such activity is hardly in doubt (Ellen 1993b). What is more controversial is the claim by Berlin (1992) and Boster (1996) that natural kinds have a different perceptual character from cultural forms, fashioned by selective pressure. As the biological world has radiated, so the human capacity to recognise the basic order in that radiation has co-evolved. Thus, in this view (with which I am in basic sympathy), nature itself – or, at least, 'the biological world' – is the product of human cognitive evolution.

A formal expression for this kind of model would be simple incremental linear aggregation: $n1 + n2 + n3\ldots = N$, where n is a culturally agreed natural kind, and N nature as a totality. But most peoples that we know of also recognise more inclusive conceptual domains such as 'plant', 'animal', 'rock' and so on, such that an aggregative model of nature should intuitively have a structure something like: animals + plants + other living things + non-living things = nature, which we might express formally as: $(n1 + n2 + n3\ldots) = N\ (\ldots)N + (\ldots)N + \ldots = N$. In order to demonstrate the plausibility of such a model we have to show that:

1. each of these generic component parts (N) is recognised;
2. they share common characteristics;
3. there is evidence to show that they are linked together to form a conceptual whole (N) – an over-arching category, in other words.

We can explore 1 and 2 by examining the Nuaulu category which glosses most closely with English 'animal'. The existence of such a category, what Brent Berlin calls a 'unique beginner', can in principle be inferred from the presence of specific terms whose reference can be shown to be coterminous with the semantic content of the domain, or, where such terms are absent, from various linguistic and cultural markers, or (up to a point) by employing sorting experiments.

There is no one commonly used or widely acknowledged Nuaulu term for all animals, though there are three possible, partial and rarely used candidates (Ellen 1993b: 96–7). So, in effect, we might say that the category is, terminologically, 'covert', or at least 'semi-covert'. But even in the absence of an unambiguous domain label we may infer the existence of a cognitive prototype marked out from other domains, and also from humans. Thus when speaking of animals, their qualities and relationships, Nuaulu employ a discourse which can be distinguished in certain small but significant respects from other discourses. It differs both lexically and in terms of appropriate semantic relationships. For example, there are different words for killing an animal (*ihunui*) and for killing a human (*atoria*), for a human voice (*mo'nyom*) and an animal call (*nioke*), and for human head hair (*hua*) and bodily hair, animal feathers or fur (*hunue*). In some cases the differences amount only to slight phonological shifts, as in *anai* (human child) and *anae* (animal young). There is also a specialised lexicon for specific activities relating to animals (e.g. *atinai*, 'to hunt cuscus', *asakaka*, to call a cuscus'), and many special anatomical terms (e.g. *mata hunua*, mollusc and insect antennae; *kihene*, wings and fins), in addition to about forty-seven such terms which humans and other animals share. The fact that forms in core animal categories are clearly similar in multiple respects, and often overlap, and that the terms are often expressed as contrast sets while animal partonyms ('head', 'heart', and so on) and other linguistic usages are present, goes some way to imply the existence of a category 'animal' (cf. Taylor 1990: 47–51). Such differences not only help to locate and maintain separate domains, in the interests of effective linguistic communion, but also serve the purposes of symbolic contrast. The core of the domain is clearly regarded as being bound by polythetic affinities, such that the unique beginner is not as arbitrary as some (e.g. Hunn 1977: 44) have suggested, although its borders may occasionally be difficult to determine.

We could undertake a similar exercise for the domain 'plant', or indeed for any other conceptual domain which aggregates identifiable parts of the human environment on the basis of similar characteristics or overall form, simply by drawing inferences from linguistic utterance and cultural practice. Once this has been done we might then order the domains themselves into more inclusive contrastive categories, using distinctive features such as those which Taylor (1990) has suggested for the Tobelo: living : non-living, sexual : non-sexual, breathing : non-breathing, and so on. Such abstract distinctions are also discernible among the Nuaulu (Ellen 1993b: 95), but have little practical bearing on their lived culture, are of no prominent symbolic significance, and certainly cannot be held to be a starting point for their classification of the natural world. In this instance, I suspect they are examples of that genre of elicited but quite ungeneralisable contrasts which are happily provided by willing informants, and at which the ethnographer is temped to grasp in some vain attempt to impose order on what otherwise looks like utter chaos.

In short, the hierarchic conception of nature typified by scientific taxonomy, and its folk-semantic extension which includes at its more comprehensive levels contrasts between unique beginners, and life and non-life, is not one which is readily yielded from the Nuaulu data. But we do not need to rely on such abstractions, irrespective of whether or not they can convincingly be shown to be emically-rooted, in order to model an aggregated or integrated concept of natural things, as conceptual domains can also be linked through their overlap (especially the overlap of their peripheries) by what various authors (e.g. Hays 1976: 502) have described for less inclusive categories as 'chaining', or 'linking'. Thus, if *a* is linked to *b*, *b* to *c* and *c* to *d* then this implies the existence of a 'group' *a-b-c-d*: an instance of polythetic resemblance.

Certain Nuaulu life-forms which are regarded as animals in phylogenetic terms have no obvious affinities with any other category. These include sponges, which are grouped with 'fungi'. Molluscs and starfish, however, are firmly perceived as animals for a combination of behavioural and morphological reasons. There is no sharp division between animals and plants and other domains, either in linguistic or conceptual terms (Lévi-Strauss 1966: 138–9; Morris 1976: 542). Some invertebrates are ambiguously animals and plants, some plants (e.g. certain fungi and lichens) are ambiguously plant and inert material; different life-forms merging together to strongly permit the inference of a life category, which itself may merge with non-life. Thus despite the cognitive imperative to distinguish domains in terms of a small number of features or cognitive prototypes, in practice there are always going to be 'problems', some of which may be culturally manifest as anomalies; and it is precisely these which serve to link domains into more inclusive groupings.

If nature is an inventory of things in this sense, then this must be linked to rules about how these things are to be identified and related: that is, order, and this order has to find some cultural legitimation. Nuaulu acknowledge that there is (indeed, must be) order in the world, an order which is in general terms comparable to the pre-Darwinian 'great chain of being'. Non-directive evidence for this might first be sought in that part of Nuaulu origin mythology which speaks of the time when the first Matoke (Lord of the Land) descended from the sky and walked throughout the earth where each natural kind was represented only by a single organism – one snake, one betel palm, one hornbill, and so on. As the Matoke came by each of these he named it, saying: 'This is a snake', This is a betel palm', 'This is a hornbill', and so on. And as he did so, the many emerged from the singular. But this is not to say that Nuaulu readily expound, even less agree upon, the principles for order, and certainly not on the identification or classification of animals for pragmatic purposes. They will simply admit to not knowing it, or at least large parts of it (Ellen 1993b: 94). Less modest individuals might dispute among themselves, but every disputed classification itself exists within an axiomatic field, the coordinates of which are assumed to be quite fixed. And the *primus inter pares* of axioms is that nature itself is finite, and that all animals have names – even if they remain unknown. In Nuaulu theory at least, names are not given arbitrarily, for economy of thought: they reveal part of an order which was laid down at the beginning of the world, but which is only partially known about, and even less understood.

Nature as an inventory of things reaches its apogee in modern Western classifications. The 'great chain of being' has already been mentioned, but it is also there in the concept of species, in the taxonomic schemes of Linnaeus and their Darwinian reinterpretation; it is there in the very idea of 'natural history', embedded within the notion of exhibitions to display nature as these emerged from cabinets of curiosity to become museums of natural history, herbaria, botanical and zoological gardens, during the eighteenth and nineteenth centuries. What is additionally significant here, and which comes through well in static displays, is that they are concerned as much with minerals (which have never lived) as with life; and equally with dead plants and animals, and the ambiguous classificatory material presented in the form of bones, fossils and the mineral extrusions and excretions of living things (such as coral). The conceptualisation of nature as a collectivity of things is, therefore, most obvious in the representations generated by Western science and those generated by anthropologists investigating the folk classifications of the natural world, where the Western paradigm is the implicit or explicit reference point. It is there also, supremely so, commoditised both in its parts and its entirety, in the slogans of environmentally inspired marketing and in the politics of ecology and biodiversity.

Nature as Space Which is not Human

Nature is often understood less as some abstracted inventory of its contents (in which items are cognitively detached from their habitat and reorganised according to a limited number of morphological or functional criteria) than in terms of its predominant spatial or phenomenological manifestation. It is this definition which is implicit in many ethnographically reported instances of the semantic congruence between forest and nature. But for different peoples, using different subsistence strategies, living in different environments the semantic congruence may be with some alternative topography ('sea' or 'desert', say, or 'mountains'), all of which have in common what is perhaps best (provisionally) construed as the quality of 'wilderness'. But 'wilderness' is the apogee of something closer and more familiar, though different. So, although for the Nuaulu the congruence is archetypically exemplified by 'forest', more routinely, perhaps, in this spatial sense, nature is 'that which is not of the village', or 'that which is not of the village or gardens'.

The 'natural otherness' of the Nuaulu concept of forest is encountered in its most mundane sense in adjectival qualifiers for animals or plants: as in the contrast between the geckoes *imasasae numa* ('house') and *imasasae ai ukune* ('tree top, tree branches, far forest'), for *Hemidactylus frenatus* and

Gekko vittatus; or in the contrast between the murids *mnaha numa/niane* ('house/village') and *mnaha wesie* ('forest'), for *Mus musculus* and *Melomys*. It is also evident in the symbolic organisation of village space (Ellen 1986), and in the differential attitudes to language and behaviour within and without the village. Thus you may 'joke', mock or use expletives involving certain animals in the village, but you may not do so outside. Among such exclamatory phrases are: *ikae nawe*, 'long fish'; *mau (w)anae*, 'kitten'; *asuani anae*, 'young cassowary'; and *hahu onate*, 'large pig'. In the village (and by extension in the gardens as well) these expletives are used extensively in ordinary discourse; in the forest they anger the spirits and bring on heavy rain. While an individual may try to escape the consequences of his utterances, he runs the risk of being swallowed up by the earth (Ellen 1993b: 175–6). Interestingly, the oath *masi mokota*, 'let the earth open up', is subject to the same taboo. The same rule – village (permissible): forest (prohibited) – applies to a wide range of other expressions, among which are included expletives derived from the names of spirits (e.g., *painakite raia*). This is significant given the classificatory similarities between animals and spirits, to which I shall turn shortly.

But it is insufficient to contrast forest and village in the abstract, since the usual personal experience is that forest, bush, or whatever its semantic approximation might be, surrounds or encompasses the village, and ultimately the self; and it is in this sense that nature comes closest to what in the Western scientific tradition has become 'environment'. Thus nature is always constructed by reference to the human domain, and is in the last instance informed by ideas and practices concerning 'self' and 'otherness'. This is not merely symbolic analogy, but an homology of experience. This should not worry us since it is a matter of fact that what is experienced and represented around us homologously is at key moments, in significant contexts, symbolically transformed into abstract binary oppositions which permit more formal analogy. Thus the Nuaulu experience of living within houses located within village spaces, which are in turn located within forest, is easily transformed into various abstract linear oppositions between, say, house and forest or village and forest, which in turn may be drawn into more complex symbolic linkages through analogy (Ellen 1986).

Nature as Inner Essence

The third dimension of the concept of nature is its sensation as an inner essence or vital energy or force, outside human control. This is the most intangible of the three. We can perceive and touch 'things' and walk through 'spaces', but inner essence is usually only experienced in terms of its sensate consequences, usually through some combination of the first two axes. However, the best physical manifestations of inner essence are those fluids and pulses associated with living things, with bodily function: blood, sweat and tears, semen, breast milk; heartbeat, breath, excretion, movement; or more generally in the environment: flow of water, heat and cold, wind, noise, growth. And this is not confined to life narrowly construed. Thus Tournefort could identify the act of creation in both seeds and mineral crystals (Atran 1990: 230). In certain clearly defined circumstances the generic cultural character of essence or energy will be clear: thus with respect to human passion we often speak of it as 'animal nature'. This is embedded in the Western notion of natural instinct, nature as opposed to nurture; Islamic *hawa nafsu* as opposed to *akal* (reason); and the widespread Indonesian idea that the process of socialisation is the progressive controlling of natural forces. But nature within need not primarily be an allusion to animality; the dynamic properties may rather be experienced as consubstantial in any number of different 'kinds of' nature. It need not be a metaphor for the social, and sometimes it might be better to speak of both natural and social phenomena – as, say, reflected in physical maturation – as wholly comparable outcomes of similar processes (Bloch 1992).

The idea of nature as an essence or force within may everywhere have associations of uncontrollability, but we cannot prescribe in advance whether its cultural expression will be positive, negative or neutral. This will very much depend on the cultural metaphors which draw upon the imagery. One set of metaphors which do so, and which have been examined extensively in the literature, are those linked to gender (MacCormack and Strathern 1980; Atkinson and Errington 1990; Valeri 1990). As it happens, the Nuaulu data fit well with the 'male is to female as culture is to nature' motif, females treated as representing a danger to the male order, the intrusion of nature into culture often physicalised with reference to menstrual blood and the act of childbirth.

Boundary Problems and Contradictions

Each of the three axes – or, if you will, dimensions or definitions – outlined is sufficient in itself to generate or define any one cultural construction of nature: all three are necessary to even begin to map out its underlying geometry. Moreover, my presentation so far has been fundamentally artificial in that I have ignored boundary problems and inner contradictions which arise once we juxtapose two or more of the axes, which is of course how we culturally experience nature. It is true that I have had to anticipate some of these, as no ethnographic data known to me present the conditions in any other way, but I have tried to limit these in the interests of clarity of exposition. It may help in reviewing these issues to imagine the three axes as related in three-dimensional space. I shall first consider the conflation of the first axis (nature as an aggregation of things) with the second (nature as outer space); I shall then consider the conflation of the first with the third (nature as inner essence); and finally, conflation of the second with the third. The justification for this order will, I hope, become apparent. Of course, there are some contexts in which all three axes have a direct bearing on what is going on.

The conflation between one and two (things and the spatial other) is best exemplified by the universal cultural recognition that humans themselves might possibly be 'things' of nature, comparable to other natural things; that the inventory of nature is not confined to 'the other' (a version of the so-called subject-object problem); and by the recognition that humans physically intrude into the space of nature. We can explore this idea in relation to Nuaulu animal classification.

In general terms, people are regarded by the Nuaulu as being in many respects like animals. People share anatomical and physiological similarities with animals, but more than this, myths inform us that animals, like their human counterparts, have societies. In the case of some species, they are represented as reflecting basically human organisation and values (e.g. Ellen 1972: 233); they are spoken of in the idiom of kinship. Animal societies, too, are bound by the Patalima-Patasiwa ('Five group'-'Nine group') division of Seramese peoples (the Nuaulu themselves being Patalima), while totemic traditions and a rich mythology underscore the idea that animals may change into humans, and vice versa (Ellen 1993b: 163–76). In short, humans impose a social classification on the world of animals. Many terms referring to behaviour and appearance which are used for humans are also used for animals. In some instances shared terms may be understood as consubstantial, while in others the allusion – at least – is to a metaphorical extension from humans. The exceptions occur – and we have examined some of these already – where there is no human model, as with 'wing', 'beak', 'tail', and so on. And, of course, none of this prevents Nuaulu from defining the domain of animals essentially in contrast to humans. Taylor (1990: 51) reports that in Tobelorese language and concepts humans are treated quite differently from 'animals'. He regards this as problematic, since 'humans' meet the defining features of the Tobelo category 'fauna'. Rather than being problematic this seems to me to be an understandable feature of all people's conceptual universes. We might ask if humans are 'animals' in British or French folk classification. The answer, of course, is that it depends, and in this respect Nuaulu beliefs are like those of many other peoples. An extension of the same problem is encountered when we consider the place in any inventory of natural things, of domesticated species, or any humanly modified part of nature (Descola 1992: 111).

The conflation between one and three (things and essences) is best exemplified in the attribution of essence to particular parts of nature. A widespread version of this idea is associated with animism – a kind of 'social objectification of nature' (Descola 1992: 114), and I have shown in Chapter 9 above that the attribution of life to the inanimate (most commonly through anthropomorphism) is basic to all human conceptualisations of the world. It is the continuity of natural kinds, as discussed above, which must, in all cultures, give plausibility to the idea that all nature is animate: animal, vegetable and mineral, the humanly modified and the humanly unmodified.

A particular aspect of this continuity is evident in my Nuaulu data dealing with the consubstantiality of spirits and animals. Nuaulu recognise spirit categories in much the same way as they recognise categories of animal; indeed, spirits are treated as natural kinds, as equally significant parts of their environment (Ellen 1993b: 176–9). People claim to hear and 'see' spirits all the time, and I have on occasions been present when the alleged discovery of a particular spirit in a tree or bush has created scenes of some excitement. Some Nuaulu spirit forms appear to describe real animals; for example, *sinne inae* (certain scarab and long-horned beetles, including *Oryctes rhinoceros* and *Mulciper linnaei*), (*kau*) *kama nahune* (edible long-horned beetles such as *Gnoma giraffe* and *Glenea corona* – *kama nahune* being the spirit of a person killed by falling from a tree in the throes of hunting cuscus), *inararai* (the frog *Litoria amboinensis*), and *rikune* (various kinds of bugs and beetles, including *Mictis*, *Oncomeris* and *Euphanta*). Perhaps we should not be surprised if it is insects which are most likely to be redefined as spirits (cf. Dentan 1968: 26–7). Other categories, such as *naka*, those mythical creatures we call dragons, are used by the Nuaulu to label certain real-world animals which they have heard of but never seen, in this case the Komodo 'dragon'. Domains become even more blurred when spirits enter the bodies of animals, influencing their behaviour, as when a *sakahatene* enters the jaws of the death adder *nanate* (*Acanthophis antarcticus*). Other spirits are modelled on particular animal prototypes to the extent that experiences of paired entities seem at times to be conflated. Thus *masenu* are compared with *tuku tuku* (probably *Otus magicus*), and *ahone* with *sakoa* (*Ninox squamipila*) in their vocalisations. These are both owls and consequently nocturnal, which is itself significant. Some animals are held to be derived from spirits, such as *isanone* ants from *isanone nanie*. So not only are there sometimes no simple breaks at domain boundaries in what we might construe as the 'real' world, there are even areas of overlap between the objectively visible and invisible.

The conflation between two and three (space and essence) is nowhere better summed up than in the notion of 'the wild', and its cognates. The natural other is not always chaotic or malign and for some peoples it might most faithfully be expressed as some kind of 'culture of the beyond' (Schefold 1988). However, as far as the Nuaulu are concerned it is unpredictable, difficult to control and with a fundamentally moral character; there are right and wrong ways in which to engage with the forest, which arise in part from the social histories of particular places within it, but also from its intrinsic mystical properties. This natural 'other' is reflected in the inferential symbolic opposition between 'nature' and 'culture' evident in most ritual, in the specific rituals conducted prior to cultivating the forest, in the charms which are used to protect travellers in the forest, in the prohibitions on certain behaviours and utterances while in the forest, and in the correct ritual disposal of its products. When humans enter the forest they carry with them what amounts to an 'aura' of culture, and when ritual is conducted in the forest, it is as if islands of culture are created to ensure its efficaciousness. Thus, in Nuaulu male initiation ceremonies platforms are erected which mimic that entity which most epitomises (indeed physicalises) culture, namely the house. Individual neophytes at this ceremony are required to stand upon blocks made of five logs, as if preventing contamination from the forest. Similar structures are used when performing land-clearing and other routine rituals. The same meeting of nature as inner force and as outer space is reflected through the prism of gender concepts in the symbolic layout of Nuaulu villages. Here, females are associated – through the location of their menstruation and birthing huts – with the outer rim of the village (nearest the forest). What is, therefore, universally significant about this conflationary aspect of nature is that it becomes a condition for knowledge, by controlling the relation between what is taken as internal nature and what is taken as external nature (Strathern 1992: 194), that which is natural and that which is of nature.

Contextual Variation

We can see, therefore, that logically the functional association of any two, or all three, of the cognitive axes specified results in conceptual complications which greatly extend and enhance the richness of the symbolic imagery of nature. But what is intriguing about human cognitive and social behaviour generally is that logical inconsistencies can be suppressed in particular circumstances, and different aspects of a multidimensional idea privileged at the expense of other aspects in any one context. Let us take a few rather different Nuaulu examples of these: forest, animal spirits and ritual killing.

As we have seen, the archetypal Nuaulu representation of the collective natural other is *wesie*, uncut primary forest (Ellen 1993a: 138–40). However, this contrasts in different ways with other land types, depending on context. It may contrast with *wasi* (owned land, which may sometimes display very mature forest growth), emphasising a jural distinction; with *nisi* (garden land), emphasising land-forms: empty as opposed to well-timbered, inhabited (dwelt) as opposed to uninhabited space, untamed as opposed to tamed space. All have various symbolic associations and practical consequences for Nuaulu consumers. Although there are no Nuaulu words for either 'nature' or 'culture', it is in the various and aggregated senses of *wesie* that the Nuaulu come closest to having such a term, and from which the existence of an abstract covert notion of 'nature' can reasonably be inferred (cf. Valeri 1990).

Thus in particular contexts the meaning of *wesie* as a natural other may be sharply dichotomised, only to appear in a different guise elsewhere, As Croll and Parkin argue (1992: 3), most peoples ascribe a somewhat capricious agency to their environment which they are obliged to interpret and negotiate, and of which they commonly regard themselves as inseparably part. In some contexts, even for the Nuaulu, the forest *is* the people, in the same way as the ancestors are, in a sense, extensions of the living. Negotiations and renegotiations take place regarding the meanings of forest and village, cleared and uncleared, cultivated and uncultivated, wild and tame. Oppositions are set up only to be transcended or merged; sometimes forest is male, sometimes female; sometimes portrayed as antagonistic, sometimes life-nurturing. These all provide alternative modes of identification (ibid., 16).

Similarly, the juxtaposition of classifications of spirits and animals not only serves to show the structural similarities and conceptual bases of categories and their relationship to each other, but also reminds us of an important difference: that spirits are in the normal way experientially incorporeal while animals are first experienced as things, even though the Nuaulu 'know' that spirits have bodies and bodies have spirits. The logic of this in one direction is that the Nuaulu must claim to see spirits for them to exist, and in the other that animals must have spirits because of the prohibitions and beliefs surrounding them. But the notion that animals have spirits is problematic if you have to kill them, and Nuaulu culture provides a very practical response to this, in rituals connected with wooden meat skewers or *asumate*.

When an animal is butchered it is generally skewered on a sharpened wooden stake, and a chip from the pointed end kept and afterwards tied to the pole. This piece is traditionally employed to butcher the killed animal, and represents its spirit; the retying to the pole is thus supposed to represent the reuniting of the soul and body of the animal killed. The purposes of the *asumate* are: to inform the ancestors that meat has been killed and that they should come and partake of it; to confer prestige, the *asumate* being placed where everyone can see it; to return the spirit to the cosmos, and therefore to ensure that finite stocks are not depleted and that hunting prospects remain good. Every time a hunter fails to plant an *asumate* the wild stock of that species is thought to be depleted by a factor of one. Such practical steps, however, if taken to their logical extreme, become highly inconvenient in the normal daily round. Far better to rely upon periodic strategic amnesia and operate with two contradictory conceptions of the animal world: one which stresses unity with humankind (and the privilege of taking life for food) and another which stresses the fundamental differences between humans and animals and which legitimates and makes easier their exploitation as food (cf. Wazir-Jahan Karim 1981: 188). Of course any cosmology motivated by animism must generate respect for other species, a respect often reinforced by prohibitions of various kinds. But this need not be inconsistent with hunting, and I suspect that there may long have been a contradiction between the doctrine of infinite renewal and the recognition that hunters could exterminate animals locally (Brightman 1987: 137).

My final example conveniently follows on from our consideration of *asumate*. All Nuaulu killing in the course of hunting takes place outside the village, in the natural other. That killing which takes place as a culmination of hunting not only takes place in nature, it involves a part of nature, and exemplifies the control of natural forces: the domination of culture over nature in nature. By contrast, animal sacrifice takes place in the village (and is therefore controlled, cultural, killing), the domination of nature in culture. In the first, the offering is a consequence of a killing for some other purpose (usually for food); in the second the food (where it is consumed) is a consequence of the offering. But meat killed outside the village is not just any kind of meat, it belongs to recognised animal categories, specific natural things. The most important of these are *peni* (the collective term for pig, deer and cassowary), simultaneously natural and cultural. *Peni* (creatures of the forest) pass, therefore, from a natural (uncontrolled) condition into a cultural (controlled) one, and in an important dual sense sustain the possibility of 'culture', being identified with the descent group and the house in which their accumulated mandibles have been stored (culture-within-nature). Animals of sacrifice, by contrast, are of domestic stock (chickens – preferably cockerels) or of the village realm by metaphoric association, as in the case of the cuscus (phalangers), which resemble humans and which, through historical convenience, have become a substitute for human heads. Such animals are, therefore, nature-within-culture (Ellen 1996a).

Conclusion

Nature is definitely not a basic category. It is more a 'higher order' category in Rappaport's sense (1971: 33–4), and for many peoples it would appear to have no clearly bounded categorical status at all. As with more inclusive units in the Linnaean hierarchy, non-basic folk categories cannot be objectively defined, and no firm distinction between perceptual and social can be sustained. Indeed, it is inconceivable that classification might proceed in ways which, to follow Geertz, 'externalise culture'. Conceptualisations of nature are not the inventions of individuals (in which case they would more closely reflect cognitive process), but arise through historical contingency, linguistic constraints, metaphorical extension, ritual prohibitions and so on. As parts of belief systems they are the productions of interactions, accretions, elaborations and condensations. That contradictions and inconsistencies exist is because nature is simultaneously an abstract symbolic and a non-basic cognitive category, variously a model 'of' the world (a representation) and a model 'for' (a plan for action) (Geertz 1966). It is precisely this ability to switch between one and the other, to engage with the environment and disengage from it, which distinguishes us from non-human primates.

Our understandings of nature are rooted in particular situations which, when their common meanings are distilled, provide us with something which has a provisional, abstract and emergent quality. Such notions of nature are the consequence of what I have elsewhere called *prehension*: those processes which through various cultural and other constraints give rise to particular classifications, designations and representations (Ellen 1993: chapter 8; see also Chapter 1 above). People bring to situations in which classifying activity takes place, and from which verbal statements about classifying behaviour result, information of diverse kinds acquired through both informal and formal socialisation of experience, of the world in general and of earlier classifying situations. How they then classify depends upon the interplay of this past knowledge (including prescriptions and preferences with regard to particular cognitive and linguistic idioms) with the material constraints of the classifying situation, the purposes of the classifying act, and upon the inputs of other interpenetrating ones.

In addition, it is important to recognise that the processing and storage of information in the brain is imperfect, and communication of that information less perfect still. Paradoxically, there is a connection between this shortcoming and the considerable capacity of the human mind to reorder information in different ways, replacing irrelevant information with that of greater and more immediate utility. As Sperber (1985: 31) has remarked, 'mental representations have a basically unstable structure: the normal fate of an idea is to become altered or to merge with other ideas; what is exceptional is the reproduction of an idea'. Following Lévi-Strauss, he insists that any epidemiology of ideas is, therefore, as much concerned with transformation as persistence. That understandings of nature are messy, cross-cutting and changing is a reflection of this. Concepts are often used and operationalised without being defined. The efficient practice which precedes theory does not require self-reflection on the operation while performing it, and much of what we learn, in fact, is learning *not* to think about operations that once needed to be thought about (Medawar 1957: 138).

All of this is to emphasise the contextual, variable and contingent way in which we use those cultural abstractions which in terms of our own emic conventions we find convenient to represent as 'nature'. But, of course, in order for communication to take place classification must have at least some intersubjective structure, agreed cultural rules, some 'doxa' (Bourdieu 1977). Much of this is possible simply because there is sufficient agreement about cultural conventions, but this is not to endorse '*a grammar* of the variety of ways in which nature is socialised' (Descola 1992: 110). Everything I have said here suggests that a grammatical analogy would be quite false, as would any attempt to confine discussion to a linguistic level of expression. Very few languages have words which easily translate as 'nature', yet some focal notion in terms of the three cognitive dimensions examined here is always present. Sometimes, as in the Nuaulu case, the resemblance to global etic nature is sufficiently close for it to be recognisable; in other cases – as among many hunter-gatherers – the resemblance is much weaker. Language only mediates – and then rather inadequately – between the many cultural appearances and the three underlying cognitive axes which generate the possible co-ordinates: the objectification of the world, the spatial other, and inner essence. Such a model of the cognitive geometry of nature as I have offered here is consistent with recent attempts – such as those of Bloch and Ingold – to go beyond linguistic representation and to situate perception within actions on the world (non-mediated forms of knowledge), and – paradoxically – to resist the imposition of our own nature-culture dualisms on data.

Notes

1. Earlier versions of this chapter were presented to a seminar at the Muséum National d'Histoire Naturelle in Paris, sponsored jointly by the CNRS and the Laboratoire d'Ethnobiologic-Biogéographie, and as a Munro Lecture at the University of Edinburgh. I would like to thank Claudine Friedberg, Cecile Barraud and Anthony Cohen for the opportunity to explore the ideas presented here in a revised and shortened form. All of the Nuaulu data referred to have been published before in the works cited, where full acknowledgement of permissions and funding bodies may be found.
2. I provide here only a few indicative references. Further examples, together with a more extensive discussion of the 'cultural construction of nature' are to be found in Ellen 1996b.
3. In a sense, my aim is to examine the extent to which it is possible to identify a category innocent of morality at a time when the prevailing inclination is to emphasise the intrinsically moral character of nature. One might, of course, demur that ultimately all categories imply rules, and all rules imply the moral force of 'right' and 'wrong'. In this I would agree.

Bibliography

Anon. 1975. 'Fetishism'. In *The New Encyclopaedia Britannica: Micropaedia*, vol. 4. Chicago: Encyclopaedia Britannica, 754

Appadurai, A., ed. 1986. 'Introduction: Commodities and the Politics of Value'. In *The Social Life of Things: Commodities in Cultural Perspective*. Cambridge: Cambridge University Press, 3–63

Ardener, E., ed. 1971. 'Introductory Essay: Social Anthropology and Language'. In *Social Anthropology and Language*. Association of Social Anthropologists Monograph 10. London: Tavistock, ix–cii

Ardener, E. 1989. *The Voice of Prophecy and Other Essays*, ed. M. Chapman. Oxford: Blackwell

Atkinson, J.M. and S. Errington, eds. 1990. *Power and Difference: Gender in Island Southeast Asia*. Stanford: Stanford University Press

Atran, S. 1985. 'The Nature of Folk-botanical Life Forms'. *American Anthropologist*, 87: 289–315

—— 1990. *Cognitive Foundations of Natural History: Towards an Anthropology of Science*. Cambridge: Cambridge University Press

—— 1998. 'Folk Biology and the Anthropology of Science: Cognitive Universals and Cultural Particulars'. *Behavioural and Brain Sciences*, 21 (4): 547–69

Aunger, R. 1993. *Biocultural Evolution and Individual Variability in Food Taboos in Zaire*. Paper presented at 92nd annual meeting of the American Anthropological Association, Washington DC, November

Aunger, R., ed. 2000. *Darwinizing Culture: The Status of Memetics as a Science*. Oxford and New York: Oxford University Press.

Balibar, E. 1973. 'Sur la dialectique historique'. *La Pensée* 170: 27–47

Barkow, J.H., L. Cosmides and J. Tooby, eds. 1992. *The Adapted Mind: Evolutionary Psychology and the Generation of Culture*. Oxford and New York: Oxford University Press

Bartlett, F.C. 1932. *Remembering: A Study in Experimental and Social Psychology*. Cambridge: Cambridge University Press

Bateson, G. 1973. *Steps to an Ecology of Mind: Collected Essays in Anthropology, Psychiatry, Evolution and Epistemology*. London: Paladin

van Bemmel, A.C.V. 1948. 'A Faunal List of the Birds of the Moluccan Islands'. *Treubia* 19: 323–402

Benedict, R. 1938. 'Religion'. In *General Anthropology*, ed. F. Boas. Boston: D.C. Heath, 627–65

Berger, P.L. and T. Luckmann. 1967. *The Social Construction of Reality*. London: Penguin

Berlin, B. 1970. 'A Universalist–Evolutionary Approach in Ethnographic Semantics'. In *Current Directions in Anthropology*, ed. A. Fisher. Bulletin of the American Anthropological Association, 3: 3–18

—— 1972. 'Speculations on the Growth of Ethnobotanical Nomenclature'. *Language in Society*, 1: 51–86

——1974. 'Folk Systematics in Relation to Biological Classification and Nomenclature'. *Annual Review of Ecology and Systematics*, 4: 259–71

——1976. 'The Concept of Rank in Ethnobiological Classification: Some Evidence from Aguarana Folk Botany'. *American Ethnologist*, 3: 381–99

——1992. *Ethnobiological Classification: Principles of Categorization of Plants and Animals in Traditional Societies*. Princeton, NJ: Princeton University Press

——2003. 'One Maya Indian's View of the Plant World: How a Folk Botanical System Can be Both Natural and Comprehensive'. *Nature Knowledge: Ethnoscience, Cognition, and Utility*, eds G. Sanga and G. Ortalli. Oxford: Berghahn

——n.d. 'Whither the Savage Mind? – Yonder, Classifying and Well, as is Its Nature'. Unpublished manuscript.

Berlin, B., D.E. Breedlove and P.H. Raven. 1966. 'Folk Taxonomies and Biological Classification'. *Science*, 154: 273–5

——1968. 'Covert Categories and Folk Taxonomies'. *American Anthropologist*, 70: 290–99

—— 1973. 'General Principles of Classification and Nomenclature in Folk Biology'. *American Anthropologist*, 75: 214–42

—— 1974. *Principles of Tzeltal Plant Classification: An Introduction to the Botanical Ethnography of a Mayan-speaking People of the Highland Chiapas*. New York: Academic Press

Bernstein, J.H. 1996. 'Higher-order Categories in Brunei Dusun Ethnobotany: the Folk-classification of Rainforest Plants'. In *Tropical Rainforest Research: Current Issues*, eds D.S. Edwards, W.E. Booth and S.C. Choy. Dordrecht, Boston and London: Kluwer, 435–50

Bernstein, J.H. and R.F. Ellen [forthcoming]. 'Licuala Palms in Brunei Dusun Ethnobotany'. *Brunei Museum Journal*.

Binet, M. 1887. 'Le fétichisme dans l'amour'. *Revue Philosophique*, 24

Bird-David, N. 1993. 'Tribal Metaphorization of Human-nature Relatedness'. In *Environmentalism: The View from Anthropology*, ed. K. Milton. Association of Social Anthropologists Monograph 32. London: Routledge, 112–25

Bloch, M. 1977. 'The Past and the Present in the Present'. *Man*, n.s. 12: 278–92

—— 1985. 'From Cognition to Ideology'. In *Power and Knowledge: Anthropological and Sociological Approaches*, ed. R. Fardon. Edinburgh: Scottish Academic Press, 21–48

—— 1991. 'Language, Anthropology and Cognitive Science'. *Man*, n.s. 26 (2): 183–98

—— 1992. 'What Goes Without Saying: The Conceptualisation of Zafimaniry Society'. In *Conceptualizing Society*, ed. A. Kuper. European Association of Social Anthropologists. London: Routledge, 127–46

—— 1993. 'Domain Specificity, Living Kinds and Symbolism'. In *Cognitive Aspects of Religious Symbolism*, ed. P. Boyer. Cambridge: Cambridge University Press, 111–20

Blust, R.A. 1974. 'Proto-Austronesian Syntax: The First Step.' *Oceanic Linguistics* 13: 1–15

Boardman, J. and E.L. Rocca. 1978. *Eros in Greece*. London: John Murray

Boden, M. [forthcoming]. *Mind as Machine: A History of Cognitive Science*. Oxford: Oxford University Press

Bonnemère, P. 1998. 'Trees and People: Some Vital Links: Tree Products and Other Agents in the Life Cycle of the Ankave-Anga of Papua Guinea'. In *The Social Life of Trees: Anthropological Perspectives on Tree Symbolism*, ed. L. Rival. Oxford: Berg, 113–31

Borges, J.L. with M. Guerrero 1969. *The Book of Imaginary Beings Revised*, enlarged and trans. N. Thomas di Giovanni in collaboration with author. London: Jonathan Cape

Boster, J. 1996. 'Human Cognition as a Product and Agent of Evolution'. In *Redefining Nature: Ecology, Culture and Domestication*, eds R.F. Ellen and K. Fukui. Oxford: Berg, 269–89

Bourdieu, P. 1977. *Outline of a Theory of Practice*, trans. R. Nice. Cambridge Studies in Social Anthropology 16. Cambridge: Cambridge University Press

Bousfield, J. 1979. 'The World Seen as a Colour Chart'. In *Classifications in Their Social Context*, eds R.F. Ellen and D. Reason. London: Academic Press, 195–220

Boyer, P. 1993. *Cognitive Aspects of Religious Symbolism*. Cambridge: Cambridge University Press

—— 2001. 'Cultural Inheritance Tracks and Cognitive Predispositions: The Example of Religious Concepts'. In *The Debated Mind: Evolutionary Psychology Versus Ethnography*, ed. H. Whitehouse. Oxford: Berg, 57–90

Brain, R. 1980. *Art and Society in Africa*. London: Longman

Brightman, R.A. 1987. 'Conservation and Resource Depletion: The Case of the Boreal Forest Algonquians'. In *The Question of the Commons: The Culture and Ecology of Communal Resources*, eds B.M. McCay and J.M. Acheson. Tucson: University of Arizona Press, 121–41

Brosses, C. de 1972 [1760]. *Du Culte des Dieux Fétiches, ou Parallèle de l'Ancienne Religion de l'Egypte avec la Religion Actuelle de Nigritie*. Farnborough: Gregg

Brown, C.H. 1977. 'Folk Botanical Life-forms: Their Universality and Growth'. *American Anthropologist*, 79: 317–42

—— 1982. 'Growth and Development of Folk-botanical Life-forms in Polynesian Languages'. *Journal of the Polynesian Society*, 91(2): 213–43

—— 1984. *Language and Living Things: Uniformities in Folk Classification and Naming*. New Brunswick, NJ: Rutgers University Press

—— 1990. 'A Survey of Category Types in Natural Language'. In *Meaning and Prototypes: Studies in Linguistic Categorisation*, ed. S.L. Tsohatzidis. London and New York: Routledge, 17–47

Brown, C.H., J. Kolar, B.J. Torrey, T. Trung-Quang and P. Volkman. 1976. 'Some General Principles of Biological and Non-biological Folk Classification'. *American Ethnologist*, 3: 73–85

Brown, P. 1981. *The Cult of the Saints: Its Rise and Function in Latin Christianity*. London: SCM Press

Bruner, J. 1996. 'Frames for Thinking: Ways of Making Meaning'. In *Modes of Thought: Explorations in Culture and Cognition*, eds D.R. Olson and N. Torrance. Cambridge: Cambridge University Press, 93–105

Bulmer, R.N.H. 1967. 'Why is the Cassowary not a Bird? A Problem of Zoological Taxonomy among the Karam of the New Guinea Highlands'. *Man*, n.s. 2: 5–25

—— 1968. 'Worms that Croak and Other Mysteries of Karam Natural History'. *Mankind*, 6, 621–39

—— 1970. 'Which came First, the Chicken or the Egg-head?' In *Échanges et Communications: mélanges offerts à Claude Lévi-Strauss*, eds J. Pouillon and P.

Maranda. The Hague and Paris: Mouton, vol. 2, 1069–91
—— 1974. 'Memoirs of a Small Game Hunter: On the Track of Unknown Animal Categories in New Guinea'. *Journal d'Agriculture Tropicale et de Botanique Appliquée*, 21: 79–99
—— 1974a. 'Folk Biology in the New Guinea Highlands'. *Social Science Information*, 13 (4–5): 9–28
—— 1978. 'Totems and Taxonomy'. In *Australian Aboriginal Concepts*, ed. L.R. Hiatt. Canberra: Australian Institute of Aboriginal Studies, 1–19
—— 1979. 'Mystical and Mundane in Kalam Classification of Birds'. In *Classifications in Their Social Context*, eds R. Ellen and D. Reason. London: Academic Press, 57–79
—— 1985. 'Trees, Grerbs, Wugs, Shwms and Quammals: The New Universal Natural History of Cecil H. Brown'. *Journal of the Polynesian Society*, 94 (4): 431–7
Bulmer, R.N.H., and M.J. Tyler. 1968. 'Karam Classification of Frogs'. *Journal of the Polynesian Society*, 81: 472–99
Buonomo, D.V. and M.M. Merzenich. 1998. 'Cortical Plasticity: From Synapses to Maps'. *Annual Reviews of Neuroscience*, 21: 149–86
Burkill, T.H. 1935. *A Dictionary of the Economic Products of the Malay Peninsula*. London, Crown Agents for the Colonies (2nd ed. Kuala Lumpur 1966)
Byrne, R. and A. Whiten, eds. 1988. *Machiavellian Intelligence: Social Expertise and the Evolution of Intellect in Monkeys, Apes and Humans*. Oxford: Clarendon Press
Casagrande, J.B. and K.L. Hale. 1967. 'Semantic Relationships in Papago Folk Definitions'. In *Studies in Southwestern Linguistics*, ed. D. Hymes. The Hague, 165–93
Changeux, J.-P. 1985. *Neuronal Man: The Biology of Mind*. Oxford: Oxford University Press
Cheney, D.L. and R.M. Seyfarth. 1990. *How Monkeys See the World: Inside the Mind of Another Species*. Chicago and London: University of Chicago Press
Christensen, H. 1996. 'Plant Names and Plant Classification in an Iban Community in Sarawak', Malaysia. Unpublished manuscript
Christian, W.A. 1981. *Local Religion in Sixteenth-century Spain*. Princeton, NJ: Princeton University Press
Clark, H.H. 1973. 'Space, Time, Semantics and the Child'. In *Cognitive Development and the Acquisition of Language*, ed. T.E. Moore, New York: Academic Press, 27–63
Clarke, D. 1968. *Analytical Archaeology*. London: Methuen
Colby, B., J. Fernandez and D. Kronenfeld. 1980. 'Toward a Convergence of Cognitive and Symbolic Anthropology'. *American Ethnologist*, 8: 422–50
Cole, M., J. Gay., J.A. Glick and D.W. Sharp. 1971. *The Cultural Context of Learning and Thinking*. London: Methuen
Collingwood, R.G. 1945. *The Idea of Nature*. Oxford: Clarendon Press
Comte, A. 1893 (1830–1832). *The Positive Philosophy of Auguste Comte*. Trans. and condensed by H. Martineau. 2 vols. London: Kegan Paul, Trench, Trubner
Conklin, H.C. 1954. The Relation of Hanunóo Culture to the Plant World. New Haven: Yale University, Ph.D. dissertation
—— 1957. *Hanunóo Agriculture, a Report on an Integral System of Shifting Cultivation in the Phillipines*. Rome: Food and Agriculture Organization of the United Nations
—— 1962. 'Lexicographical Treatment of Folk Taxonomies'. *International Journal of American Linguistics*, 28: 119–41. Also in *Problems in Lexicography*, eds F.W. Householder and S. Saporta. Publication 21. Bloomington: Indiana University Research Center in Anthropology, Folklore and Linguistics

—— 1964. 'Ethnogenealogical Method'. In *Explorations in Cultural Anthropology*, ed. W.H. Goodenough. New York: McGraw-Hill, 25–55
—— 1972. *Folk Classification: A Topically Arranged Bibliography of Contemporary and Background References Through 1971*. New Haven: Yale University, Department of Anthropology
Corner, E.J.H. 1966. *The Natural History of Palms*. London: Weidenfeld and Nicolson
Coxon, A.P.M. and C.L. Jones. 1979. 'Images and Predication: The Use of Subjective Occupational Hierarchies'. *Quality and Quantity*, 13: 121–40
Croll, E. and D. Parkin. 1992. 'Cultural Understandings of the Environment'. In *Bush Base: Forest Farm: Culture, Environment and Development*, eds E. Croll and D. Parkin. London: Routledge, 11–56
D'Andrade, Roy 1995. *The Development of Cognitive Anthropology*. Cambridge: Cambridge University Press
Davidson, I. and W. Noble. 1989. 'The Archaeology of Perception: Traces of Depiction and Language'. *Current Anthropology*, 30 (2): 125–55
Dawkins, R. 1976. *The Selfish Gene*. Oxford: Oxford University Press
Deleuze, G. and F. Guattari. 1987. *A Thousand Plateaus: Capitalism and Schizophrenia*, trans. B. Massumi. London: Athlone
Dentan, R.K. 1968. 'Notes on Semai Ethnoentomology'. *Malayan Nature Journal*, 16: 17–28
Descola, P. 1992. 'Societies of Nature and the Nature of Society'. In *Conceptualizing Society*, ed. A. Kuper. European Association of Social Anthropologists. London: Routledge, 107–26
Diamond, J. 1966. 'Zoological Classification System of a Primitive People'. *Science*, 151: 1102–4
Donald, M. 1993. *Origins of the Modern Mind: Three Stages in the Evolution of Culture and Cognition*. Cambridge, MA: Harvard University Press
Dougherty, J.W.D. 1979. 'Learning Names for Plants and Plants for Names'. *Anthropological Linguistics*, 21: 298–315
Douglas, M. 1966. *Purity and Danger*. London: Routledge and Kegan Paul
—— 1970. *Natural Symbols: Explorations in Cosmology*. London: Barrie and Rockliffe
—— 1971. 'Do Dogs Laugh? A Cross-cultural Approach to Body Symbolism'. *Journal of Psychosomatic Research*, 15: 387–90
—— 1972. 'Self Evidence'. *Proceedings of the Royal Anthropological Institute of Great Britain and Ireland for 1972*, 27–44
—— 1973. *Rules and Meanings: An Anthropology of Everyday Knowledge*. Harmondsworth: Penguin
—— 1975. *Implicit Meanings: Essays in Anthropology*. London and Boston: Routledge and Kegan Paul
—— 1993. 'Hunting the Pangolin [correspondence]'. *Man*, n.s. 28 (1): 161–5
Douglas, M. and D. Hull, eds. 1992. *How Classification Works*. Edinburgh: Edinburgh University Press
Dove, M.R. 1985. *Swidden Agriculture in Indonesia: The Subsistence Strategies of the Kalimantan Kantu*. Berlin: Mouton
Dunbar, R.I.M. 1993. 'Coevolution of Neocortical Size, Group Size, and Language in Humans'. *The Behavioural and Brain Sciences*, 16: 681–735
—— 1995. *The Trouble with Science*. London: Faber and Faber
Durkheim, E. 1915. *The Elementary Forms of the Religions of Life*. Trans. from French by J.W. Swain. London: George Allen and Unwin
Durkheim, E. and M. Mauss. 1901–2. 'De quelques formes primitives de classification'. *Année sociologique*, 6

—— 1963. *Primitive Classification*. Trans. R. Needham. London: Cohen and West
Dwyer, P.D. 1976. 'An Analysis of Rofaifo Mammal Taxonomy'. *American Ethnologist*, 3: 425–45
—— 1976a. 'Beetles, Butterflies and Bats: Species Transformation in New Guinea Folk Classification'. *Oceania*, 46: 188–205
Edelman, G.M. 1987. *Neuronal Darwinism*. New York: Basic Books
—— 1992. *Bright Air, Brilliant Fire: On the Matter of the Mind*. London: Penguin
Ellen, R.F. 1972. 'The Marsupial in Nuaulu Ritual Behaviour'. *Man*, n. s. 7: 223–38
—— 1975. 'Variable Constructs in Nuaulu Zoological Classification'. *Social Science Information*, 14 (3/4): 201–28
—— 1977. 'Polythetic Classification [correspondence]'. *Man*, n. s. 12: 177
—— 1977a. 'Anatomical Classification and the Semiotics of the Body'. In *The Anthropology of the Body*, ed. J. Blacking. Association of Social Anthropologists, Monograph 15. London: Tavistock, 343–73
—— 1977b. 'The Place of Sago in the Subsistence Economics of Seram'. In *Sago-76: Papers of the First International Sago Symposium*, ed. Tan Koonlin. Kuala Lumpur: Kemajuan Kanji, 105–11
—— 1978. 'Restricted Faunas and Ethnozoological Inventories in Wallacea'. In *Nature and Man in Southeast Asia*, ed. P.A. Stott. London: School of Oriental and African Studies, 142–64
—— 1978a. *Nuaulu Settlement and Ecology: An Approach to the Environmental Relations of an Eastern Indonesian Community*. Verhandelingen van het Koninklijk Institut voor Taal-, Land- en Volkenkunde, 83. The Hague: Martinus Nijhoff
—— 1979. 'Omniscience and Ignorance: Variation in Nuaulu Knowledge, Identification and Classification of Animals'. *Language in Society*, 8: 337–64
—— 1979a. 'Introductory Essay'. In *Classifications in Their Social Context*, eds R.F. Ellen and D. Reason. London: Academic Press, 1–32
—— 1985. 'Comment on Mode of Subsistence and Folk Biological Taxonomy by C.H. Brown'. *Current Anthropology*, 26 (1): 55–6
—— 1986. 'Ethnobiology, Cognition and the Structure of Prehension: Some General Theoretical Notes'. *Journal of Ethnobiology*, 6 (1): 83–98
—— 1986a. 'Microcosm, Macrocosm and the Nuaulu House: Concerning the Reductionist Fallacy as Applied to Metaphorical Levels'. *Bijdragen tot de Taal-, Land- en Volkenkunde*, 142, 1: 1–30
—— 1986b. 'What Black Elk Left Unsaid: On the Illusory Images of Green Primitivism'. *Anthropology Today*, 2 (6): 8–12
—— 1987. 'Review of Language and Living things by C.H. Brown'. *Language in Society*, 16: 123–30
—— 1988. 'Foraging, Starch Extraction and the Sedentary Lifestyle in the Lowland Rainforest of Central Seram'. In *History, Evolution and Social Change in Hunting and Gathering Societies*, eds J. Woodburn., T. Ingold and D. Riches. London: Berg, 117–34
—— 1988a. 'Fetishism', *Man*, n. s. 23: 1–23
—— 1990. 'Nuaulu Sacred Shields: The Reproduction of Things or the Reproduction of Images'. *Etnofoor*, 3 (1): 5–25
—— 1991. 'Nuaulu Betel Chewing: Ethnobotany, Technique, and Cultural Significance'. *Cakalele: Maluku Research Journal*, 2 (2): 97–122
—— 1993. *The Cultural Relations of Classification: An Analysis of Nuaulu Animal Categories from Central Seram*. Cambridge Studies in Social and Cultural Anthropology, 91. Cambridge: Cambridge University Press
—— 1993a. 'Rhetoric, Practice and Incentive in the Face of the Changing Times: A

Case Study of Nuaulu Attitudes to Conservation and Deforestation'. In *Environmentalism: The View from Anthropology*, ed. K. Milton. Association of Social Anthropologists, Monograph 32. London: Routledge, 126–43

—— 1993b. *Nuaulu Ethnozoology: A Systematic Inventory*. Centre for Social Anthropology and Computing Monograph 6. University of Kent at Canterbury: CSAC in co-operation with the Centre for South-East Asian Studies

—— 1994. 'Hunting the Pangolin [correspondence]'. *Journal of the Royal Anthropological Institute*, 29 (1): 1–2

—— 1994a. 'Review of Berlin, Ethnobiological Classification'. *Journal of the Royal Anthropological Institute*, 29 (1): 223–4

—— 1996. 'Cuscus and Cockerels: Killing Rituals and Ritual Killing amongst the Nuaulu of Seram'. In *For the Sake of Our Future: Sacrificing in Eastern Indonesia*, ed. S. Howell. CNWS Publication 42. Leiden: Research School CNWS and Koninklijk Instituut voor Taal-, Land- en Volkenkunde, 263–81

—— 1996a. 'Introduction'. In *Redefining Nature: Ecology, Culture and Domestication*, eds R.F. Ellen and K. Fukui. New York and Oxford: Berg, 1–36

—— 1996b. 'Individual Strategy and Cultural Regulation in Nuaulu Hunting'. In *Redefining Nature: Ecology, Culture and Domestication*, eds R.F. Ellen, and K. Fukui. New York and Oxford: Berg, 597–635

—— 1996c. 'The Cognitive Geometry of Nature: A Contextual Approach'. In *Nature and Society: Anthropological Perspectives*, eds P. Descola and G. Palsson. London: Routledge, 103–23

—— 1998. 'Doubts about a Unified Cognitive Theory of Taxonomic Knowledge and Its Memic Status'. *Behavioural and Brain Sciences*, 21 (4): 572–3

—— 1999. 'Modes of Subsistence and Ethnobiological Knowledge: Between Extraction and Cultivation in Southeast Asia'. In *Folkbiology: A Synthesis*, eds D.L. Medin and S. Atran. Cambridge, MA: MIT Press, 91–117

—— 2003. 'Variation and Uniformity in the Construction of Biological Knowledge across Cultures'. In *Nature Across Cultures: Views of Nature and the Environment in non-Western Cultures*, ed. H. Selin. London: Kluwer, 47–74

—— 2003a. 'Arbitrariness and Necessity in Ethnobiological Classification: Notes on Some Persisting Issues'. In *Nature Knowledge: Ethnoscience, Cognition and Utility*, eds G. Sanga and G. Ortalli. Oxford: Berghahn, 47–56

Ellen, R.F. and H. Harris. 2000. 'Introduction'. In *Indigenous Environmental Knowledge and its Transformations: Critical Anthropological Perspectives*, eds R.F. Ellen, P. Parkes and A. Bicker. Amsterdam: Harwood, 1–33

Ember, M. 1973. 'Taxonomy in Comparative Studies'. In *A Handbook of Method in Cultural Anthropology*, eds R. Naroll and R. Cohen. New York and London: Columbia University Press, 697–706

Engels, F. 1934. *The Dialectics of Nature*. Moscow: Progress Press

Evans-Pritchard, E.E. 1956. *Nuer Religion*. Oxford: Oxford University Press

—— 1965. *Theories of Primitive Religion*. Oxford: Clarendon Press

Fantz, R.L. 1961. 'The Origin of Form Perception'. *Scientific American*, 204: 66–72

Finucane, R.C. 1977. *Miracles and Pilgrims: Popular Beliefs in Medieval England*. London: Dent

Firth, R.F. 1967 [1939]. *The Work of the Gods in Tikopia*. London School of Economics and Political Science Monographs in Social Anthropology 1–2. London: Athlone

—— 1973. *Symbols: Public and Private*. London: Allen and Unwin

Fischer, M.D. 2003. 'Powerful Knowledge: Applications in a Cultural Context'. In *Development and Local Knowledge: New Approaches to Issues in Natural Resources*

Management, Conservation and Agriculture, eds A. Bicker, P. Sillitoe and J. Pottier. Studies in Environmental Anthropology 9. London and New York: Routledge, 19–30

—— 2004. 'Integrating Anthropological Approaches to the Study of Culture: The "Hard" and the "Soft"'. *Cybernetics and Systems*, 35

Fodor, J.A. 1983. *The Modularity of the Mind*. Cambridge, MA: MIT Press

Foucault, M. 1970. *The Order of Things: An Archaeology of the Human Sciences*. London: Tavistock

—— 1972. *The Archaeology of Knowledge*. London: Tavistock

Fox, J.J. 1971. 'Sister's Child as Plant: Metaphors in an Idiom of Consanguinity'. In *Rethinking Kinship and Marriage*, ed. R. Needham. Association of Social Anthropologists Monograph 11. London: Tavistock., 219–52

—— 1975. 'On Binary Categories and Primary Symbols: Some Rotinese Perspectives'. In *The Interpretation of Symbolism*, ed. R. Willis. Association of Social Anthropologists Studies 3. London: Malaby, 99–132

—— 1977. *Harvest of the Palm: Ecological Change in Eastern Indonesia*. Cambridge, MA: Harvard University Press

Fox, R.1979. 'Kinship Categories as Natural Categories'. In *Evolutionary Biology and Human Social Behaviour*, eds N. Chagnon and W. Irons. North Scituate, MA: Duxbury Press, 132–44

—— 1980. *The Red Lamp of Incest*. London: Hutchinson

—— 1986. 'The Passionate Mind: Brain, Dreams, Memory, and Social Categories'. *Zygon*, 21 (1): 31–46

Frake, C.O. 1961. 'The Diagnosis of Disease among the Subanun of Mindanao'. *American Anthropologist*, 63: 113–32

—— 1962. 'The Ethnographic Study of Cognitive Systems'. In *Anthropology and Human Behaviour*, eds T. Gladwin and W.C. Sturtevant. Washington DC: The Anthropological Society of Washington. Repr. 1969 in *Cognitive Anthropology*, ed. S.A. Tyler. New York: Holt, Rinehart and Winston, 28–41 and 1980 in *Language and Cultural Description: Essays by Charles O. Frake*, ed. Anwar S. Dil. Stanford: Stanford University Press, 1–17

—— 1964. 'Notes on Queries in Ethnography'. *American Anthropologist*, 66 (3): 132–45 Repr. 1969 in *Cognitive Anthropology*, ed. S.A. Tyler. New York: Holt, Rinehart and Winston, 123–37

Franklin, K.J. 1963. 'Kewa Ethnolinguistic Concepts of Body Parts'. *Southwestern Journal of Anthropology*, 19 (1): 54–63

Frazer, J.G. 1922 [1925]. *The Golden Bough*. London: Macmillan

Freud, S. 1954. *The Interpretation of Dreams*, trans. J. Strachey. London: Allen and Unwin

—— 1964 [1940]. 'Splitting of the Ego in the Process of Defence'. In *The Complete Works of Sigmund Freud*, standard edn. London: The Hogarth Press, 275–8

—— 1977. *On Sexuality: Three Essays on the Theory of Sexuality and Other Works*. Harmondsworth: Penguin

Friedberg, C. 1968. 'Les méthodes d'enquête en ethnobotanique'. *Journal d'Agriculture Tropicale et de Botanique Appliquée*, 15: 297–324

—— 1970. 'Analyse de quelques groupements de végétaux comme introduction à l'étude de la classification botanique Bunaq'. In *Échanges et Communications: Mélanges Offerts à Claude Lévi-Strauss*, eds J. Pouillon and P. Maranda, vol. 2. The Hague and Paris: Mouton, 1092–1131

—— 1979. 'Socially Significant Plant Species and Their Taxonomic Position among the Bunaq of Central Timor'. In *Classifications in Their Social Context*, eds R.F. Ellen and D. Reason. London: Academic Press, 81–101

—— 1990. *Le savoir botanique des Bunaq: percevoir et classer dans le haut Lamaknen (Timor, Indonesie)*. Mémoires du Museum National d'Histoire Naturelle, Botanique 32. Paris
—— 1995. Review of Ellen, 'Cultural Relations of Classification'. *Journal of the Royal Anthropological Institute*, 1 (1): 209–10
Friedman, J. 1974. 'The Place of Fetishism and the Problem of Materialist Interpretations'. *Critique of Anthropology*, 1: 26–62
—— 1979. *System, Structure and Contradiction: The Evolution of 'Asiatic' Social Formations*. Social Studies in Oceania and Southeast Asia, 2. Copenhagen: National Museum of Denmark
Friedrich, P. 1969. 'Metaphor-like Relations between Referential Subsets'. *Lingua*, 24 (1): 1–10
Frith, H.J. 1962. *The Mallee Fowl*. Sydney: Angus and Robertson
de Garine, I. 1994. 'The Diet and Nutrition of Human Populations'. In *Companion Encyclopedia of Anthropology: Humanity, Culture and Social Life*, ed. T. Ingold. London: Routledge, 226–64
Gebherd, P.H. 1971. 'Human Sexual Behaviour: A Summary Statement'. In *Human Sexual Behaviour: Variations in the Ethnographic Spectrum*, eds D.S. Marshall and R.C. Suggs. Englewood Cliffs, NJ: Prentice-Hall
—— 1976. 'Fetishism and Sado-masochism'. In *Sex Research: Studies from the Kinsey Institute*, ed. M.S. Weinberg. Oxford: Oxford University Press, 156–66
Geertz, C. 1966. 'Religion as a Cultural System'. In *Anthropological Approaches to the Study of Religion*, ed. M. Banton. Association of Social Anthropologists Monograph 3. London: Tavistock, 1–46
—— 1973. *The Interpretation of Cultures: Selected Essays by Clifford Geertz*. London: Hutchinson
Gell, A. 1975. *Metamorphosis of the Cassowaries: Umeda society, Language and Ritual*. London School of Economics Monograph on Social Anthropology 51. London: Athlone
George, W. and B. Yapp. 1991. *The Naming of Beasts: Natural History in the Medieval Bestiary*. London: Duckworth
Giambelli, R.A. 1998. 'The Coconut, the Body and the Human Being: Metaphors of Life and Growth in Nusa Penida and Bali'. In *The Social Life of Trees: Anthropological Perspectives on Tree Symbolism*, ed. L. Rival. Oxford: Berg, 133–57
Gianno, R. 1990. *Semelai Culture and Resin Technology*. Connecticut Academy of Arts and Sciences Memoir 22. New Haven, CT.
Giddens, A. 1986. *The Constitution of Society: Outline of the Theory of Structuration*. London: Polity
Godelier, M. 1970. 'Économie marchande, fétichisme, magie et science selon Marx dans «Le Capital»' *La Nouvelle Revue de Psychanalyse*, 2 (automne): 197–213
—— 1977. *Perspectives in Marxist Anthropology*. Cambridge Studies in Social and Cultural Anthropology. Cambridge: Cambridge University Press
Goodenough, W.H. 1963. *Co-operation in Change*. New York: Russell Sage
Goody, J. 1968. 'Introduction'. In *Literacy in Traditional Societies*, ed. J. Goody. Cambridge: Cambridge University Press, 1–26
Goody, J. and I. Watt. 1968. 'The Consequences of Literacy'. In *Literacy in Traditional Societies*, ed. J. Goody. Cambridge: Cambridge University Press, 27–68
Gosselin, C. and G. Wison. 1980. *Sexual Variations: Fetishism, Sado-masochism and Transvestism*. London: Faber & Faber
Griaule, M. 1965. *Conversations with Ogotemmêli: An Introduction to Dogon Religious Ideas*, intro. Germaine Dieterlen. London: Oxford University Press

van Gulik, R.H. 1974. *Sexual Life in Ancient China: A Preliminary Survey of Chinese Sex and Society from ca. 1500* BC *till 1644* AD. Leiden: E.J. Brill
Gumperz, J.J. 1969. 'Communication in Multilingual Societies'. In *Cognitive Anthropology*, ed. S.A. Tyler. New York: Holt, Rinehart and Winston, 435–49
Haddon, A.C. 1921. *Magic and Fetishism*. London: Constable
Hallpike, C.R. 1969. 'Social Hair', *Man*, n.s. 4 (2): 256–67
Harré, R. 1986. 'Is the Body a Thing?' *International Journal of Moral and Social Studies*, 1 (3): 189–203
Harris, D.R. 1977. 'Alternative Pathways toward Agriculture'. In *Origins of Agriculture*, ed. C.A. Reed. The Hague: Mouton, 179–243
Harris, M. 1969. *The Rise of Anthropological Theory: A History of Theories of Culture*. London: Routledge and Kegan Paul
—— 1970. 'Referential Ambiguity in the Calculus of Brazilian Racial Identity', *Southwestern Journal of Anthropology*, 26: 1–14
—— 1975. *Cows, Pigs, Wars and Witches: The Riddles of Culture*. New York: Vintage Books, Random House
——1978. *Cannibals and Kings: The Origins of Culture*. New York: Vintage Books, Random House
Harris, P. and P. Heelas. 1979. 'Cognitive Processes and Collective Representations'. *European Journal of Sociology*, 20: 211–41
Hastings, J. 1963. *Dictionary of the Bible*, vol. 3 (2nd edn). London: Clark
Haudricourt, A. 1973. 'Botanical Nomenclature and Its Translation'. In *Changing Perspectives in the History of Science: Essays in Honour of Joseph Needham*, eds M. Teich and R. Young. London: Heinemann, 265–73
Hays, T.E. 1976. 'An Empirical Method for the Identification of Covert Categories in Ethnobiology'. *American Ethnologist*, 8: 489–507
—— 1979. 'Plant Classification and Nomenclature in Ndumba, Papua New Guinea Highlands'. *Ethnology*, 18: 253–270
—— 1982. 'Utilitarian/adaptationist Explanations of Folk Biological Classification: Some Cautionary Notes'. *Journal of Ethnobiology*, 2 (1): 89–94
Hegel, G.W.F. 1975 [1830]. 'Introduction: Reason in History'. *Lectures on the Philosophy of World History*. Cambridge: Cambridge University Press
Heider, E.R. 1972. 'Probabilities, Sampling and Ethnographic Methods: The Case of Dani Colour Names', *Man*, n.s. 7 (3): 448–66. [See also Rosch 1977]
Hempel, C.G. 1965. *Aspects of Scientific Explanation*, ed. C.G. Hempel. New York: Free Press
Henderson, A., G. Galeano and R. Bernal. 1989. *Field Guide to Palms of the Americas*. Princeton NJ: Princeton University Press
Heppell, D. 1990. 'Unveiled: Satan's Murky Origins'. *The Independent*, Monday 30 July, 13
Herdt, G. 1982. 'Fetish and Fantasy in Sambis Initiation'. In *Rituals of Manhood*, ed. G. Herdt. Berkeley, CA: University of California Press, 44–98
Hernnstein, R.D. 1985. 'Riddles of Natural Classification'. *Philosophical Transactions of the Royal Society (London) B*, 308: 129–43
Hernnstein, R.J., D.H. Loveland and C. Cable. 1976. 'Natural Concepts in Pigeons'. *Journal of Experimental Psychology: Animal Behavior Processes*, 2: 285–302
Holland, D. and N. Quinn., eds. 1987. *Cultural Models in Language and Thought*. Cambridge: Cambridge University Press
Horigan, S. 1988. *Nature and Culture in Western Discourses*. London: Routledge
Howell, S. 1998 '"May Blessings Come, May Mischiefs Go!" Living Kinds as Agents of Transitions and Transformation in an Eastern Indonesian Setting'. In *The Social Life of Trees: Anthropological Perspectives on Tree Symbolism*, ed. L.

Rival. Oxford: Berg, 159–75
Hull, D. 1992. 'Biological Species: An Inductivist's Nightmare'. In *How Classification Works: Nelson Goodman among the Social Sciences*, eds. M. Douglas and D. Hull. Edinburgh: Edinburgh University Press, 42–68
Hunn, E. 1975. 'The Tenejapa Tzeltal Version of the Animal Kingdom'. *Anthropological Quarterly*, 48: 14–30
—— 1975a. 'A Measure of the Degree of Correspondence of Folk to Scientific Biological Classification'. *American Ethnologist*, 2: 309–27
—— 1976. 'Toward a Perceptual Model of Folk Biological Classification'. *American Ethnolologist*, 3: 508–24
—— 1977. *Tzeltal Folk Zoology: The Classification of Discontinuities in Nature*. London: Academic Press
—— 1979. 'The Abominations of Leviticus Revisited: A Commentary on Anomaly in Symbolic Anthropology'. In *Classifications in Their Social Context*, eds R.F. Ellen and D. Reason. London: Academic Press, 103–16
—— 1982. 'The Utilitarian Factor in Folk Biological Classification'. *American Anthropologist*, 84: 830–47
—— 1987. 'Science and Common Sense: A Reply to Atran'. *American Anthropologist*, 89: 146–9
Ingold, T. 1986. *The Appropriation of Nature: Essays on Human Ecology and Social Relations*. Manchester: Manchester University Press
—— 1992. 'Culture and the Perception of the Environment'. In *Bush Base: Forest Farm, Culture, Environment and Development*, eds E. Croll and D. Parkin. London: Routledge, 39–56
—— 2001. 'From the Transmission of Representations to the Education of Attention'. In *The Debated Mind: Evolutionary Psychology Versus Ethnography*, ed. H. Whitehouse. Oxford. Berg, 113–53
Inhelder, B. and J. Piaget. 1964. *The Early Growth of Logic in the Child*, trans. E.A. Lunzer and D. Papert. London: Routledge and Kegan Paul
Jansen, H.J. 1933. 'Inheensche groepen-systemen in de Ambonsche Molukkan', *Adatrechtbundels*, 36: 445–59
Jellicoe, G., S. Jellicoe, P. Goode and M. Lancaster, eds. 1986. *The Oxford Companion to Gardens*. Oxford: Oxford University Press
Johnson-Laird, P. 1982. *Mental Models*. Cambridge: Cambridge University Press
Jones, D.E. 2002. *An Instinct for Dragons*. London: Routledge
Jung, C.G. 1958. *Psyche and Symbol*, ed. Violet S. de Laszlo. New York: Doubleday
Kay, P.D. 1969. 'Comments on Colby'. In *Cognitive Anthropology*, ed. S.A. Tyler. New York: Holt, Rinehart and Winston, 78–90
—— 1971. 'On Taxonomy and Semantic Contrast'. *Language*, 47: 886–7
Kay, P.D. and W. Kempton 1984. 'What is the Sapir-Whorf Hypothesis?' *American Anthropologist*, 86: 65–79
Kay, P.D. and C.K. McDaniel. 1978. 'The Linguistic Meanings of Basic Color Terms'. *Language*, 54: 610–46
Knight, D. 1981. *Ordering the World: A History of Classifying Man*. London: Burnett
Kocher Schmid, C. 1991. *Of People and Plants: A Botanical Ethnography of Nokopo Village, Madang and Morobe Provinces, Papua New Guinea*. Basler Beiträge zur Ethnologie 33. Basel: Ethnologisches Seminar der Universität und Museum für Völkerkunde, Wepf and Co. AG Verlag
von Krafft-Ebing, R. 1894. *Psychopathia Sexualis*, trans. C.G. Chaddock. Philadelphia, MD: F.A. Davis
Laderman, C. 1981. 'Symbolic and Empirical Reality: A New Approach to the Analysis of Food Avoidances'. *American Ethnologist*, 8 (3): 468–93

Lakoff, G. 1972. 'Hedges: A Study in Meaning Criteria and the Logic of Fuzzy Concepts'. In *Papers from the Eighth Regional Meeting,* Chicago: Chicago Linguistic Society

Lakoff, G. and M. Johnson. 1980. *Metaphors We Live By*. Chicago: Chicago University Press

Lamarck, J.B. 1963. *Zoological Philosophy: An Exposition with Regard to the Natural History of Animals,* trans. with intro. H. Eliot. New York and London: Hafner Publishing Company

Lancy, D.F. and A.J. Strathern 1981. 'Making Twos: Pairing as an Alternative to the Taxonomic Mode of Representation'. *American Anthropologist,* 83: 773–95

Langer, J. 1993. 'Comparative Cognitive Development'. In *Tools, Language and Cognition in Human Evolution,* eds K.R. Gibson and T. Ingold. Cambridge: Cambridge University Press, 300–13

Laughlin, C.D., J. McManus and E. d'Aguili. 1992. *Brain, Symbol and Experience: Toward a Neurophenomenology of Human Consciousness.* New York: Columbia University Press

Lave, J. 1988. *Cognition in Practice: Mind, Mathematics and Culture in Everyday Life.* Cambridge: Cambridge University Press

Lawrence, E., ed. 1985. *The Illustrated Book of Trees and Shrubs.* London: Octopus

Leach, E.R. 1954. *Political Systems of Highland Burma: A Study of Kachin Social Structures.* London: Bell, London School of Economics and Political Science

Leach, E.R., ed. 1961. 'Rethinking Anthropology'. In *Rethinking Anthropology.* London School of Economics Monographs on Social Anthropology 22. London: Athlone, 1–27

—— 1964. 'Anthropological Aspects of Language: Animal Categories and Verbal Abuse'. In *New Directions in the Study of Language,* ed. E. Lenneberg. Cambridge, MA: MIT Press, 23–63

—— 1966. 'Correspondence: Twins, Birds and Vegetables'. *Man,* n.s. 1 (4): 557–8

—— 1976. *Social Anthropology: A Natural Science of Society?* From the Proceedings of the British Academy 62. Oxford: Oxford University Press

Lehrer, A. 1974. *Semantic Field and Lexical Structure.* Amsterdam: North Holland

Lemonnier, P. 1992. *Elements for an Anthropology of Technology.* Anthropological Papers, Museum of Anthropology 88. Ann Arbor, MI: University of Michigan

Lenormand, M.H. 1950. 'Connaissance du corps et de la personne chez le Melanesian de Lifou (Iles Loyalty)'. *Journal de la Société des Océanistes,* 6: 33–65

Lepowsky, M. 1985. 'Food Taboos, Malaria, and Dietary Change: Infant Feeding and Cultural Adaptation on a Papua New Guinea Island'. *Ecology of Food and Nutrition,* 16 (2): 105–26

Lévi-Strauss, C. 1962. *Le Totémisme Aujourd'hui.* Paris: Presses Universitaires de France

—— 1964. *Totemism,* trans. R. Needham. London: Merlin Press

—— 1966. *The Savage Mind.* London: Weidenfeld and Nicholson

Lewis, G. 1974. 'Gnau Anatomy and Vocabulary for Illness'. *Oceania,* 45 (1): 50–78

Lienhardt, G. 1961. *Divinity and Experience.* Oxford: Clarendon Press

Lowie, R.H. 1934. *An Introduction to Cultural Anthropology.* New York: Farrar and Rinehart

Lubbock, J. 1870. *The Origin of Civilisation and the Primitive Condition of Man: Mental and Social Conditions of Savages.* London: Longmans, Green

Mabberley, D. J. 1987. *The Plant-book: A Portable Dictionary of the Higher Plants.* Cambridge: Cambridge University Press

MacCormack, C. and M. Strathern, eds. 1980. *Nature, Culture and Gender.* Cambridge: Cambridge University Press

McDougall, L. 1977. 'Symbols and Somatic Structures'. In *The Anthropology of the Body*, ed. J. Blacking. Association of Social Anthropologists, Monograph 15. London: Academic Press, 391–406
MacLean, P.D. 1973. *The Triune Concept of the Brain and Behaviour*. Toronto: University of Toronto Press
McLean, R.C. and W.R. Ivimey-Cook. 1956. *Textbook of Theoretical Botany*, vol. 2. London: Longman
McManus, C. 2003. *Right Hand, Left Hand: The Origins of Symmetry*. London: Weidenfeld and Nicolson
MacRae, D.G. 1975. 'The Body and Social Metaphor'. In *The Body as a Medium of Expression*, eds J. Benthall and T. Polhemus. London: Allen Lane, 59–73
—— 1976. 'The Naming of Names'. Review of *Implicit Meanings* by M. Douglas. *Observer Review*, 25 January, 30
Mahr, A.C. 1960. 'Anatomical Terminology of the Eighteenth-century Delaware Indians: A Study in Semantics'. *Anthropological Linguistics*, 2 (5): 1–65
Marcus, G.E. 1991. 'Notes and Quotes Concerning the Further Collaboration of Ian Saem Majnep and Ralph Bulmer: Saem becomes a Writer'. In *Man and a Half: Essays in Pacific Anthropology and Ethnobiology in Honour of Ralph Bulmer*, ed. Andrew Pawley. Auckland: The Polynesian Society, 37–45
Marsh, G.H., and W.S. Laughlin. 1956. 'Human Anatomical Knowledge among the Aleutian Islanders'. *Southwestern Journal of Anthropology*, 12: 38–78
Marx, K. 1970 [1887]. *Marx-Engels Gesamtausgabe*, part 1, vol. 1 (2). Glashütten im Taunus: Verlag Detlev Auvermann KG
—— 1970a [1867]. *Capital*. London: Lawrence and Wishart
—— 1975. *Collected Works: Karl Marx-Frederick Engels*, vol. 1: Karl Marx, 1835–43. London: Lawrence and Wishart
—— 1977 [1844]. *Economic and Philosophic Manuscripts of 1844*. Moscow: Progress Publishers
Mauss, M. 1954. *The Gift: Forms and Functions of Exchange in Archaic Societies*, trans. I. Cunnison. London: Cohen and West
—— 1973. 'Techniques of the Body'. Trans. B. Brewster. *Economy and Society*, 2 (1): 70–88
Medawar, P.B. 1957. *The Uniqueness of the Individual*. London: Methuen
Mendelson, M. 1967. 'The "uninvited guest": Ancilla to Lévi-Strauss on Totemism and Primitive Thought'. In *The Structural Study of Myth and Totemism*, ed. E.R Leach. Association of Social Anthropologists Monograph 5. London: Tavistock, 119–39
Merrill, E.D. 1954 [1946]. *Plant Life of the Pacific World*. New York: Macmillan
Miller, G. 1956. 'The Magical Number Seven, Plus or Minus Two: Some Limits on Our Capacity for Processing Information'. *Psychological Review*, 63: 81–97
Mithen, S. 1996. *The Prehistory of the Mind: A Search for the Origins of Art, Religion and Science*. London: Thames and Hudson
Moerman, M. 1969. 'A Little Knowledge'. In *Cognitive Anthropology*, ed. S. Tyler. New York: Holt, Rinehart and Winston, 449–69
Morris, B. 1976. 'Whither the Savage Mind? Notes on the Natural Taxonomies of a Hunting and Gathering People'. *Man*, n.s. 11: 542–57
—— 1979. 'Symbolism and Ideology: Thoughts Around Navaho Taxonomy and Symbolism'. In *Classifications in Their Social Context*, eds R.F. Ellen and D. Reason. London: Academic Press, 117–38
Moscovici, S. 1981. 'On Social Representation'. In *Social Cognition: Perspectives on Everyday Understanding*, ed. J.P. Forgas. London: Academic Press, 181–209
Mulkay, M.J. 1972. *The Social Process of Innovation: A Study in the Sociology of*

Sciences. London: Macmillan
Nagel, E. 1961. *The Structure of Science: Problems in the Logic of Scientific Explanation*. New York: Harcourt
Nassau, R.H. 1969 [1904)]. *Fetishism in West Africa*. New York: Negro Universities Press
Needham, J. 1962. *Science and Civilization in China, vol. 2: History of a Scientific Thought*. Cambridge: Cambridge University Press
Needham, R. 1963. 'Introduction'. In *Primitive Classification*, eds E. Durkheim and M. Mauss, trans. R. Needham. London: Cohen and West, vii–xlviii
—— 1971. 'Introduction'. In *Rethinking Kinship and Marriage*, ed. R. Needham. Association of Social Anthropologists Monograph 11. London: Tavistock, xiii–cxvii
—— 1975. 'Polythetic Classification: Convergence and Consequences'. *Man*, n.s. 10: 349–69
—— 1979. *Symbolic Classification*. Santa Monica, CA: Goodyear
Needham, R., ed. 1973. *Right and Left: Essays on Dual Symbolic Classification*. Chicago and London: University of Chicago Press
Nilsson, S. 1868. *The Primitive Inhabitants of Scandinavia*. London: Longmans, Green
Ohnuki-Tierney, E. 1981. 'Phases in Human Perception/cognition/symbolization Processes: Cognitive Anthropology and Symbolic Classification'. *American Ethnologist*, 8 (2): 451–67
Orians, G.H. and J.H. Heerwagen. 1992. 'Evolved Responses to Landscapes'. In *The Adapted Mind: Evolutionary Psychology and the Generation of Culture*, eds J.H. Barkow, L. Cosmides, and J. Tooby. Oxford and New York: Oxford University Press, 555–579.
Peck, A.L. 1965. 'Introduction'. In *Aristotle: Historia Animalium*, trans. A.L. Peck. London: Heinemann
Peeters, A. 1979. 'Nomenclature and Classification in Rumphius's Herbarium Amboinense'. In *Classifications in Their Social Context*, eds R.F. Ellen and D. Reason. London: Academic Press, 145–66
Perchonak, N. and O. Werner. 1969. 'Navaho Systems of Classification: Some Implications for Ethnoscience'. *Ethnology*, 8 (3): 229–43
Perey, A. 1975. 'Body and World in Oksaomin Kin Terms'. *Oceania*, 45 (3): 235–6
Phillips, R. 1978. *Trees in Britain, Europe and North America*. London: Ward Lock
Piaget, J. 1971. *Structuralism*, trans. and ed. C. Maschler. London: Routledge and Kegan Paul
—— 1971a. *Biology and Knowledge: An Essay on the Relations between Organic Regulations and Cognitive Processes*, trans. B. Walsh. Edinburgh: Edinburgh University Press
Pigeaud, T.G.T. 1977 [1928]. 'Javanese Divination and Classification'. In *Structural Anthropology in the Netherlands*, ed. P.E. de Josselin de Jong. Koninklijk Institut voor Taal-, Land- en volkenkunde Translation Series 17. The Hague: Martinus Nijhoff, 61–82
Platt, B.S. 1962. *Tables of Representative Values of Foods Commonly Used in Tropical Countries*. London: HMSO. Medical Research Council Special Report Series 302.
Pouillon, J. 1975 [1970]. *Fétiches sans Fétichisme*. Paris: François Maspero
Premack, D. 1976. *Intelligence in Ape and Man*. Hillsdale, NJ: Lawrence Erlbaum Associates
—— 1983. 'The Codes of Man and Beast'. *Behavioural and Brain Sciences*, 6: 125–67
—— 1986. *Gavagai*. Cambridge, MA: MIT, Bradford Books

Price-Williams, D.R. 1962. 'Abstract and Concrete Modes of Classsification in a Primitive Society'. *British Journal of Educational Psychology*, 32: 50–61

Radcliffe-Brown, A.R. 1957. *A Natural Science of Society*. Foreword by F. Eggan. Glencoe, IL: The Falcon's Wing Press

Rand, A.L. and E.T. Gilliard. 1967. *Handbook of New Guinea Birds*. London: Weidenfeld and Nicolson

Randall, R.A. 1976. 'How Tall is a Taxonomic Tree? Some Evidence for Dwarfism'. *American Ethnologist*, 8: 229–42

—— 1987. 'The Nature of Highly Inclusive Folk-botanical Categories'. *American Anthropologist*, 89: 143–6

Randall, R.A. and E.S. Hunn. 1984. 'Do Life-forms Emerge or Do Uses for Life? Some Doubts about Brown's Universals Hypotheses'. *American Ethnologist*, 11: 329–49

Rappoport, R. 1971. 'Ritual, Sanctity and Cybernetics', *American Anthropologist*, 73: 73–6

Reed, E.S. 1988. 'The Affordances of the Animate Environment: Social Science from the Ecological Point of View'. In *What is an Animal?* ed. T. Ingold. London: Unwin Hyman, 110–26

Revel, N. 1990. *Fleurs de Paroles: Histoire Naturelle Palawan*, vol. 1: *Les dons de Nagsalad*. Société pour l'Etude des Langues Africaines 314. Paris: Editions Peeters

Reyna, S.P. 2002. *Connections: Mind and Culture in a Social Anthropology*. London: Routledge

Richards, G. 1989. 'Human Behavioural Evolution: A Physiomorphic Model'. *Current Anthropology*, 30 (2): 244–55

Ridley, M. 2003. *Nature via Nurture: Genes, Experience and What Makes us Human*. London: Fourth Estate

Ritvo, H. 1997. *The Platypus and the Mermaid as Figments of the Classifying Imagination*. London: Harvard University Press

Rival, L. 1993. 'The Growth of Family Trees: Understanding Huaorani Perceptions of the Forest'. *Man*, n.s. 28 (4): 635–52

Robertson-Smith, W. 1884. *Lectures on the Religion of the Semites*. London: Adam and Charles Black

Robins, R.H. 1971. 'Malinowski, Firth and the Context of Situation'. In *Social Anthropology and Language*, ed. E. Ardener. Association of Social Anthropologists Monographs 10. London: Tavistock, 33–46

Rosaldo, M. and J.M. Atkinson. 1975. 'Man the Hunter and Woman: Metaphors For the Sexes in Ilongot Magical Spells'. In *The Interpretation of Symbolism*, ed. R. Willis. Association of Social Anthropologists Studies 3. London: Malaby, 43–75

Rosch, E. 1977. 'Human Categorisation'. In *Studies in Cross-cultural Psychology*, vol. 1, ed. N. Warren. London: Academic Press, 1–49

Rubel, M., and M. Manale. 1975. *Marx without Myth: A Chronological Study of His Life and Work*. Oxford: Basil Blackwell

Ruddle, K., D. Johnson, P. Townsend and J. Rees. 1978. *Palm Sago: A Tropical Starch from Marginal Lands*. Honolulu: University Press of Hawaii

Sacks, O. 1995. *An Anthropologist on Mars: Seven Paradoxical Tales*. London: Picador

Schefold, R. 1988. 'De wildernis als cultuur van zijde; tribale concepten van de "Natuur" in Indonesië'. *An Anthropologische Verkenningen*, 7 (4): 5–22

Scherner, K.A. 1861. *Das Leben des Traumes – Entdeckungen auf dem Gebiet de Seele*. Berlin: Schindler

Shigeta, M. 1996. 'Creating Landrace Diversity: The Case of the Ari People and

Ensete (Ensete ventricosum) in Ethiopia'. In *Redefining Nature: Ecology, Culture and Domestication*, eds R.F. Ellen and K. Fukui. Oxford: Berg, 233–68
Sillitoe, P. 1995. 'An Ethnobotanical Account of the Plant Resources of the Wola Region, Southern Highlands Province, Papua New Guinea'. *Journal of Ethnobiology*, 15 (2): 201–35
Singer, C. 1957. *A Short History of Anatomy and Physiology from the Greeks to Harvey*. New York: Dover
Skeat, W.W. 1953 [1879–82] *An Etymological Dictionary of the English Language*. Oxford: Clarendon Press
Skoyles, J.R. and D. Sagan. 2002. *Up from Dragons: The Evolution of Human Intelligence*. New York: McGraw-Hill
van Slooten, D.F. 1959. 'Rumphius as an Economic Botanist'. In *Rumphius Memorial Volume*, ed. H.C.D. de Wit. Baarn: Hollandia NV, 295–338
Sokal, R.R. and P.H. Sneath. 1963. *Principles of Numerical Taxonomy*. San Francisco and London: Freeman
le Souef, A.S. and H. Burrell. 1926. *The Wild Animals of Australasia*. London: Harrap
Sperber, D. 1975. *Rethinking Symbolism*, trans. A.L. Morton. Cambridge: Cambridge University Press
—— 1975a. 'Pourquoi les animaux parfaits, les hybrids et les monstres sont-ils bons a penser symboliquement?' *L'Homme*, 15: 5–34
—— 1985. 'Anthropology and Psychology: Towards an Epidemiology of Representations'. *Man*, n.s. 20: 73–89
—— 1996. *Explaining Culture: A Naturalistic Approach*. Oxford: Blackwell
Spicker, S.F. 1970. *The Philosophy of the Body*. Chicago: Quadrangle Books
Stark, L.R. 1969. 'The Lexical Structure of Quechua Body-parts', *Anthropological Linguistics*, 11 (1): 1–15
Steiner, F. 1967 [1956]. *Taboo*. London: Penguin
Strathern, M. 1992. *After Nature: English Kinship in the Late Twentieth Century*. Cambridge: Cambridge University Press
Strauss, C. 1992. 'Models and Motives'. In *Human Motives and Cultural Models*, eds R. d'Andrade and C. Strauss. Cambridge: Cambridge University Press, 1–20
Sturtevant, W.C. 1964. 'Studies in Ethnoscience'. In *Transcultural Studies in Cognition*, eds A.K. Romney and R.G. d'Andrade. Also in *American Anthropologist*, 66: 99–131
Sumption, J. 1975. *Pilgrimage: An Image of Medieval Religion*. London: Faber and Faber
Swartz, M.J. 1960. 'Situational Determinants of Kinship Terminology', *South Western Journal of Anthropology*, 16: 393–7
Tallis, R. 2003. *The Hand: A Philosophical Enquiry into Human Being*. Edinburgh: Edinburgh University Press
Tambiah, S.J. 1969. 'Animals are Good to Think and Good to Prohibit'. *Ethnology*, 8: 424–59
Taussig, M.T. 1980. *The Devil and Commodity Fetishism in South America*. Chapel Hill, NC: University of North Carolina Press
Taylor, P.M. 1990. *The Folk Biology of the Tobelo People: A Study in Folk Classification*. Smithsonian Contributions to Anthropology 34. Washington DC: Smithsonian Institution Press
Thomas, K. 1983. *Man and the Natural World: Changing Attitudes in England, 1500–1800*. London: Allen Lane
Torrance, J., ed. 1992. *The Concept of Nature: The Herbert Spencer Lectures*. Oxford: Clarendon Press
Trager, G.L. 1939. '"Cottonwood" = "tree": a Southwestern Linguistic Trait.'

International Journal of American Linguistics, 9: 117–18
Traube, E.G. 1986. *Cosmology and Social Life: Ritual Exchange among the Mambai of East Timor*. Chicago: University of Chicago Press
Tulving, E. 1983. *Elements of Episodic Memory*. Oxford: Oxford University Press
Turner, V.W. 1966. 'The Syntax of Symbolism in an African Religion'. In *Philosophical Transactions of the Royal Society B*, 772, vol. 251: 295–303
—— 1966a. 'Colour Classification in Ndembu Ritual'. In *Anthropological Approaches to the Study of Religion*, ed. M. Banton. Association of Social Anthropologists Monograph 3. London: Tavistock, 47–84
—— 1983. 'Body, Brain and Culture'. *Zygon*, 18 (3): 221–45
Tyler, S.A., ed. 1969. *Cognitive Anthropology*. New York: Holt, Rinehart and Winston
—— 1969a. 'Introduction'. In *Cognitive Anthropology*, ed. S. Tyler. New York: Holt, Rinehart and Winston, 1–23
—— 1969b. 'Relevance: Context: Introduction'. In *Cognitive Anthropology*, ed. S. Tyler. New York: Holt, Rinehart and Winston, 433–4
—— 1969c. 'Context and Variation in Koya Kinship Terminology'. In *Cognitive Anthropology*, ed. S. Tyler. New York: Holt, Rinehart and Winston, 487–503
Tylor, E.B. 1878. *Researches into the Early History of Mankind and the Development of Civilisation*, 3rd edn. London: Murray
—— 1924 [1871]. *Primitive Culture: Researches into the Development of Mythology, Philosophy, Religion, Language, Art and Custom*, vol. 2. New York: Brentano's
Ucko, P.J. 1969. 'Penis Sheaths: A Comparative Study'. *Proceedings of the Royal Anthropological Institute for 1969*, 27–67
Uhl, N.W. and J. Dransfield. 1987. *Genera Palmarum: A Classification of Palms Based on the Work of Harold E. Moore*. The L.H. Bailey Hortorium and the International Palm Society. Lawrence, KS: Allen Press
Valeri, V. 1990. 'Both Nature and Culture: Reflections on Menstrual and Parturitional Taboos in Huaulu (Seram)'. In *Power and Difference: Gender in Island Southeast Asia*, eds J.M. Atkinson and S. Errington. Stanford, CA Stanford University Press, 235–72
—— 1992. 'If We Feed Them, We Do Not Feed on Them: A Principle of Huaulu Taboo and Its Application'. *Ethnos*, 57 (3–4): 149–67
—— 1995. 'Review of Ellen: The Cultural Relations of Classification'. *Ethnos*, 60 (1–2): 123–6
Varela, F.J., E.T. Thompson and E. Rosch. 1993. *The Embodied Mind: Cognitive Science and Human Experience*. Boston: MIT Press
Voget, F.W. 1975. *A History of Ethnology*. New York: Holt, Rinehart and Winston
Warren, D.M, L.J. Slikkerveer and D. Brokensha, eds. 1995. *The Cultural Dimension of Development: Indigenous Knowledge Systems*. London: Intermediate Technology Publications
Wazir-Jahan Karim 1981. 'Ma Betisek Concepts of Humans, Plants and Animals'. *Bijdragen tot de Taal, Land- en Volkenkunde*, 137: 35–60
Weitzmen, K. 1978. *The Icon: Holy Images, Sixth to Fourteenth Century*. London: Chatto and Windus
Werner, O. and K.Y. Begishe. 1970. 'A Lexemic Typology of Navajo Anatomical Terms I. The Foot', *International Journal of American Linguistics*, 36: 247–65
Werner, O. and J. Fenton. 1973. 'Method and Theory in Ethnoscience or Ethno-epistemology'. In *A Handbook of Method in Cultural Anthropology*, eds R. Naroll and R. Cohen. New York and London: Columbia University Press, 537–78
Whitehouse, H. 2001. 'Conclusion: Towards a Reconciliation'. In *The Debated Mind: Evolutionary Psychology Versus Ethnography*, ed. H. Whitehouse. Oxford: Berg,

203–23
Whitely, W.F. 1966. 'Social Anthropology, Meaning and Linguistics', *Man*, n.s. 1 (2): 139–57
Whorf, B.L. 1956. *Language, Thought and Reality*. Boston, MA: MIT Press
Wierzbicka, A. 1985. *Lexicography and Conceptual Analysis*. Ann Arbor, MI: Karoma Publishers
Williams, N.M. and G. Baines, eds. 1993. *Traditional Ecological Knowledge: Wisdom for Sustainable Development*. Canberra: Centre for Resource and Environmental Studies, Australian National University
Willis, R. 1974. *Man and Beast*. London: Paladin
Winnicott, D.W. 1974. *Playing and Reality*. Harmondsworth: Penguin
de Wit, H.C.D. 1959. 'A Checklist to Rumphius's Herbarium Amboinense'. In *Rumphius Memorial Volume*, ed. H.C.D. de Wit. Baarn: Hollandia NV, 339–460
Witkowski, S.R., C.H. Brown and P.K. Chase. 1981. 'Where Do Tree terms come from?' *Man*, n.s. 16: 1–14.
Worsley, P. 1956. 'Emile Durkheim's Theory of Knowledge'. *Sociological Review*, 4: 47–62

Index

Printed in the United States
108409LV00002BA/121-198/P

9 781845 451554